CREATED BY **JOSS WHEDON**

JORDIE **BELLAIRE** JEREMY **LAMBERT** ANDRÉS **GENOLET**
RAMON **BACHS** ELEONORA **CARLINI**

Buffy the Vampire Slayer™

VOLUME SIX **SECRETS OF THE SLAYER**

Published by
BOOM! STUDIOS

Series Designer
Michelle Ankley

Collection Designer
Marie Krupina & **Scott Newman**

Assistant Editor
Gavin Gronenthal

Associate Editor
Jonathan Manning

Editor
Jeanine Schaefer

Special Thanks to **Sierra Hahn**,
Becca J. Sadowsky, and **Nicole Spiegel**, & **Carol Roeder**.

CD
YAGN
741.5973
BEL
v.6

Ross Richie CEO & Founder
Joy Huffman CFO
Matt Gagnon Editor-in-Chief
Filip Sablik President, Publishing & Marketing
Stephen Christy President, Development
Lance Kreiter Vice President, Licensing & Merchandising
Bryce Carlson Vice President, Editorial & Creative Strategy
Kate Henning Director, Operations
Spencer Simpson Director, Sales
Scott Newman Manager, Production Design
Elyse Strandberg Manager, Finance
Sierra Hahn Executive Editor
Dafna Pleban Senior Editor
Shannon Watters Senior Editor
Eric Harburn Senior Editor
Sophie Philips-Roberts Associate Editor
Amanda LaFranco Associate Editor
Jonathan Manning Associate Editor
Gavin Gronenthal Assistant Editor
Gwen Waller Assistant Editor
Allyson Gronowitz Assistant Editor

Ramiro Portnoy Assistant Editor
Kenzie Rzonca Assistant Editor
Shelby Netschke Editorial Assistant
Michelle Ankley Design Lead
Marie Krupina Production Designer
Grace Park Production Designer
Chelsea Roberts Production Designer
Samantha Knapp Production Design Assistant
José Meza Live Events Lead
Stephanie Hocutt Digital Marketing Lead
Esther Kim Marketing Lead
Breanna Sarpy Live Events Coordinator
Amanda Lawson Marketing Assistant
Morgan Perry Retail Sales Lead
Megan Christopher Operations Coordinator
Rodrigo Hernandez Operations Coordinator
Zipporah Smith Operations Coordinator
Jason Lee Senior Accountant
Sabrina Lesin Accounting Assistant
Lauren Alexander Administrative Assistant

BOOM! STUDIOS | **20th** TELEVISION

BUFFY THE VAMPIRE SLAYER Volume Six, July 2021.
Published by BOOM! Studios, a division of Boom Entertainment,
Inc. © 2021 20th Television. Originally published in single magazine
form as BUFFY THE VAMPIRE SLAYER No. 21-22, BUFFY
THE VAMPIRE SLAYER: FAITH No. 1. © 2021 20th Television.
BOOM! Studios™ and the BOOM! Studios logo are trademarks
of Boom Entertainment, Inc., registered in various countries and
categories. All characters, events, and institutions depicted herein
are fictional. Any similarity between any of the names, characters,
persons, events, and/or institutions in this publication to actual
names, characters, and persons, whether living or dead, events,
and/or institutions is unintended and purely coincidental. BOOM!
Studios does not read or accept unsolicited submissions of ideas,
stories, or artwork.

BOOM! Studios, 5670 Wilshire Boulevard, Suite 400, Los Angeles,
CA 90036-5679 Printed in China. First Printing.

ISBN: 978-1-68415-687-0, eISBN: 978-1-64668-231-7

AUGUST 2021

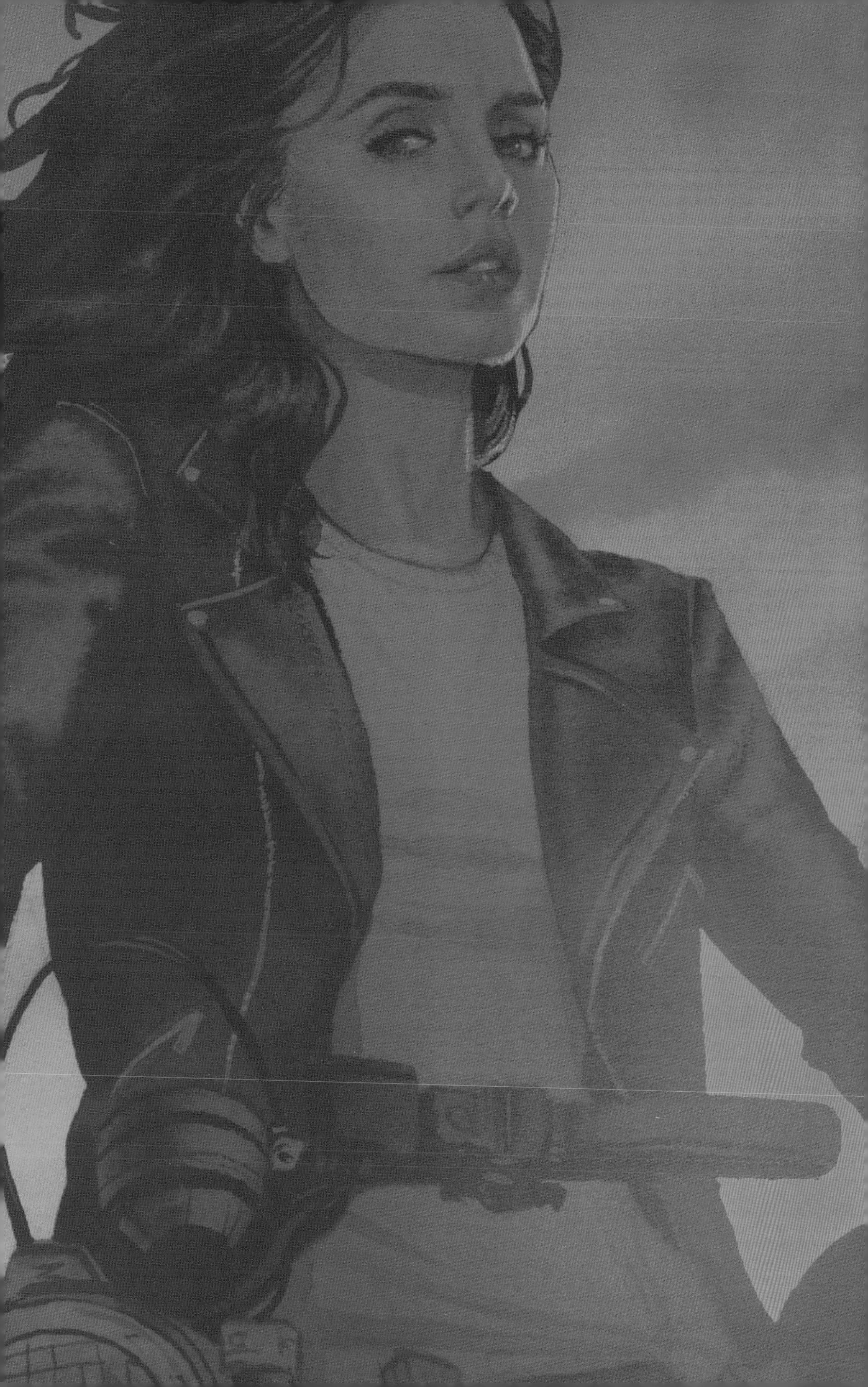

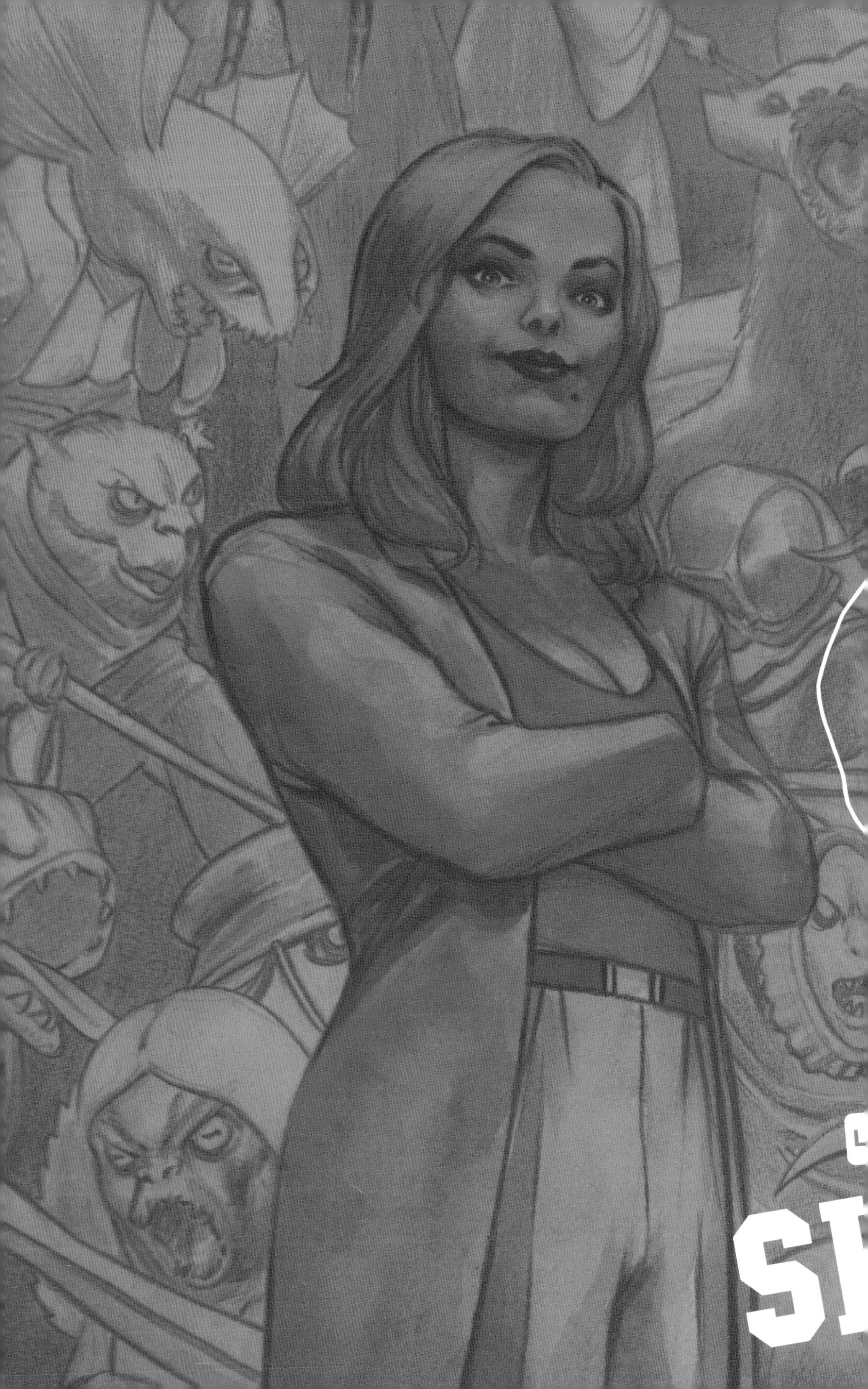

Created by
Joss Whedon

Written by
Jordie Bellaire
& Jeremy Lambert

Illustrated by
Andrés Genolet (Chapter 21)
Ramon Bachs (Chapter 22)
Eleonora Carlini (Faith)

Colored by
Raúl Angulo
Mattia Iacono (Faith)

Lettered by
Ed Dukeshire
Jim Campbell (Faith)

Cover by
David López

CHAPTER
TWENTY-ONE

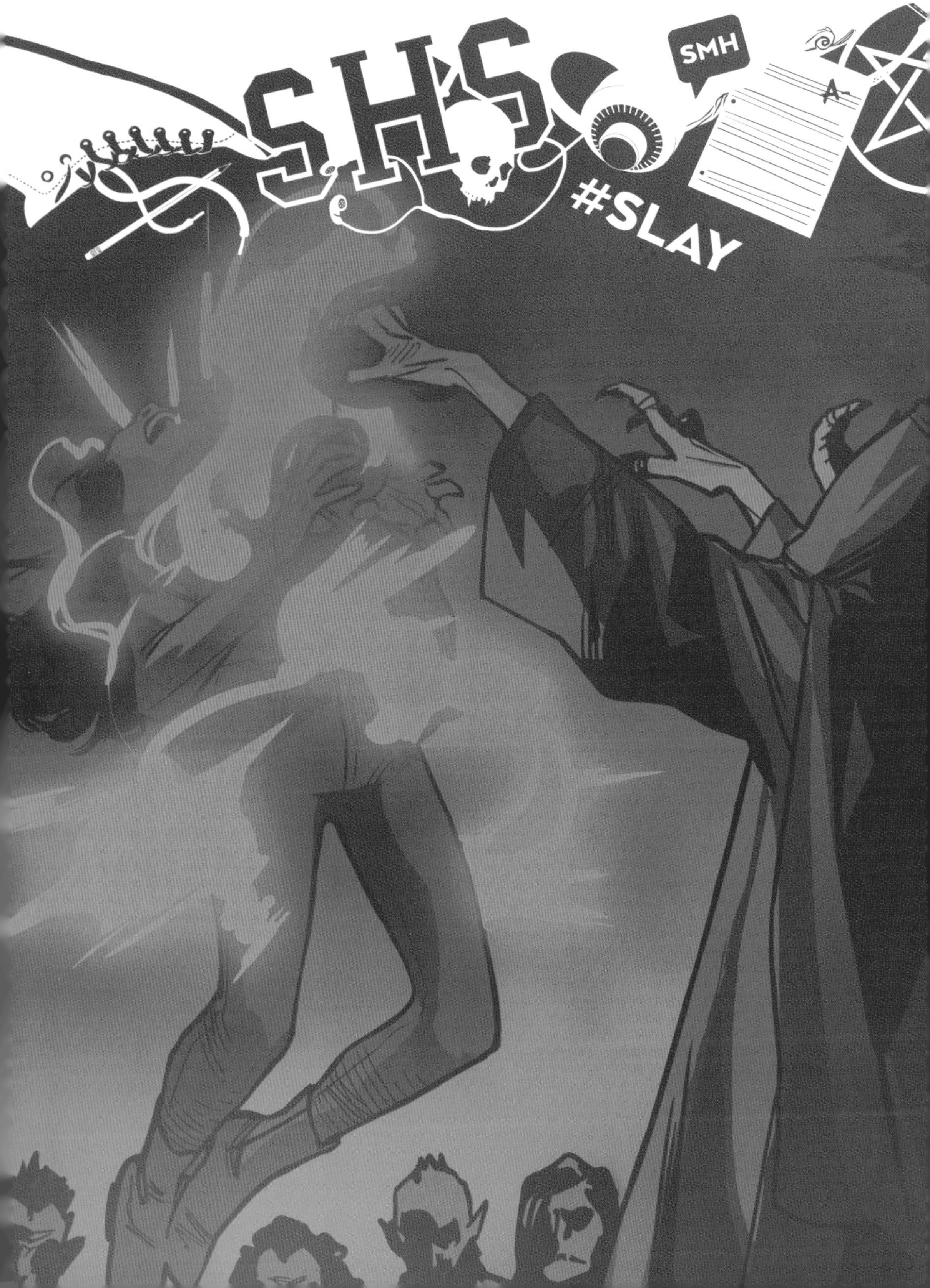
S.H.S.
SMH
A
#SLAY

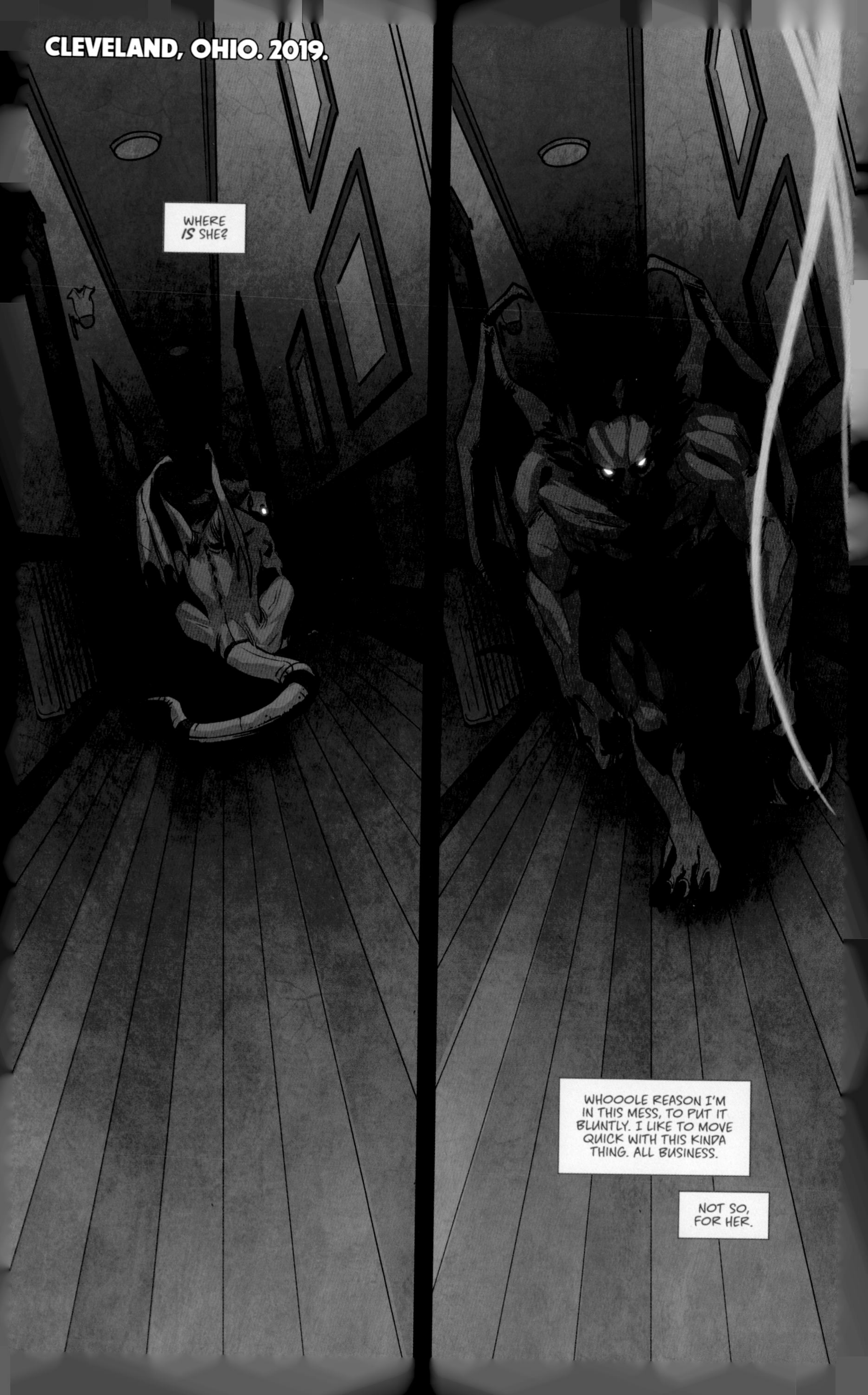
CLEVELAND, OHIO. 2019.
WHERE *IS* SHE?
WHOOOLE REASON I'M IN THIS MESS, TO PUT IT BLUNTLY. I LIKE TO MOVE QUICK WITH THIS KINDA THING. ALL BUSINESS.
NOT SO, FOR HER.

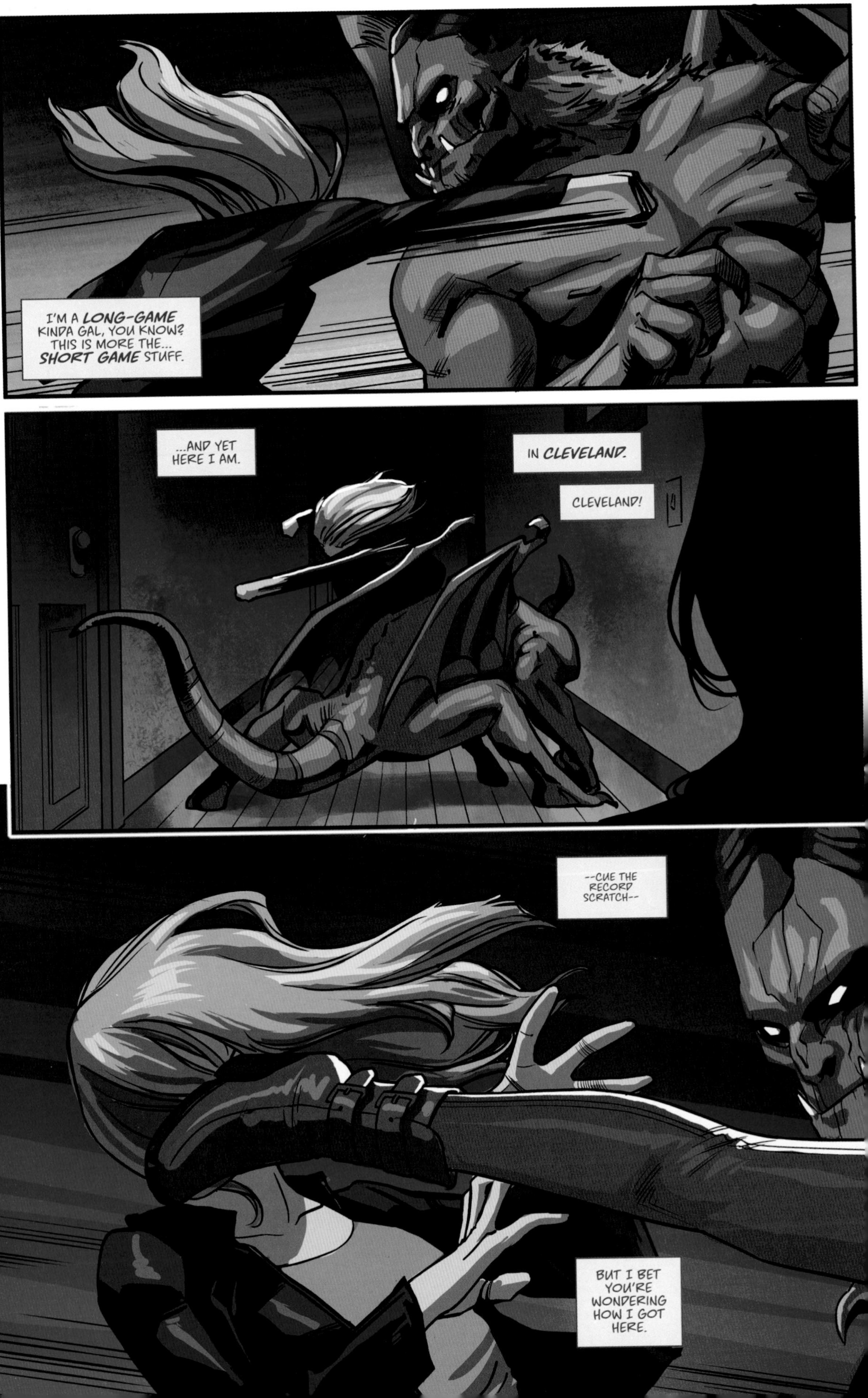
I'M A LONG-GAME KINDA GAL, YOU KNOW? THIS IS MORE THE... SHORT GAME STUFF.
...AND YET HERE I AM.
IN CLEVELAND.
CLEVELAND!
--CUE THE RECORD SCRATCH--
BUT I BET YOU'RE WONDERING HOW I GOT HERE.

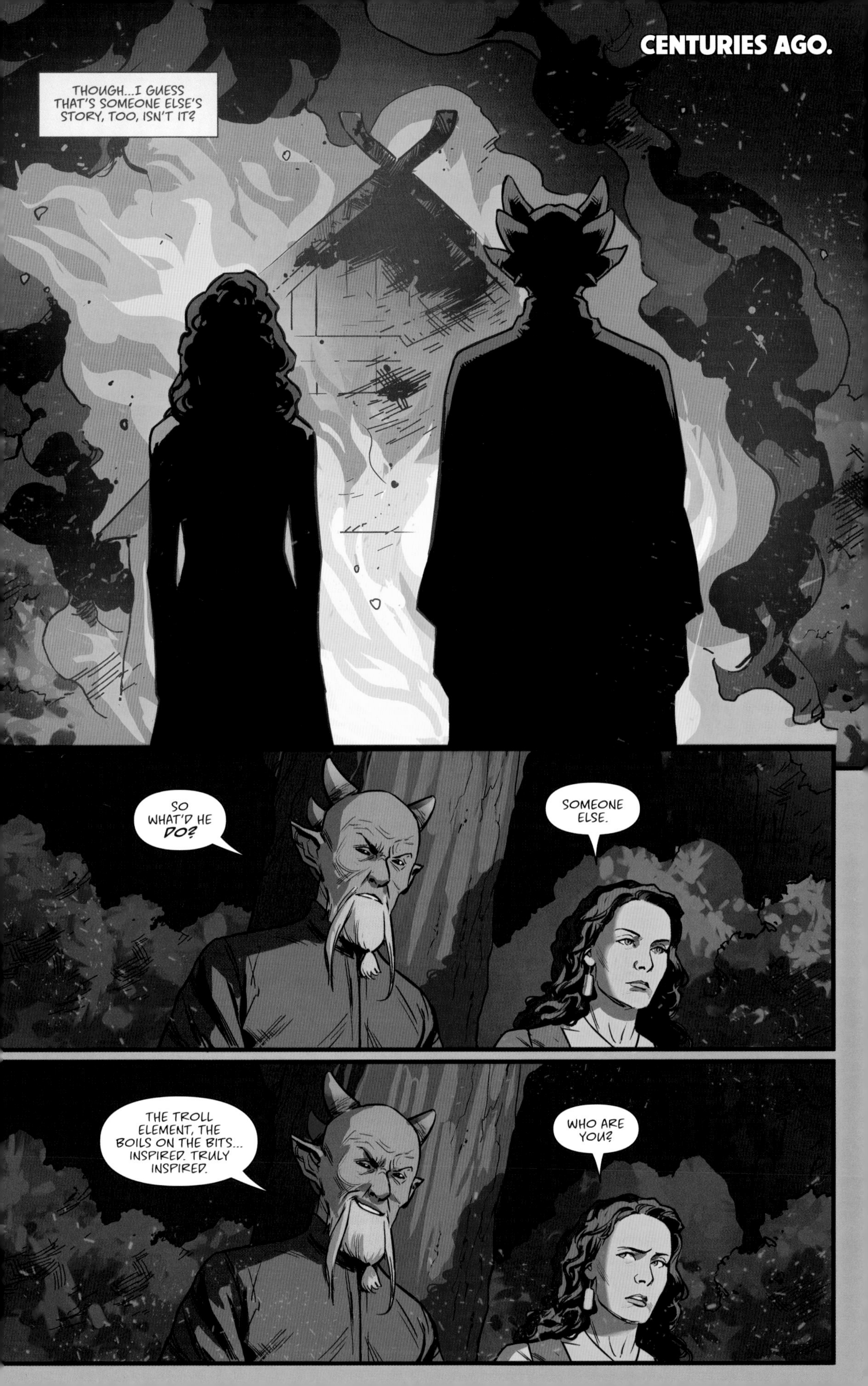
CENTURIES AGO.
THOUGH...I GUESS THAT'S SOMEONE ELSE'S STORY, TOO, ISN'T IT?
SO WHAT'D HE *DO?*
SOMEONE ELSE.
THE TROLL ELEMENT, THE BOILS ON THE BITS... INSPIRED. TRULY INSPIRED.
WHO ARE YOU?

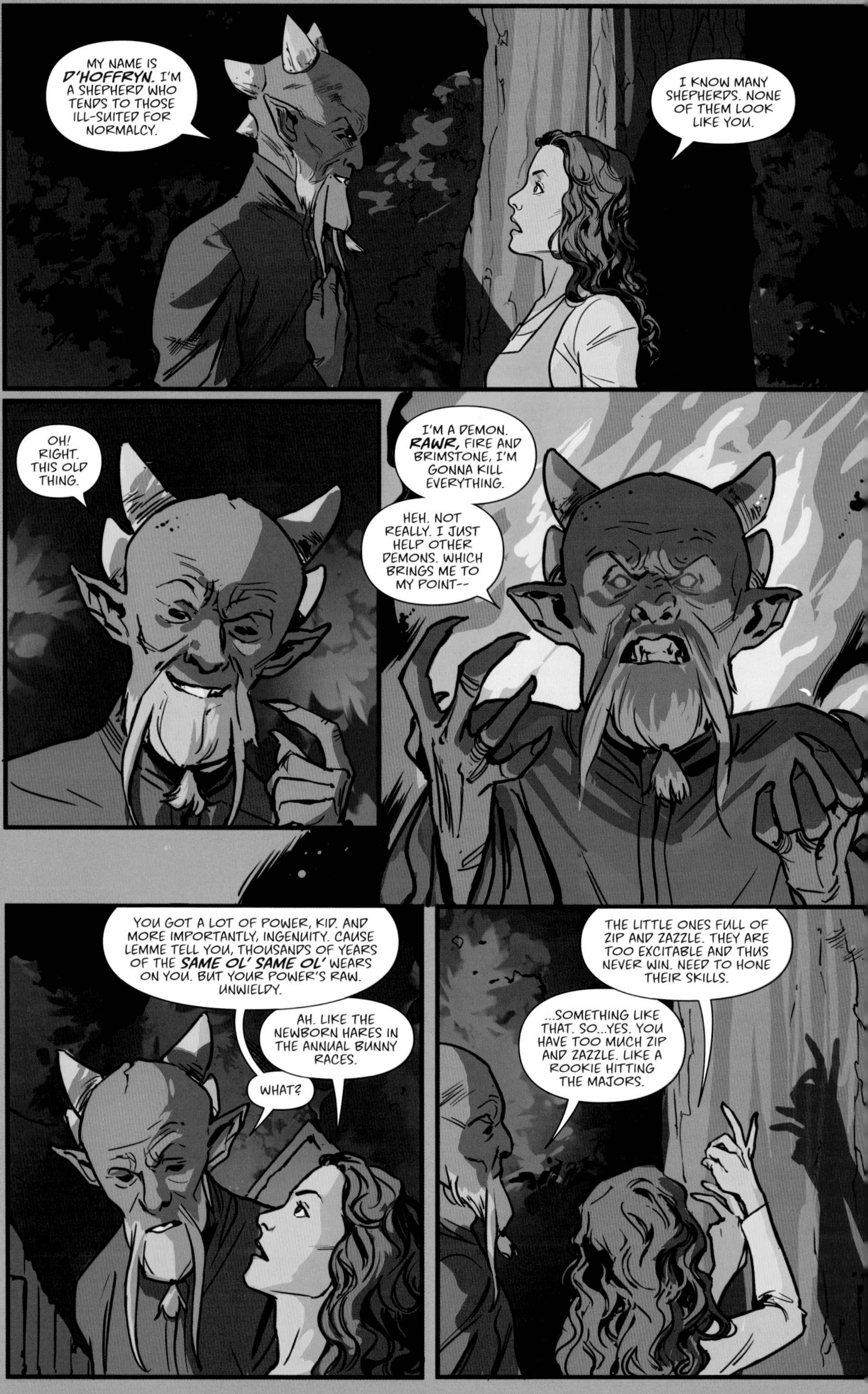
MY NAME IS *D'HOFFRYN.* I'M A SHEPHERD WHO TENDS TO THOSE ILL-SUITED FOR NORMALCY.
I KNOW MANY SHEPHERDS. NONE OF THEM LOOK LIKE YOU.
OH! RIGHT. THIS OLD THING.
I'M A DEMON. *RAWR,* FIRE AND BRIMSTONE, I'M GONNA KILL EVERYTHING.
HEH. NOT REALLY. I JUST HELP OTHER DEMONS. WHICH BRINGS ME TO MY POINT--
YOU GOT A LOT OF POWER, KID. AND MORE IMPORTANTLY, INGENUITY. CAUSE LEMME TELL YOU, THOUSANDS OF YEARS OF THE *SAME OL' SAME OL'* WEARS ON YOU. BUT YOUR POWER'S RAW. UNWIELDY.
AH. LIKE THE NEWBORN HARES IN THE ANNUAL BUNNY RACES.
WHAT?
THE LITTLE ONES FULL OF ZIP AND ZAZZLE. THEY ARE TOO EXCITABLE AND THUS NEVER WIN. NEED TO HONE THEIR SKILLS.
...SOMETHING LIKE THAT. SO...YES. YOU HAVE TOO MUCH ZIP AND ZAZZLE. LIKE A ROOKIE HITTING THE MAJORS.

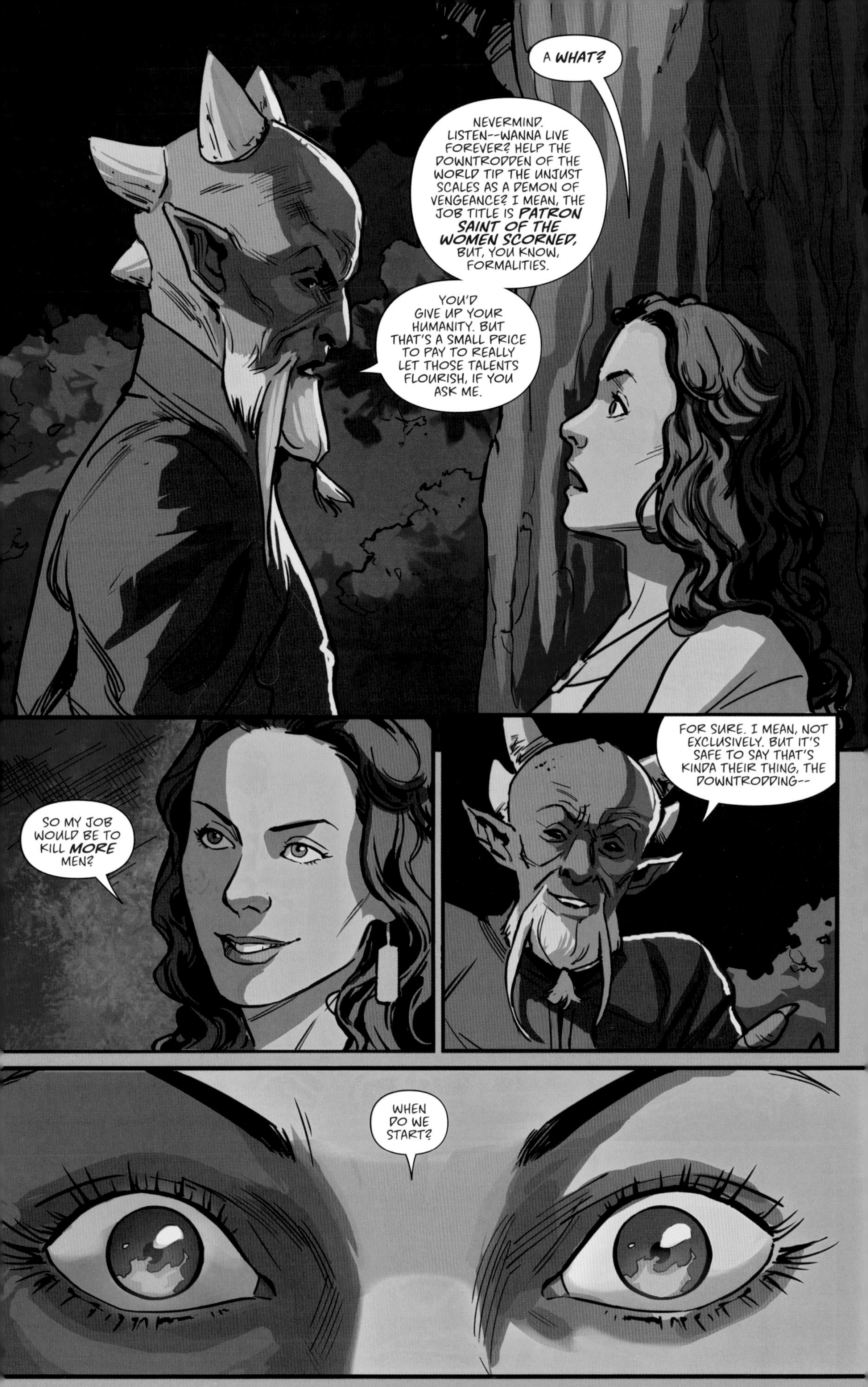
A WHAT?
NEVERMIND. LISTEN--WANNA LIVE FOREVER? HELP THE DOWNTRODDEN OF THE WORLD TIP THE UNJUST SCALES AS A DEMON OF VENGEANCE? I MEAN, THE JOB TITLE IS PATRON SAINT OF THE WOMEN SCORNED, BUT, YOU KNOW, FORMALITIES.
YOU'D GIVE UP YOUR HUMANITY. BUT THAT'S A SMALL PRICE TO PAY TO REALLY LET THOSE TALENTS FLOURISH, IF YOU ASK ME.
SO MY JOB WOULD BE TO KILL MORE MEN?
FOR SURE. I MEAN, NOT EXCLUSIVELY. BUT IT'S SAFE TO SAY THAT'S KINDA THEIR THING, THE DOWNTRODDING--
WHEN DO WE START?

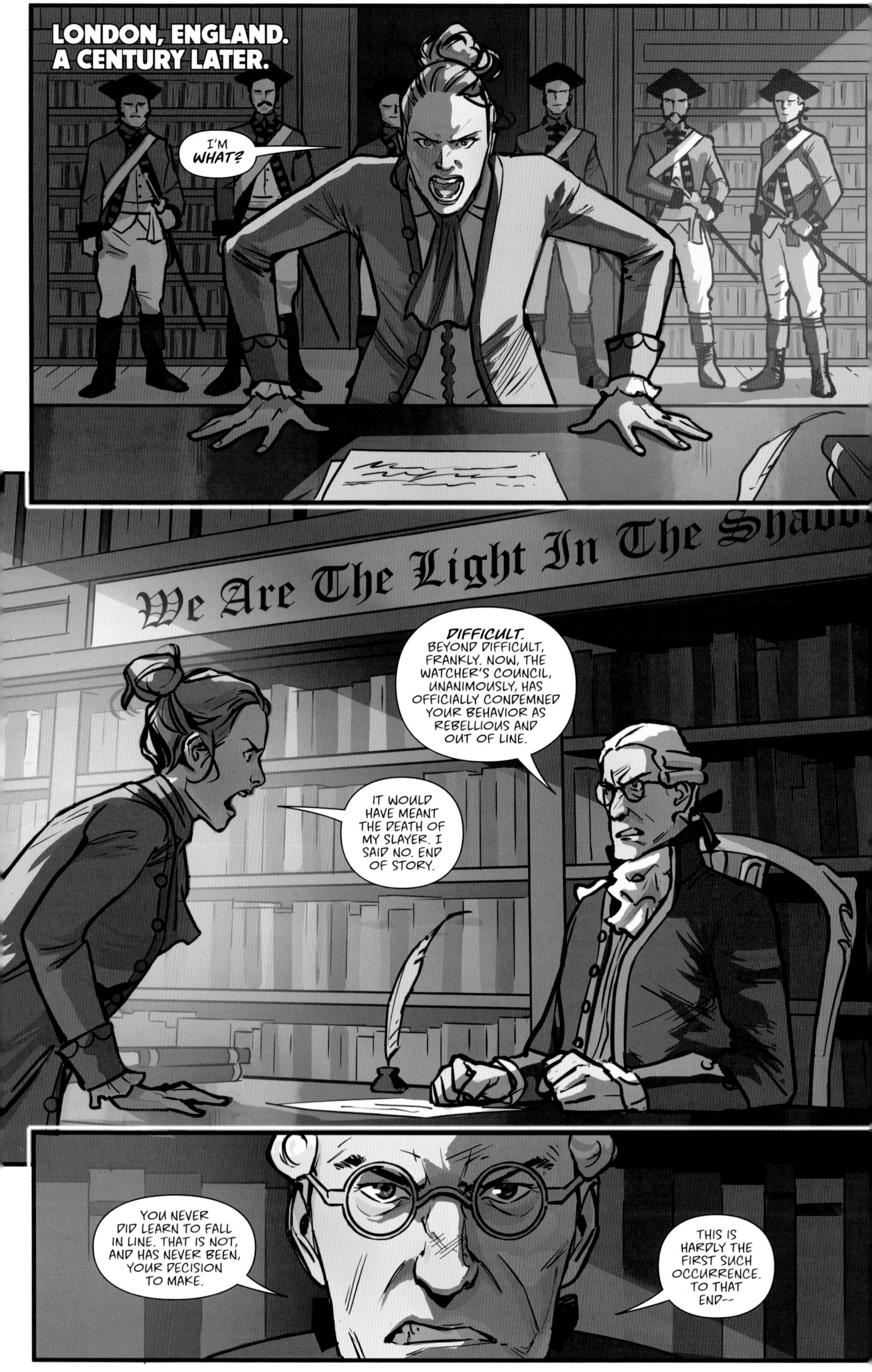
LONDON, ENGLAND. A CENTURY LATER.
I'M WHAT?
We Are The Light In The Shado
DIFFICULT. BEYOND DIFFICULT, FRANKLY. NOW, THE WATCHER'S COUNCIL, UNANIMOUSLY, HAS OFFICIALLY CONDEMNED YOUR BEHAVIOR AS REBELLIOUS AND OUT OF LINE.
IT WOULD HAVE MEANT THE DEATH OF MY SLAYER. I SAID NO. END OF STORY.
YOU NEVER DID LEARN TO FALL IN LINE. THAT IS NOT, AND HAS NEVER BEEN, YOUR DECISION TO MAKE.
THIS IS HARDLY THE FIRST SUCH OCCURRENCE. TO THAT END--

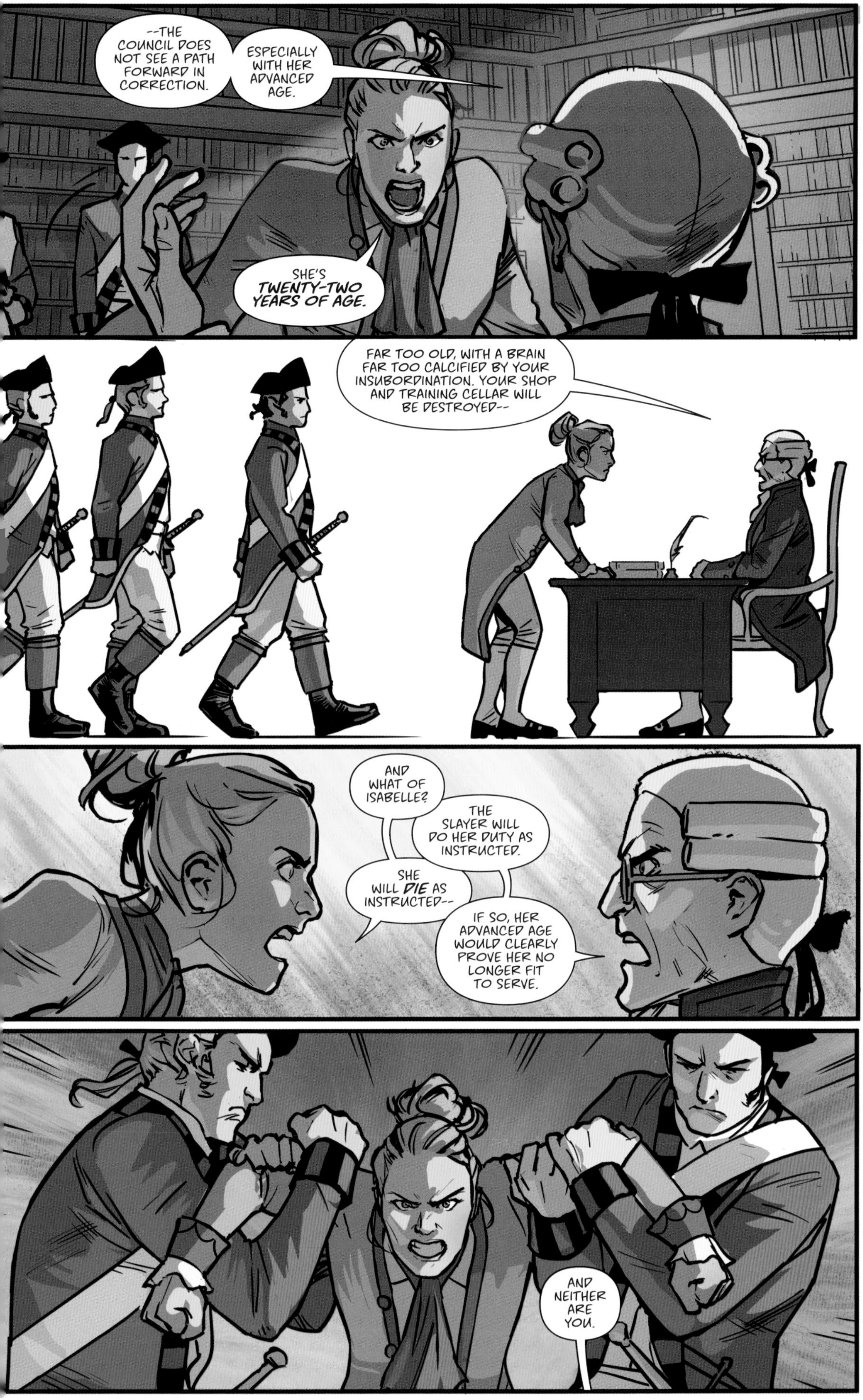
--THE COUNCIL DOES NOT SEE A PATH FORWARD IN CORRECTION.
ESPECIALLY WITH HER ADVANCED AGE.
SHE'S *TWENTY-TWO YEARS OF AGE.*
FAR TOO OLD, WITH A BRAIN FAR TOO CALCIFIED BY YOUR INSUBORDINATION. YOUR SHOP AND TRAINING CELLAR WILL BE DESTROYED--
AND WHAT OF ISABELLE?
THE SLAYER WILL DO HER DUTY AS INSTRUCTED.
SHE WILL *DIE* AS INSTRUCTED--
IF SO, HER ADVANCED AGE WOULD CLEARLY PROVE HER NO LONGER FIT TO SERVE.
AND NEITHER ARE YOU.

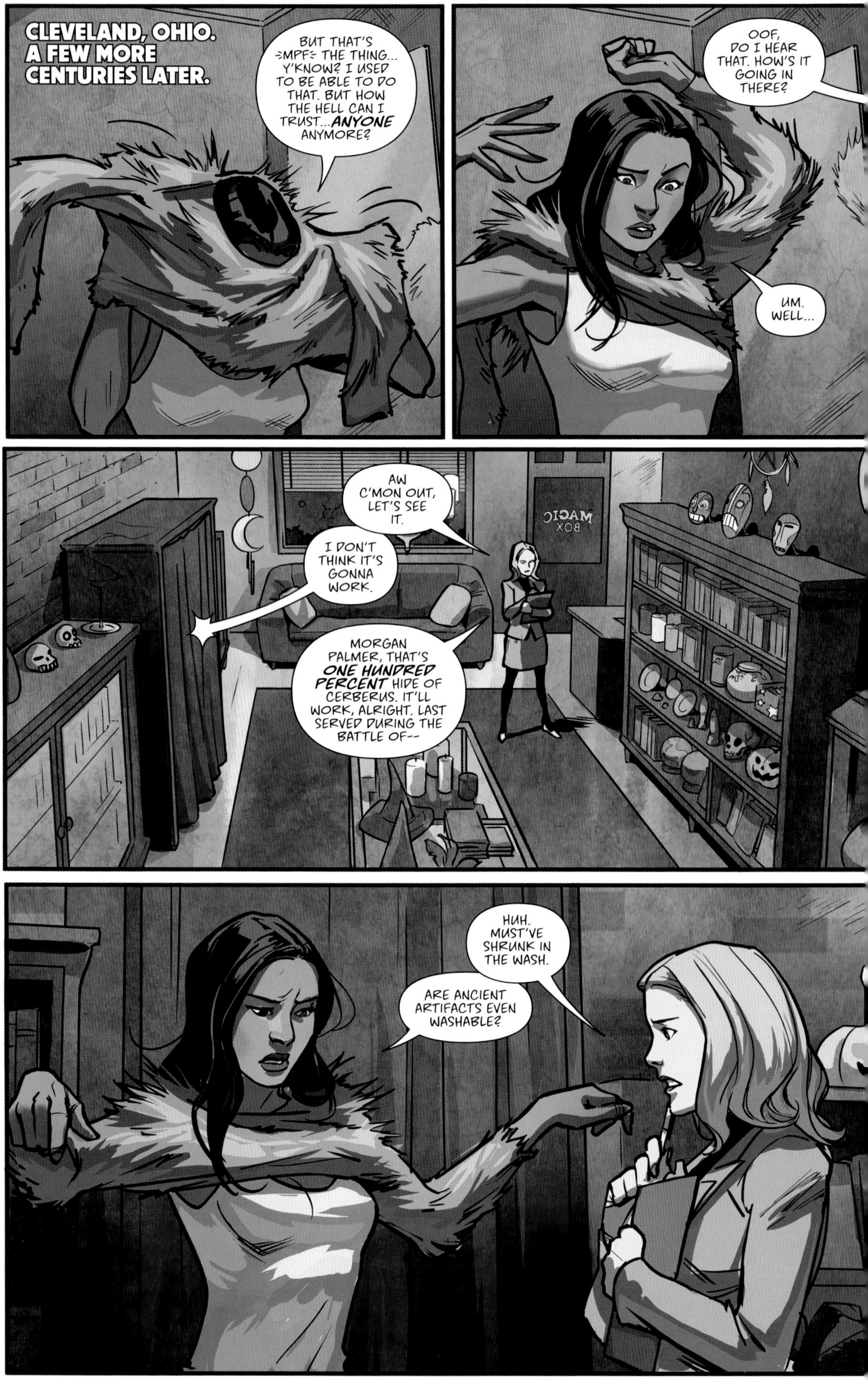

CLEVELAND, OHIO. A FEW MORE CENTURIES LATER.
BUT THAT'S =MPF= THE THING... Y'KNOW? I USED TO BE ABLE TO DO THAT. BUT HOW THE HELL CAN I TRUST... ANYONE ANYMORE?
OOF, DO I HEAR THAT. HOW'S IT GOING IN THERE?
UM. WELL...
AW C'MON OUT, LET'S SEE IT.
I DON'T THINK IT'S GONNA WORK.
MORGAN PALMER, THAT'S ONE HUNDRED PERCENT HIDE OF CERBERUS. IT'LL WORK, ALRIGHT. LAST SERVED DURING THE BATTLE OF--
MAGIC BOX
HUH. MUST'VE SHRUNK IN THE WASH.
ARE ANCIENT ARTIFACTS EVEN WASHABLE?

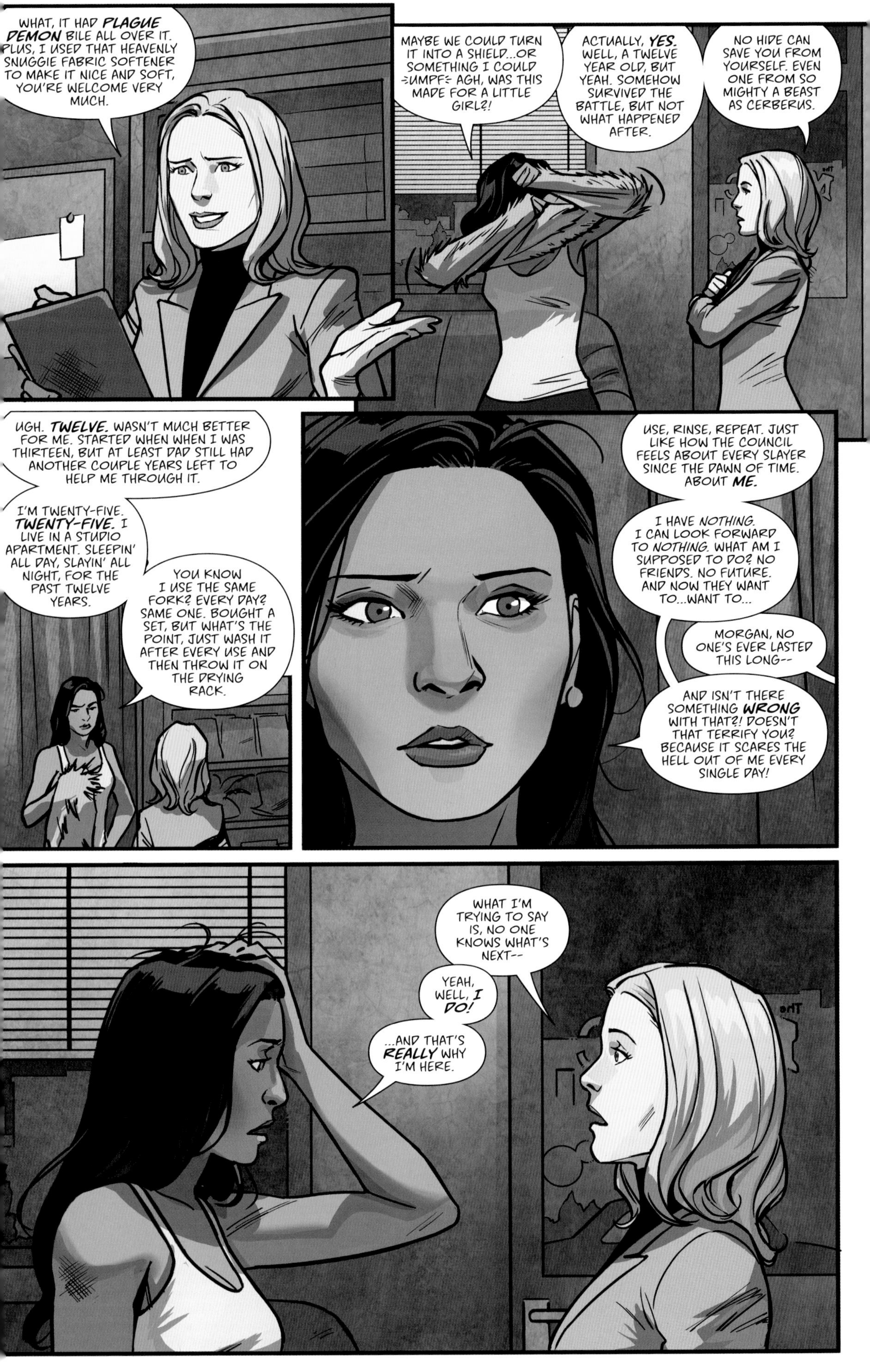
WHAT, IT HAD PLAGUE DEMON BILE ALL OVER IT. PLUS, I USED THAT HEAVENLY SNUGGIE FABRIC SOFTENER TO MAKE IT NICE AND SOFT, YOU'RE WELCOME VERY MUCH.
MAYBE WE COULD TURN IT INTO A SHIELD...OR SOMETHING I COULD =UMPF= AGH, WAS THIS MADE FOR A LITTLE GIRL?!
ACTUALLY, YES. WELL, A TWELVE YEAR OLD, BUT YEAH. SOMEHOW SURVIVED THE BATTLE, BUT NOT WHAT HAPPENED AFTER.
NO HIDE CAN SAVE YOU FROM YOURSELF. EVEN ONE FROM SO MIGHTY A BEAST AS CERBERUS.
UGH. TWELVE. WASN'T MUCH BETTER FOR ME. STARTED WHEN WHEN I WAS THIRTEEN, BUT AT LEAST DAD STILL HAD ANOTHER COUPLE YEARS LEFT TO HELP ME THROUGH IT.
I'M TWENTY-FIVE. TWENTY-FIVE. I LIVE IN A STUDIO APARTMENT. SLEEPIN' ALL DAY, SLAYIN' ALL NIGHT, FOR THE PAST TWELVE YEARS.
YOU KNOW I USE THE SAME FORK? EVERY DAY? SAME ONE. BOUGHT A SET, BUT WHAT'S THE POINT, JUST WASH IT AFTER EVERY USE AND THEN THROW IT ON THE DRYING RACK.
USE, RINSE, REPEAT. JUST LIKE HOW THE COUNCIL FEELS ABOUT EVERY SLAYER SINCE THE DAWN OF TIME. ABOUT ME.
I HAVE NOTHING. I CAN LOOK FORWARD TO NOTHING. WHAT AM I SUPPOSED TO DO? NO FRIENDS. NO FUTURE. AND NOW THEY WANT TO...WANT TO...
MORGAN, NO ONE'S EVER LASTED THIS LONG--
AND ISN'T THERE SOMETHING WRONG WITH THAT?! DOESN'T THAT TERRIFY YOU? BECAUSE IT SCARES THE HELL OUT OF ME EVERY SINGLE DAY!
WHAT I'M TRYING TO SAY IS, NO ONE KNOWS WHAT'S NEXT--
YEAH, WELL, I DO!
...AND THAT'S REALLY WHY I'M HERE.

THEY WANT TO KILL ME.

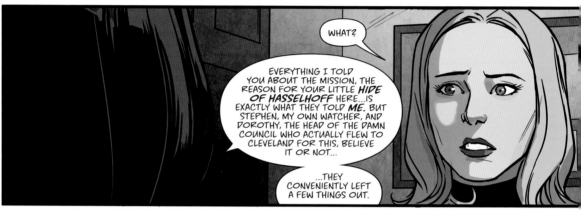

WHAT?

EVERYTHING I TOLD YOU ABOUT THE MISSION, THE REASON FOR YOUR LITTLE *HIDE OF HASSELHOFF* HERE...IS EXACTLY WHAT THEY TOLD *ME*. BUT STEPHEN, MY OWN WATCHER, AND DOROTHY, THE HEAD OF THE DAMN COUNCIL WHO ACTUALLY FLEW TO CLEVELAND FOR THIS, BELIEVE IT OR NOT...

...THEY CONVENIENTLY LEFT A FEW THINGS OUT.

IT'S NOT A VAMP NEST. NOT JUST A NEST, I MEAN. THERE'S A DEMON THAT RUNS IT, ONE THAT'S ALL ABOUT THE CHAOS MAGICK AND HE'S SUPPOSED TO MAKE ME...*VANISH*. RIGHT INTO THIN AIR. LIKE I NEVER EXISTED. LIKE IT'S ALL BEEN PLANNED.

THEY THOUGHT THEY WERE ALONE. THEY WEREN'T. I FOLLOWED. I HEARD EVERYTHING. AND IT WAS STEPHEN'S IDEA. THEY WANT TO KILL ME AND MAKE IT LOOK LIKE IT WAS JUST...PART OF THE *JOB*.

JUST...WHAT, *FULFILLING MY PURPOSE?* I MEAN, DO SLAYERS EVEN GET TO HAVE FUTURES? OTHER THAN SLAY AND TRY TO STAY ALIVE.

I GUESS YOU JUST CAN'T STOP FATE, HUH? *HELL* ALWAYS CATCHES UP TO YOU.

THEY'LL JUST SAY MORGAN MUST'VE SLIPPED IN HER ANCIENT CRONE AGE OF HER *MID-TWENTIES.* SO THEY CAN GET SOMEONE ELSE. SOMEONE NEW. YOUNG. SOMEONE WHO DOESN'T AS QUESTIONS. SOMEONE WHO ISN'T...ISN'T...

DIFFICULT.

...SOMEONE WHO ISN'T *ME.*

YEAH.

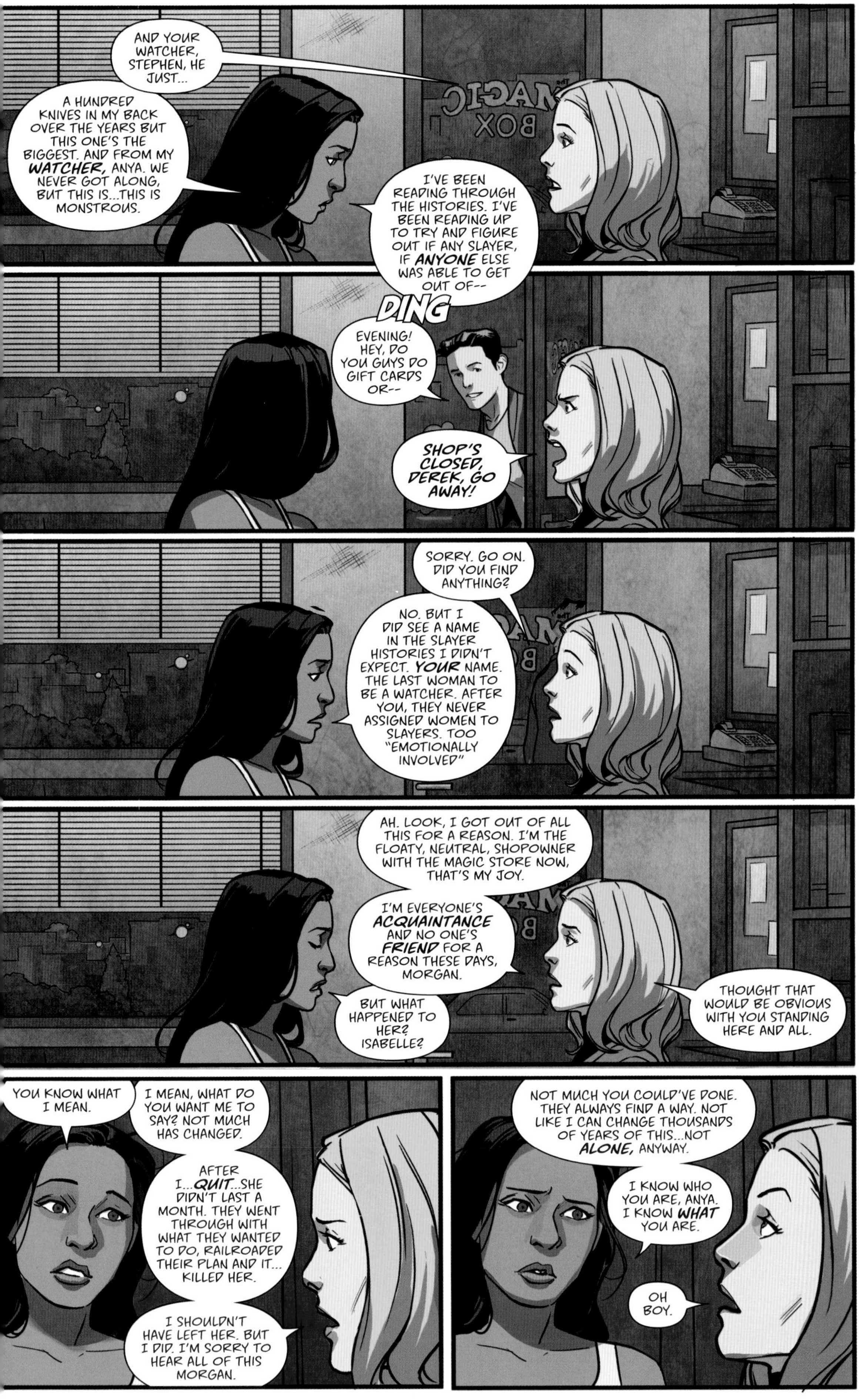
AND YOUR WATCHER, STEPHEN, HE JUST...
A HUNDRED KNIVES IN MY BACK OVER THE YEARS BUT THIS ONE'S THE BIGGEST. AND FROM MY WATCHER, ANYA. WE NEVER GOT ALONG, BUT THIS IS...THIS IS MONSTROUS.
MAGIC BOX
I'VE BEEN READING THROUGH THE HISTORIES. I'VE BEEN READING UP TO TRY AND FIGURE OUT IF ANY SLAYER, IF ANYONE ELSE WAS ABLE TO GET OUT OF--
DING
EVENING! HEY, DO YOU GUYS DO GIFT CARDS OR--
SHOP'S CLOSED, DEREK, GO AWAY!
SORRY. GO ON. DID YOU FIND ANYTHING?
NO. BUT I DID SEE A NAME IN THE SLAYER HISTORIES I DIDN'T EXPECT. YOUR NAME. THE LAST WOMAN TO BE A WATCHER. AFTER YOU, THEY NEVER ASSIGNED WOMEN TO SLAYERS. TOO "EMOTIONALLY INVOLVED"
AH. LOOK, I GOT OUT OF ALL THIS FOR A REASON. I'M THE FLOATY, NEUTRAL, SHOPOWNER WITH THE MAGIC STORE NOW, THAT'S MY JOY.
I'M EVERYONE'S ACQUAINTANCE AND NO ONE'S FRIEND FOR A REASON THESE DAYS, MORGAN.
BUT WHAT HAPPENED TO HER? ISABELLE?
THOUGHT THAT WOULD BE OBVIOUS WITH YOU STANDING HERE AND ALL.
YOU KNOW WHAT I MEAN.
I MEAN, WHAT DO YOU WANT ME TO SAY? NOT MUCH HAS CHANGED.
AFTER I...QUIT...SHE DIDN'T LAST A MONTH. THEY WENT THROUGH WITH WHAT THEY WANTED TO DO, RAILROADED THEIR PLAN AND IT... KILLED HER.
I SHOULDN'T HAVE LEFT HER. BUT I DID. I'M SORRY TO HEAR ALL OF THIS MORGAN.
NOT MUCH YOU COULD'VE DONE. THEY ALWAYS FIND A WAY. NOT LIKE I CAN CHANGE THOUSANDS OF YEARS OF THIS...NOT ALONE, ANYWAY.
I KNOW WHO YOU ARE, ANYA. I KNOW WHAT YOU ARE.
OH BOY.

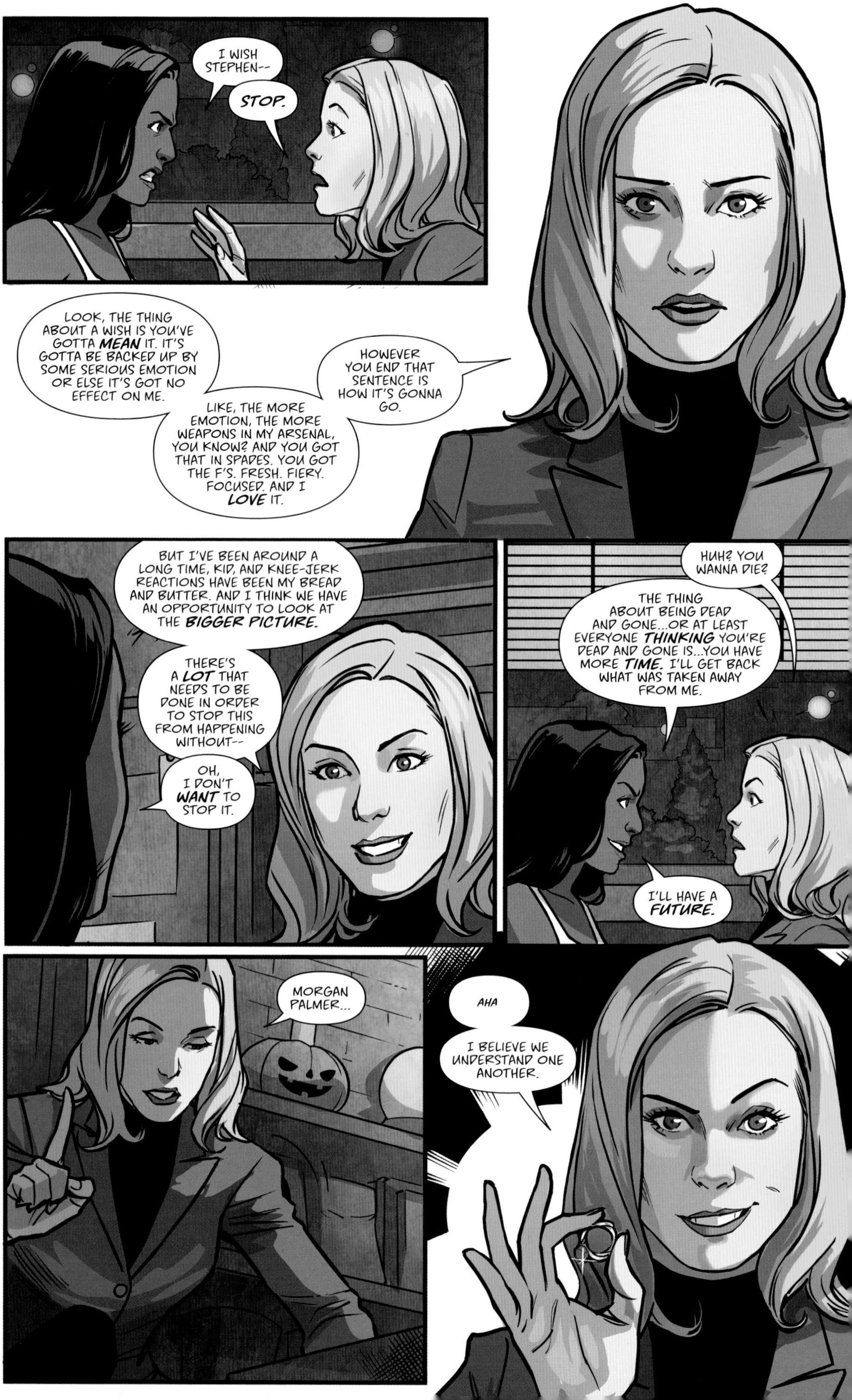
I WISH STEPHEN--
STOP.
LOOK, THE THING ABOUT A WISH IS YOU'VE GOTTA MEAN IT. IT'S GOTTA BE BACKED UP BY SOME SERIOUS EMOTION OR ELSE IT'S GOT NO EFFECT ON ME.
LIKE, THE MORE EMOTION, THE MORE WEAPONS IN MY ARSENAL, YOU KNOW? AND YOU GOT THAT IN SPADES. YOU GOT THE F'S. FRESH. FIERY. FOCUSED. AND I LOVE IT.
HOWEVER YOU END THAT SENTENCE IS HOW IT'S GONNA GO.
BUT I'VE BEEN AROUND A LONG TIME, KID, AND KNEE-JERK REACTIONS HAVE BEEN MY BREAD AND BUTTER. AND I THINK WE HAVE AN OPPORTUNITY TO LOOK AT THE BIGGER PICTURE.
THERE'S A LOT THAT NEEDS TO BE DONE IN ORDER TO STOP THIS FROM HAPPENING WITHOUT--
OH, I DON'T WANT TO STOP IT.
HUH? YOU WANNA DIE?
THE THING ABOUT BEING DEAD AND GONE...OR AT LEAST EVERYONE THINKING YOU'RE DEAD AND GONE IS...YOU HAVE MORE TIME. I'LL GET BACK WHAT WAS TAKEN AWAY FROM ME.
I'LL HAVE A FUTURE.
MORGAN PALMER...
AHA
I BELIEVE WE UNDERSTAND ONE ANOTHER.

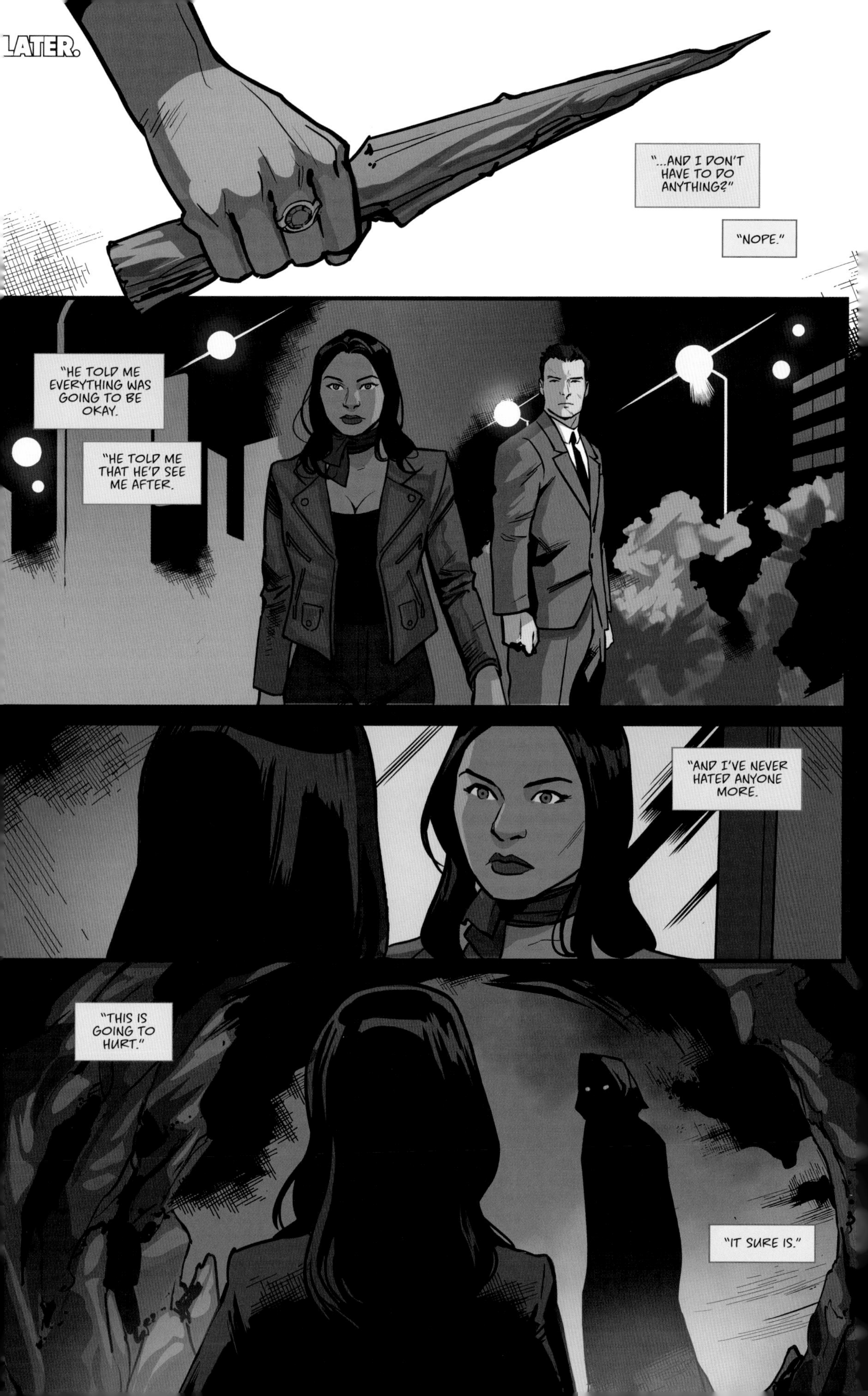
LATER.
"...AND I DON'T HAVE TO DO ANYTHING?"
"NOPE."
"HE TOLD ME EVERYTHING WAS GOING TO BE OKAY.
"HE TOLD ME THAT HE'D SEE ME AFTER.
"AND I'VE NEVER HATED ANYONE MORE.
"THIS IS GOING TO HURT."
"IT SURE IS."

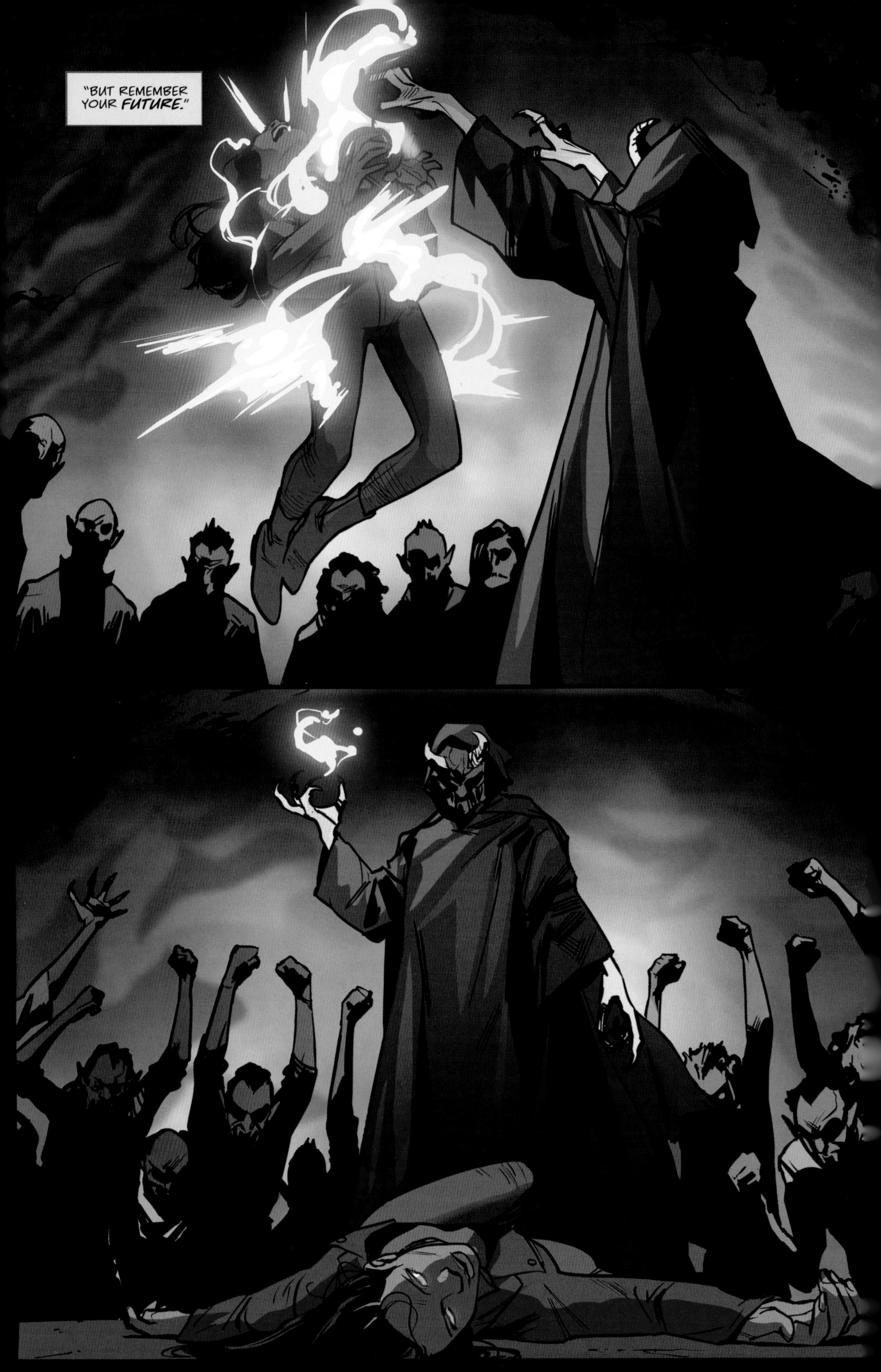
"BUT REMEMBER YOUR FUTURE."

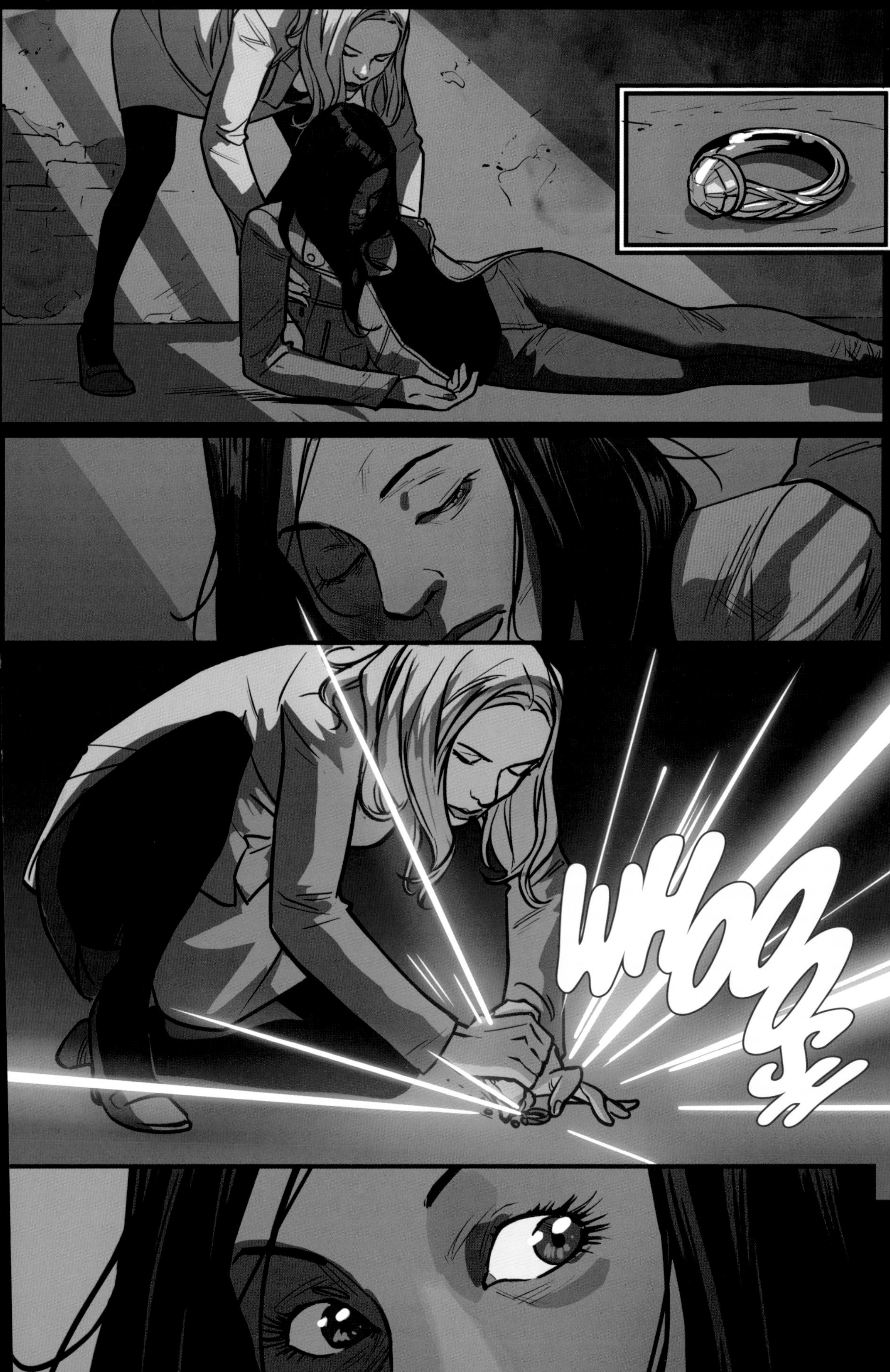
WHOOSH

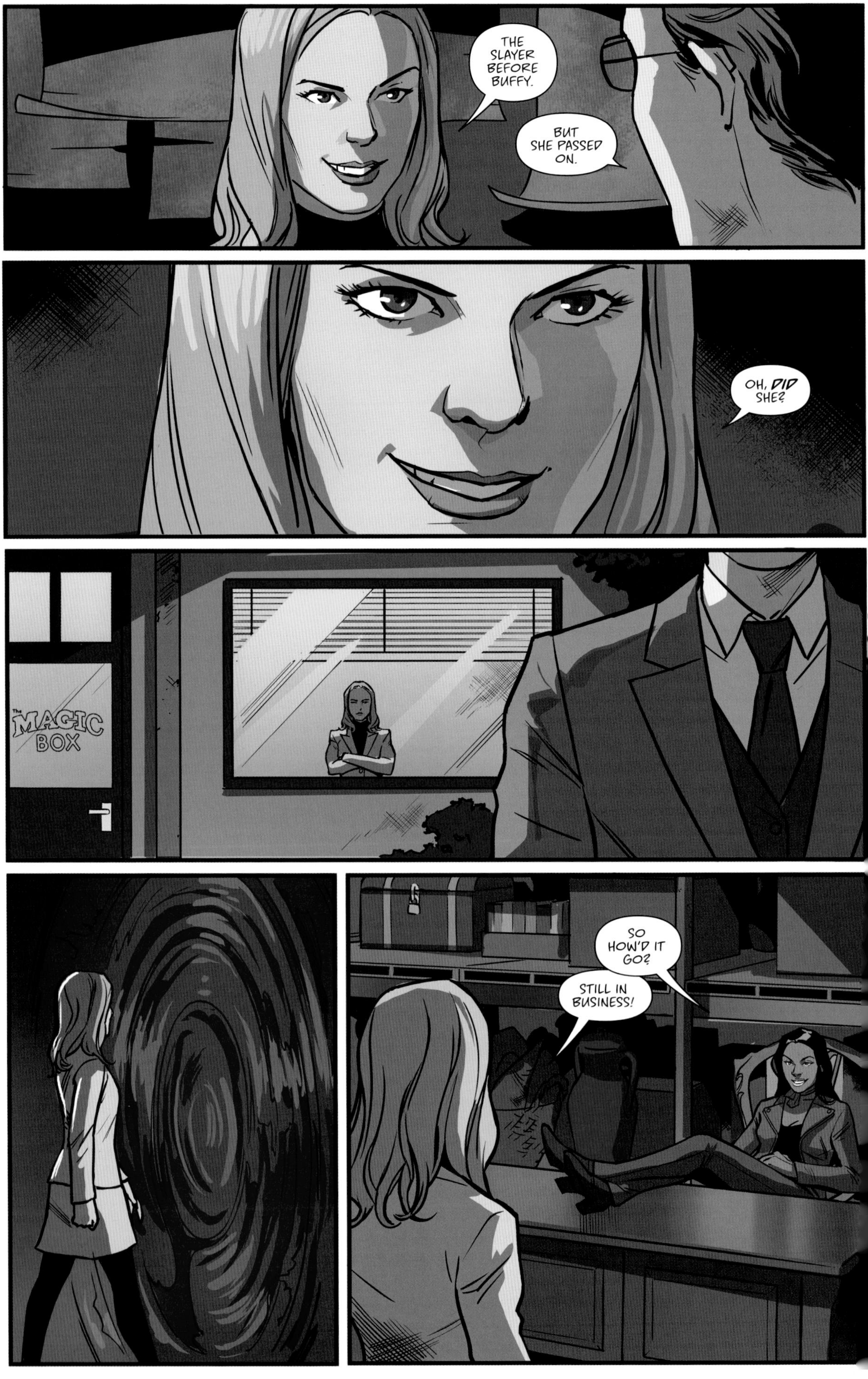
THE SLAYER BEFORE BUFFY.
BUT SHE PASSED ON.
OH, DID SHE?
The MAGIC BOX
SO HOW'D IT GO?
STILL IN BUSINESS!

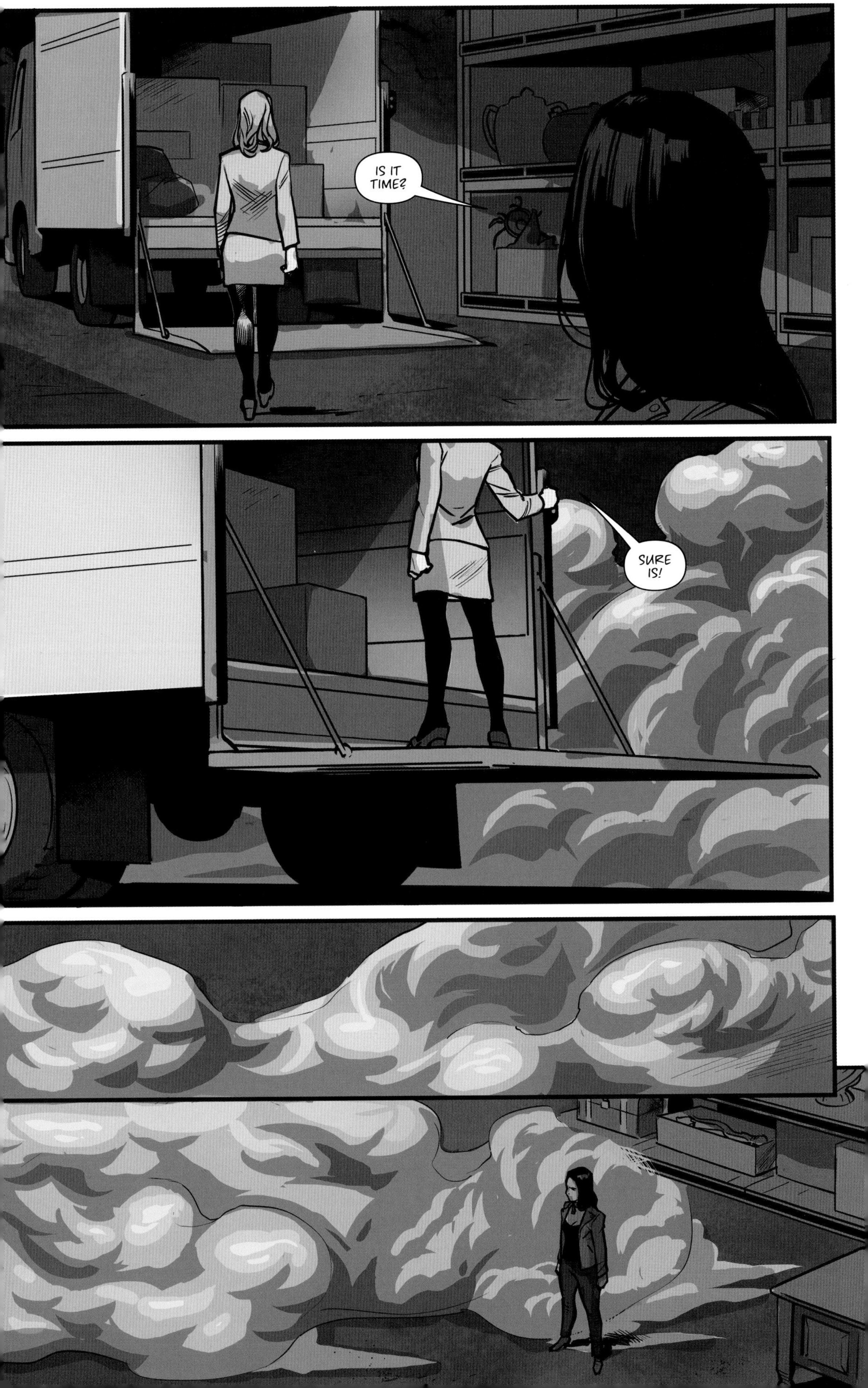
IS IT TIME?
SURE IS!

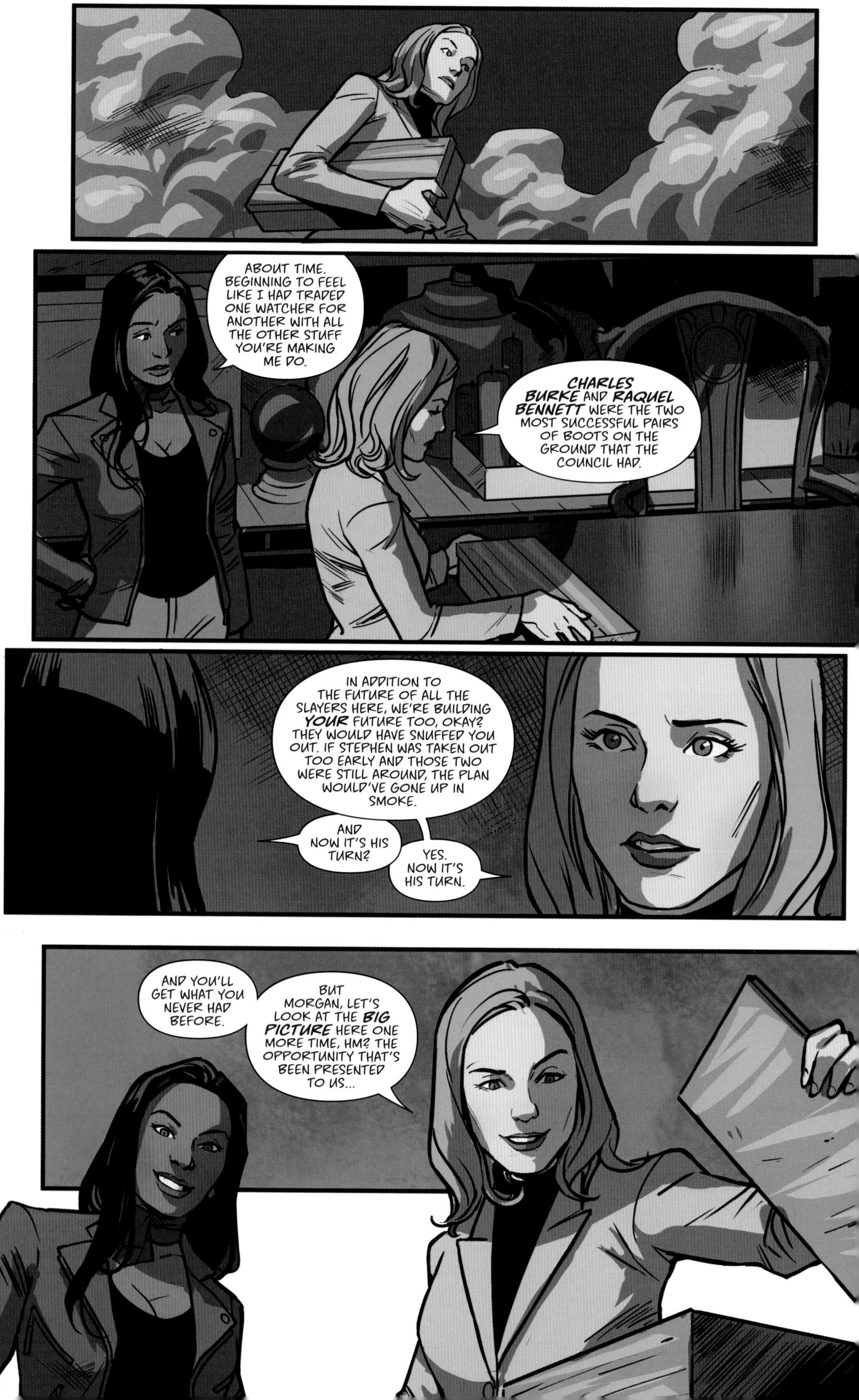
ABOUT TIME. BEGINNING TO FEEL LIKE I HAD TRADED ONE WATCHER FOR ANOTHER WITH ALL THE OTHER STUFF YOU'RE MAKING ME DO.
CHARLES BURKE AND RAQUEL BENNETT WERE THE TWO MOST SUCCESSFUL PAIRS OF BOOTS ON THE GROUND THAT THE COUNCIL HAD.
IN ADDITION TO THE FUTURE OF ALL THE SLAYERS HERE, WE'RE BUILDING YOUR FUTURE TOO, OKAY? THEY WOULD HAVE SNUFFED YOU OUT. IF STEPHEN WAS TAKEN OUT TOO EARLY AND THOSE TWO WERE STILL AROUND, THE PLAN WOULD'VE GONE UP IN SMOKE.
AND NOW IT'S HIS TURN?
YES. NOW IT'S HIS TURN.
AND YOU'LL GET WHAT YOU NEVER HAD BEFORE.
BUT MORGAN, LET'S LOOK AT THE BIG PICTURE HERE ONE MORE TIME, HM? THE OPPORTUNITY THAT'S BEEN PRESENTED TO US...

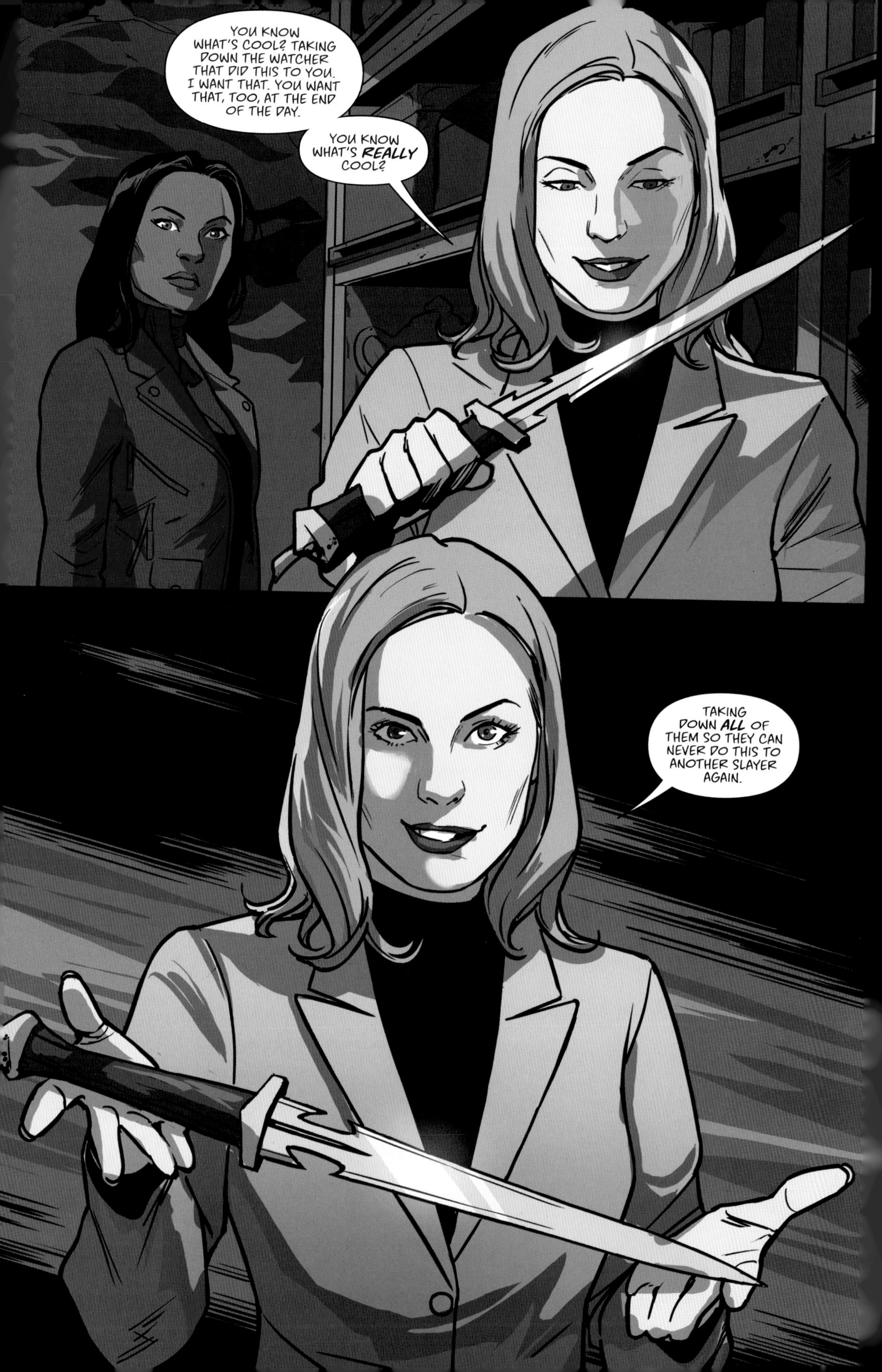
YOU KNOW WHAT'S COOL? TAKING DOWN THE WATCHER THAT DID THIS TO YOU. I WANT THAT. YOU WANT THAT, TOO, AT THE END OF THE DAY.
YOU KNOW WHAT'S REALLY COOL?
TAKING DOWN ALL OF THEM SO THEY CAN NEVER DO THIS TO ANOTHER SLAYER AGAIN.

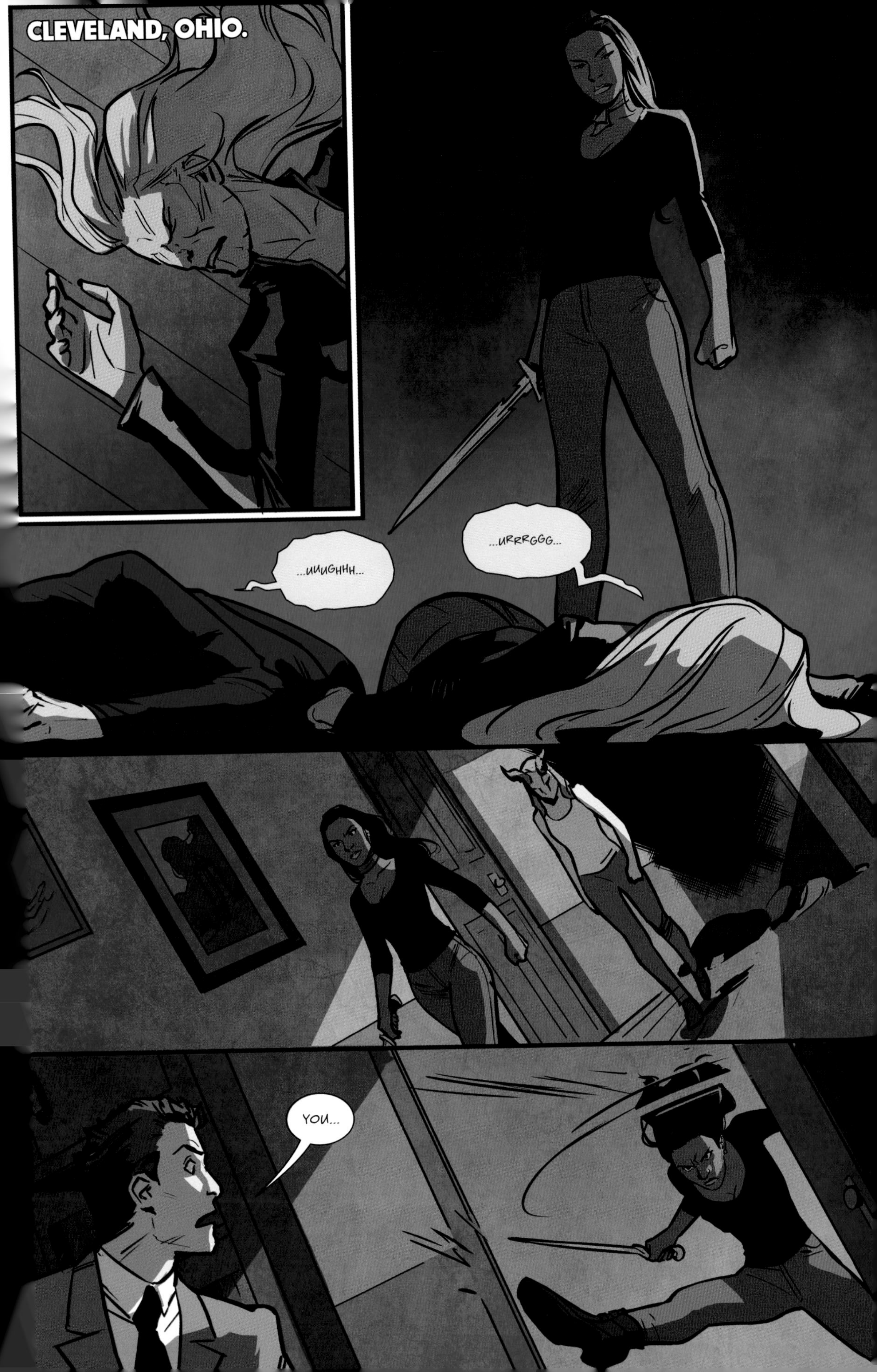

CLEVELAND, OHIO.
...UUUGHHH...
...URRRGGG...
YOU...

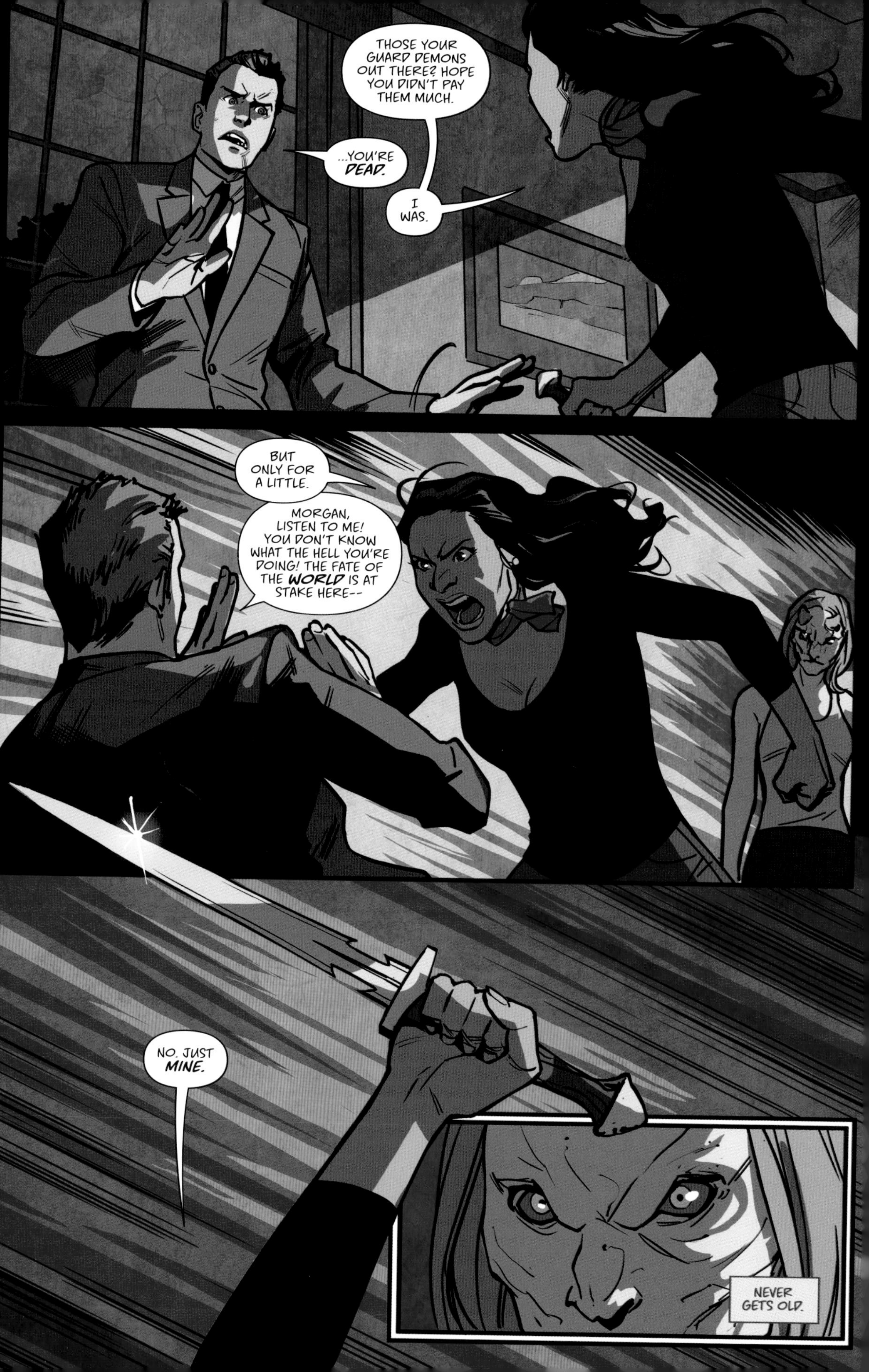
THOSE YOUR GUARD DEMONS OUT THERE? HOPE YOU DIDN'T PAY THEM MUCH.
...YOU'RE DEAD.
I WAS.
BUT ONLY FOR A LITTLE.
MORGAN, LISTEN TO ME! YOU DON'T KNOW WHAT THE HELL YOU'RE DOING! THE FATE OF THE WORLD IS AT STAKE HERE--
NO. JUST MINE.
NEVER GETS OLD.

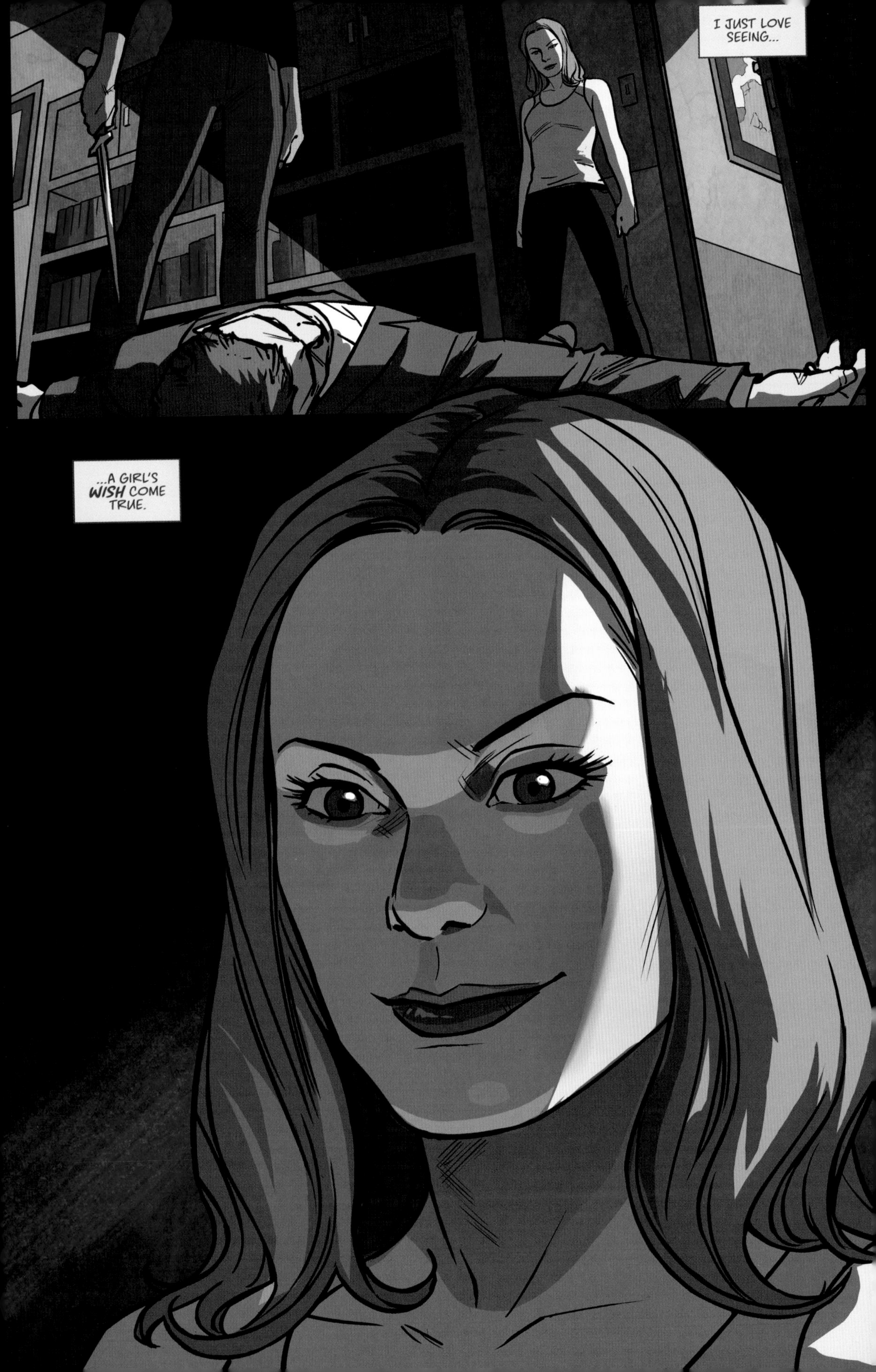
I JUST LOVE SEEING...
...A GIRL'S WISH COME TRUE.

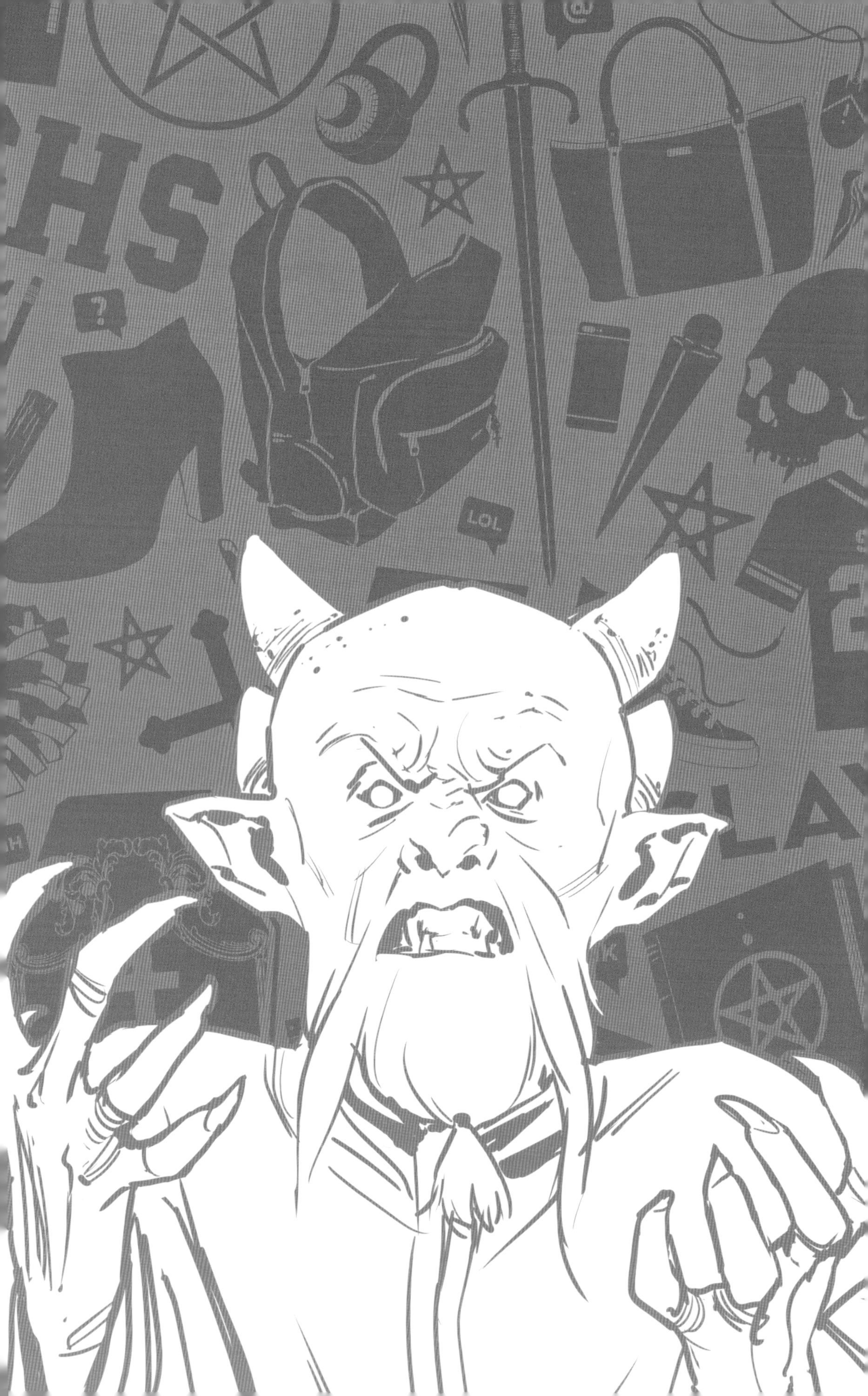
LOL

CHAPTER
TWENTY-TWO

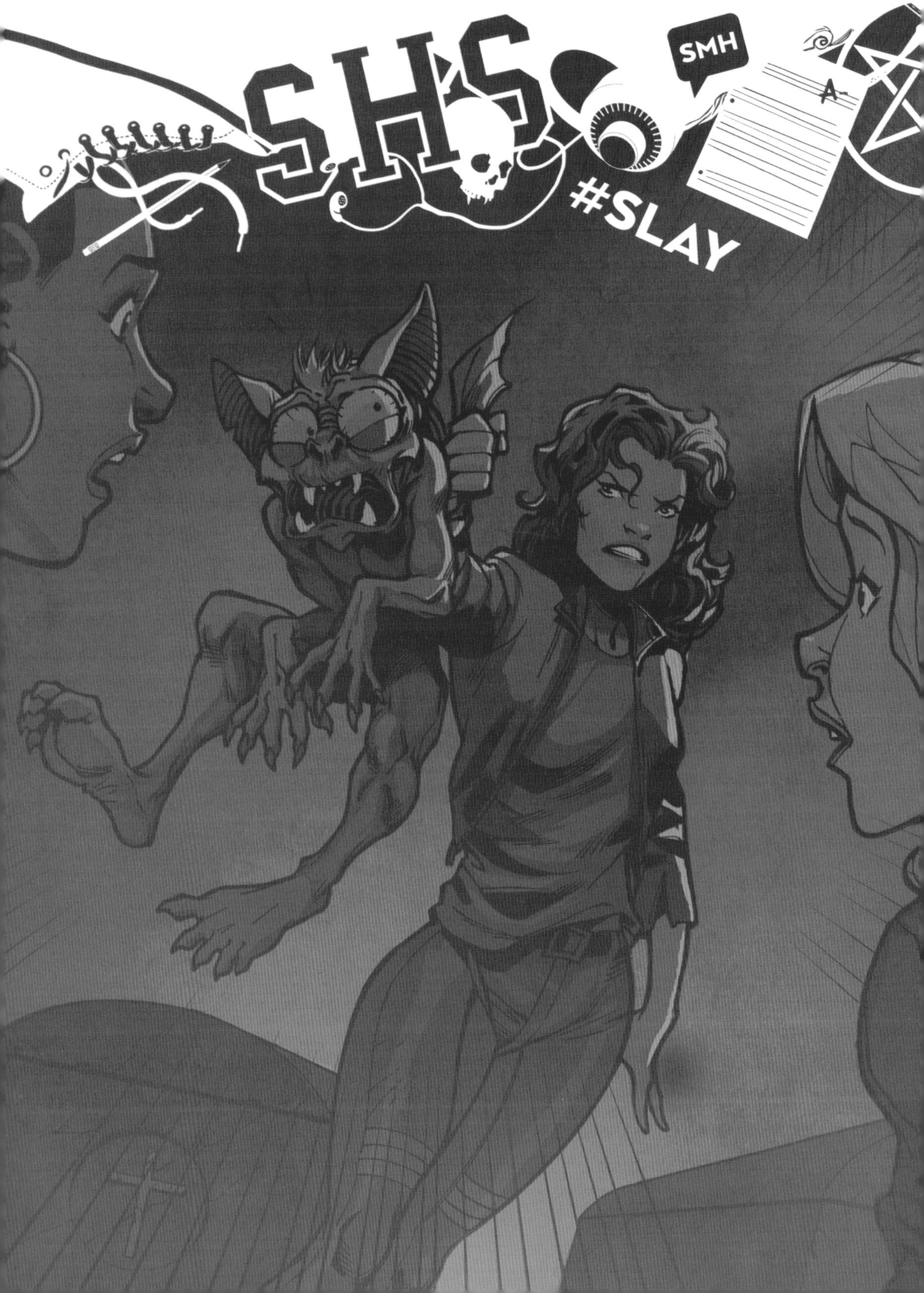

S.H.S.
SMH
#SLAY

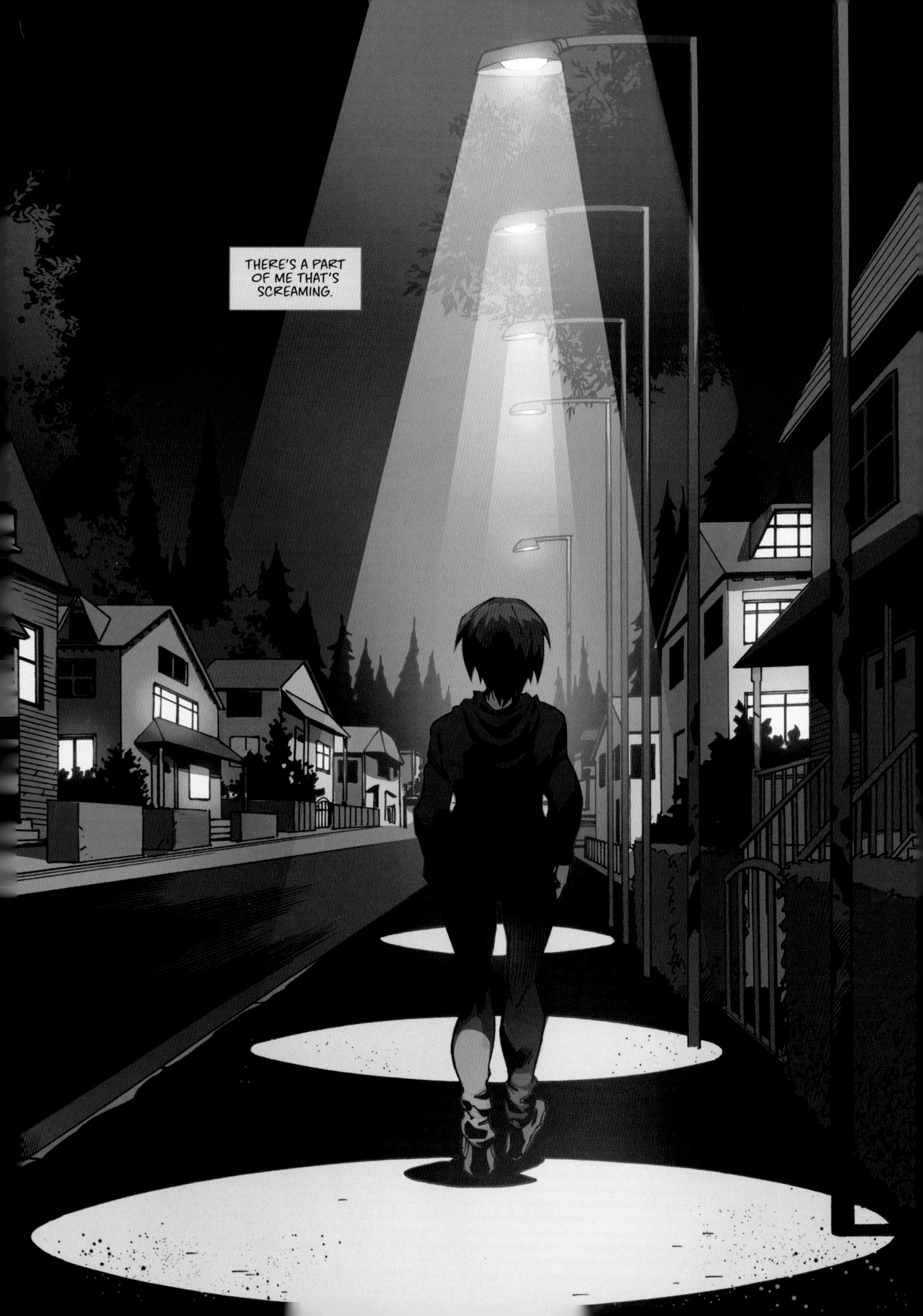
THERE'S A PART OF ME THAT'S SCREAMING.

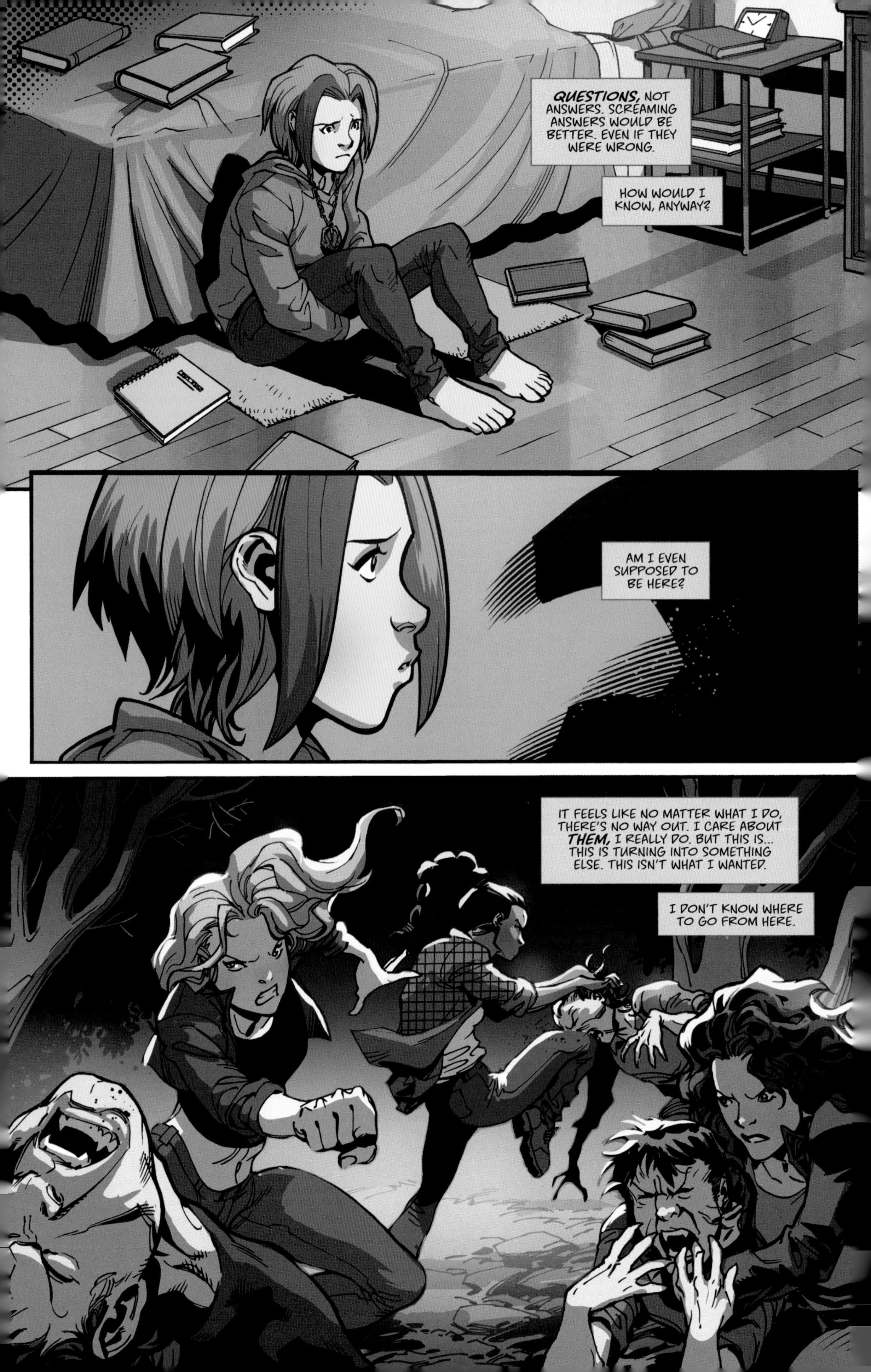
QUESTIONS, NOT ANSWERS. SCREAMING ANSWERS WOULD BE BETTER. EVEN IF THEY WERE WRONG.
HOW WOULD I KNOW, ANYWAY?
AM I EVEN SUPPOSED TO BE HERE?
IT FEELS LIKE NO MATTER WHAT I DO, THERE'S NO WAY OUT. I CARE ABOUT THEM, I REALLY DO. BUT THIS IS... THIS IS TURNING INTO SOMETHING ELSE. THIS ISN'T WHAT I WANTED.
I DON'T KNOW WHERE TO GO FROM HERE.

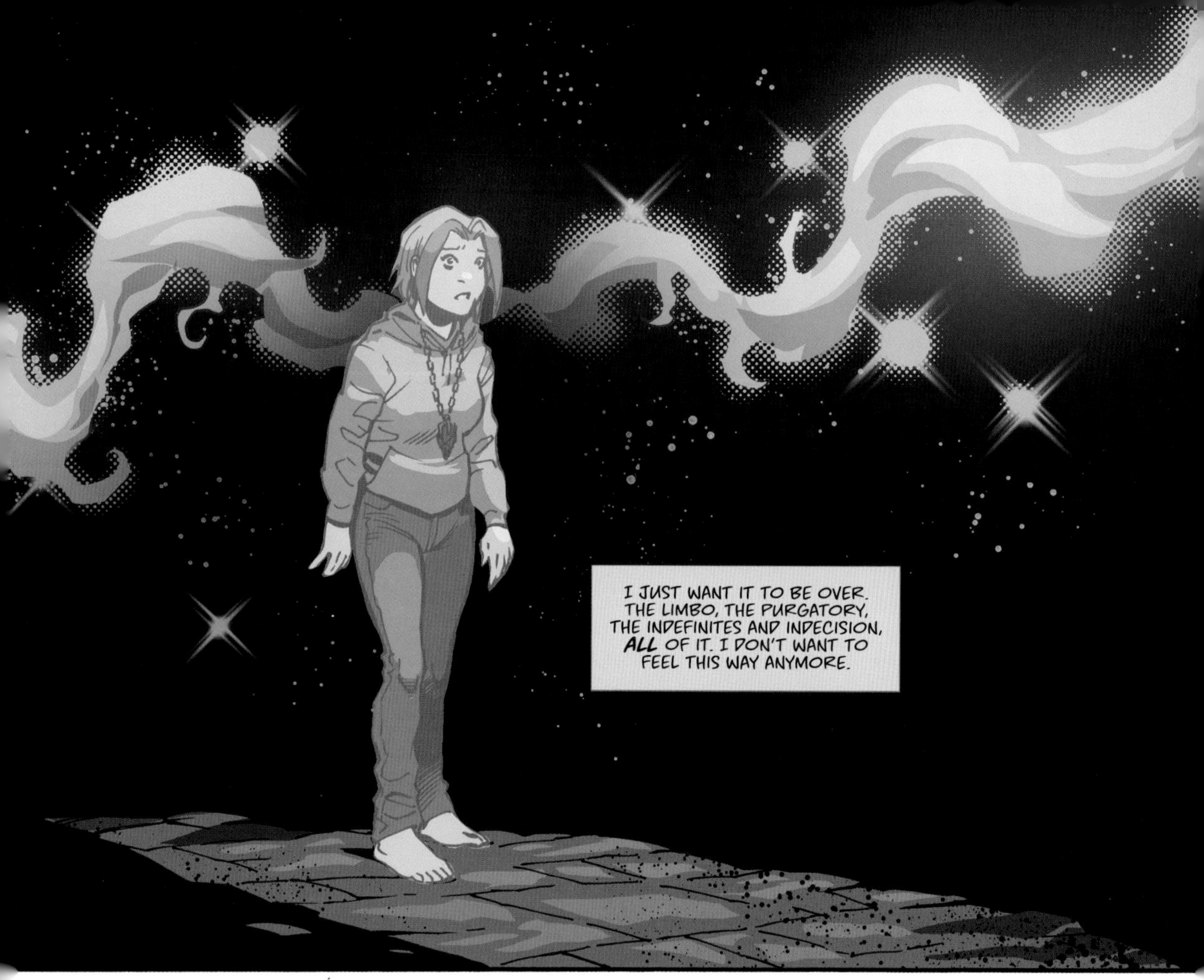
I JUST WANT IT TO BE OVER. THE LIMBO, THE PURGATORY, THE INDEFINITES AND INDECISION, ***ALL*** OF IT. I DON'T WANT TO FEEL THIS WAY ANYMORE.

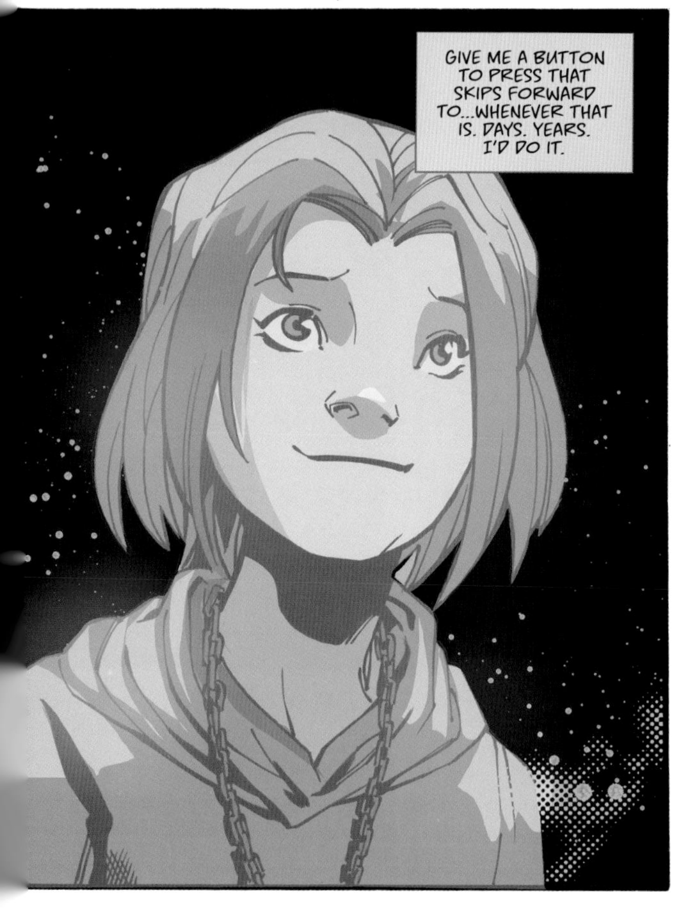
GIVE ME A BUTTON TO PRESS THAT SKIPS FORWARD TO...WHENEVER THAT IS. DAYS. YEARS. I'D DO IT.

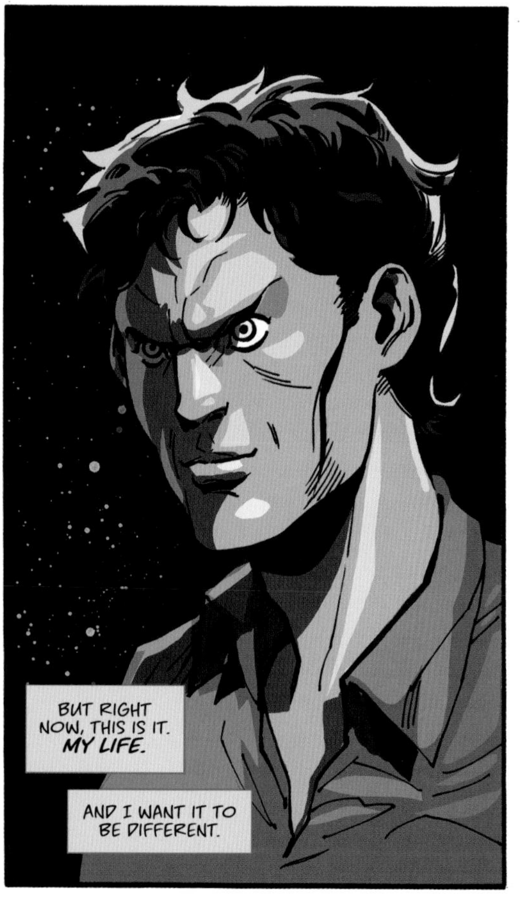
BUT RIGHT NOW, THIS IS IT. ***MY LIFE.***
AND I WANT IT TO BE DIFFERENT.

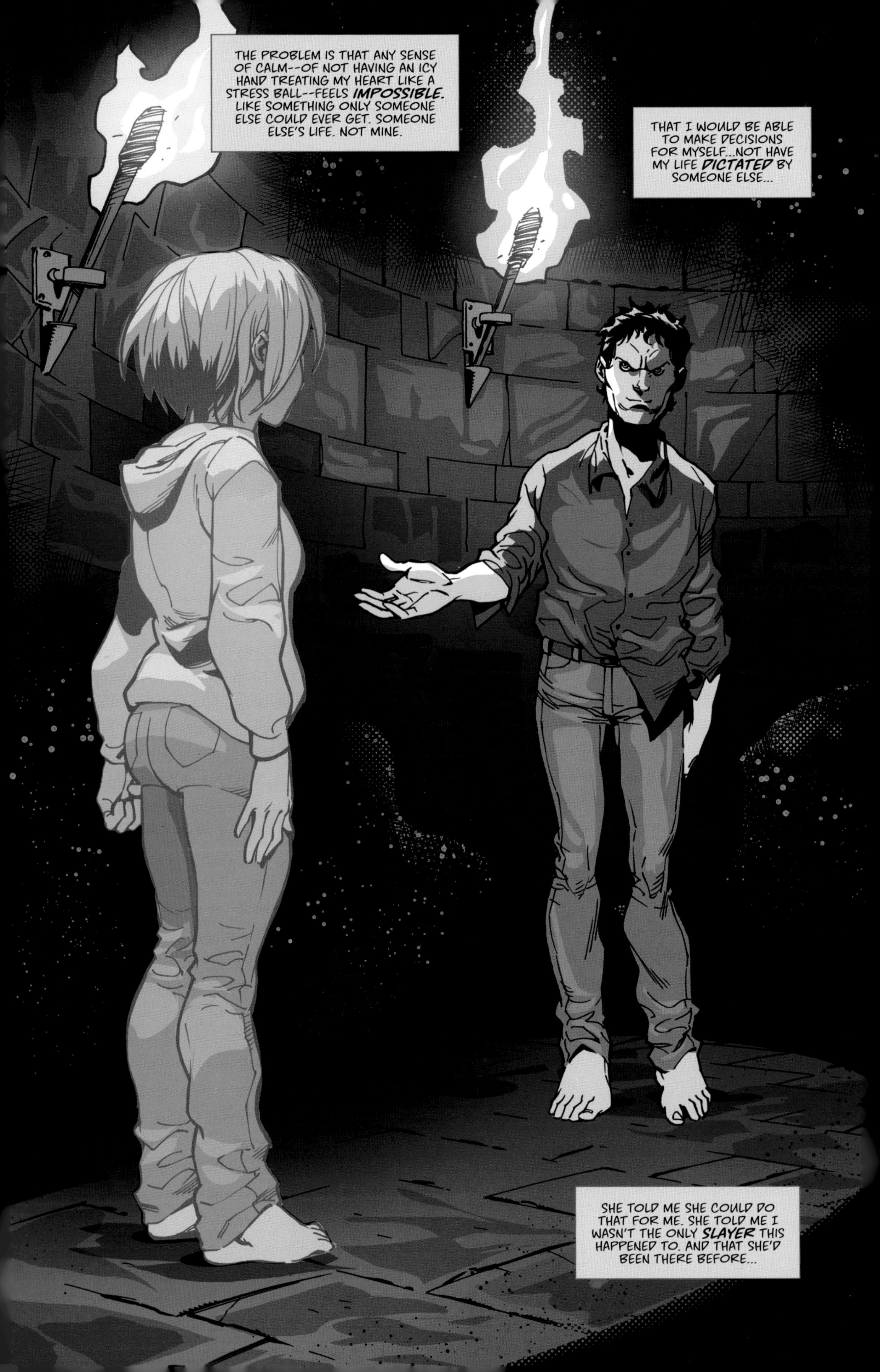
THE PROBLEM IS THAT ANY SENSE OF CALM--OF NOT HAVING AN ICY HAND TREATING MY HEART LIKE A STRESS BALL--FEELS IMPOSSIBLE. LIKE SOMETHING ONLY SOMEONE ELSE COULD EVER GET. SOMEONE ELSE'S LIFE. NOT MINE.
THAT I WOULD BE ABLE TO MAKE DECISIONS FOR MYSELF...NOT HAVE MY LIFE DICTATED BY SOMEONE ELSE...
SHE TOLD ME SHE COULD DO THAT FOR ME. SHE TOLD ME I WASN'T THE ONLY SLAYER THIS HAPPENED TO. AND THAT SHE'D BEEN THERE BEFORE...

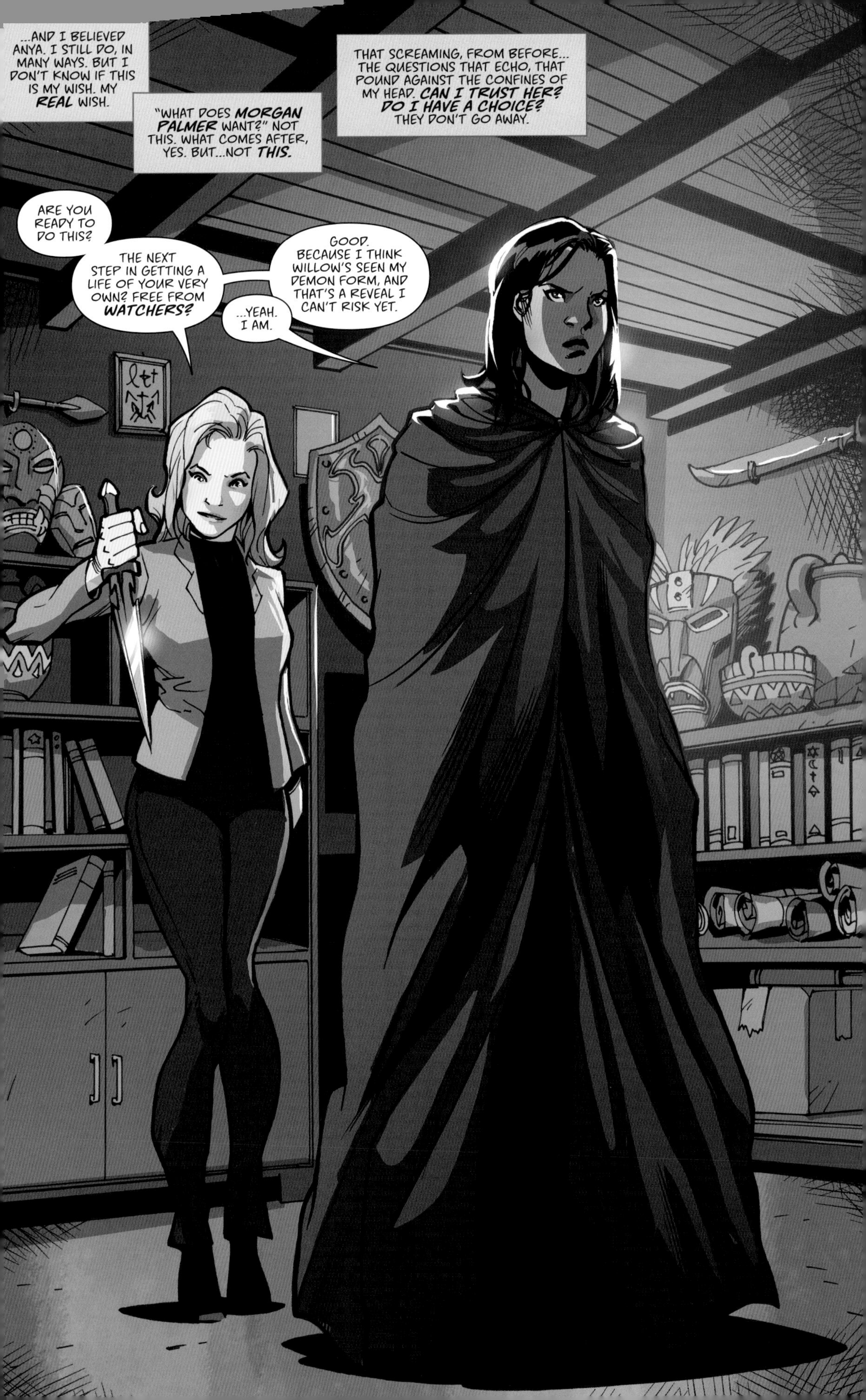
...AND I BELIEVED ANYA. I STILL DO, IN MANY WAYS. BUT I DON'T KNOW IF THIS IS MY WISH. MY REAL WISH.
"WHAT DOES MORGAN PALMER WANT?" NOT THIS. WHAT COMES AFTER, YES. BUT...NOT THIS.
THAT SCREAMING, FROM BEFORE... THE QUESTIONS THAT ECHO, THAT POUND AGAINST THE CONFINES OF MY HEAD. CAN I TRUST HER? DO I HAVE A CHOICE? THEY DON'T GO AWAY.
ARE YOU READY TO DO THIS?
THE NEXT STEP IN GETTING A LIFE OF YOUR VERY OWN? FREE FROM WATCHERS?
...YEAH. I AM.
GOOD. BECAUSE I THINK WILLOW'S SEEN MY DEMON FORM, AND THAT'S A REVEAL I CAN'T RISK YET.

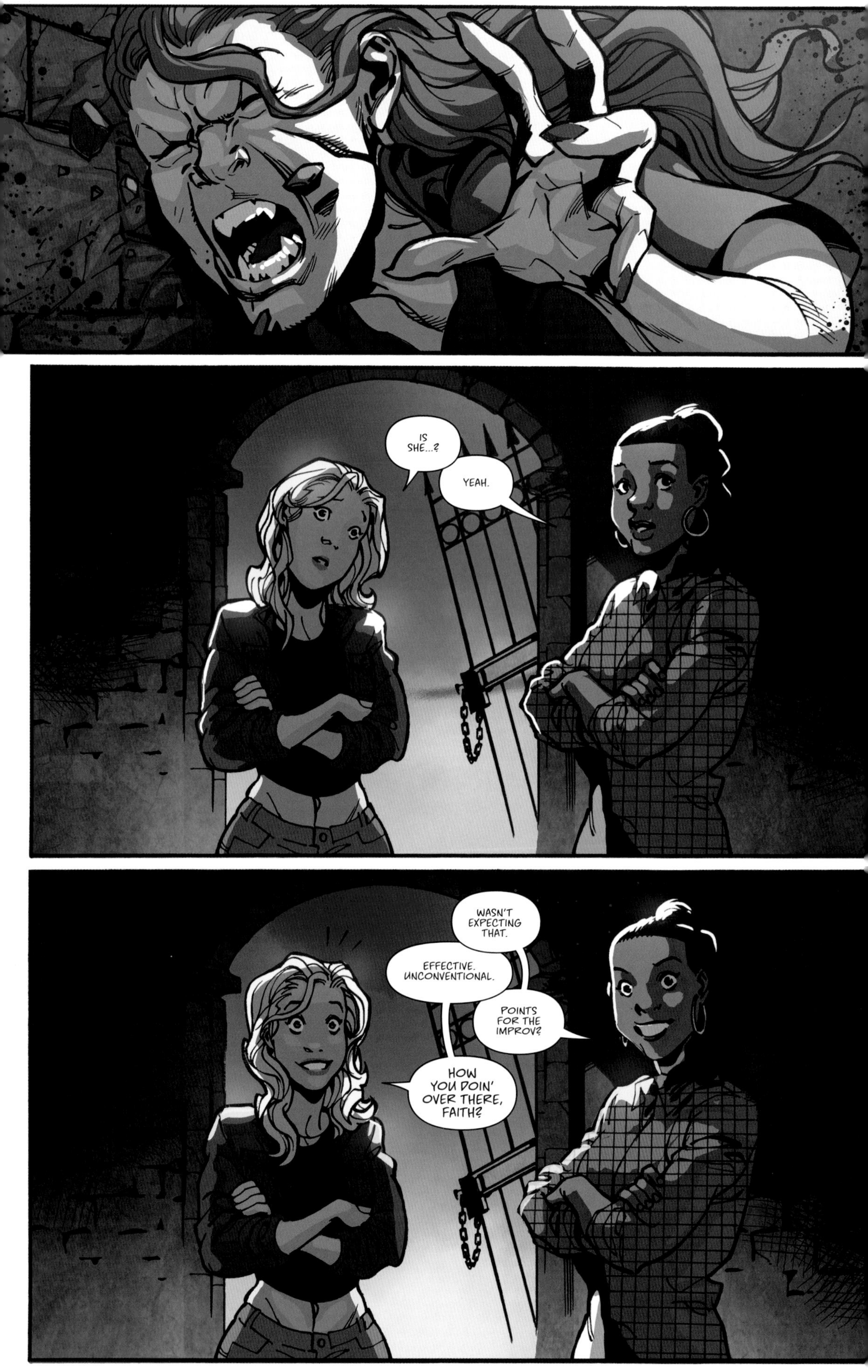
IS SHE...?
YEAH.
WASN'T EXPECTING THAT.
EFFECTIVE. UNCONVENTIONAL.
POINTS FOR THE IMPROV?
HOW YOU DOIN' OVER THERE, FAITH?

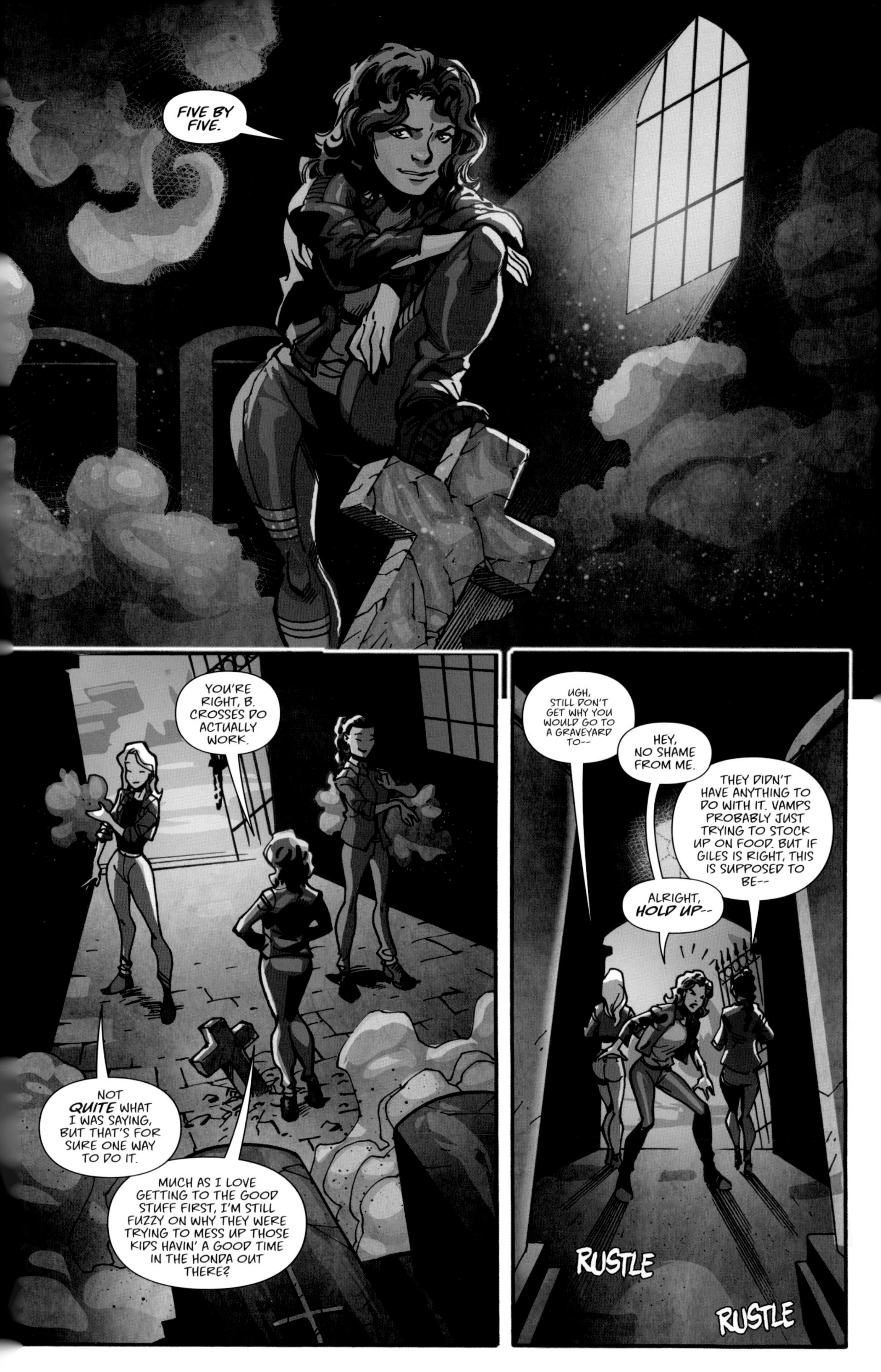
FIVE BY FIVE.
YOU'RE RIGHT, B. CROSSES DO ACTUALLY WORK.
NOT QUITE WHAT I WAS SAYING, BUT THAT'S FOR SURE ONE WAY TO DO IT.
MUCH AS I LOVE GETTING TO THE GOOD STUFF FIRST, I'M STILL FUZZY ON WHY THEY WERE TRYING TO MESS UP THOSE KIDS HAVIN' A GOOD TIME IN THE HONDA OUT THERE?
UGH, STILL DON'T GET WHY YOU WOULD GO TO A GRAVEYARD TO--
HEY, NO SHAME FROM ME.
THEY DIDN'T HAVE ANYTHING TO DO WITH IT. VAMPS PROBABLY JUST TRYING TO STOCK UP ON FOOD. BUT IF GILES IS RIGHT, THIS IS SUPPOSED TO BE--
ALRIGHT, HOLD UP--
RUSTLE
RUSTLE

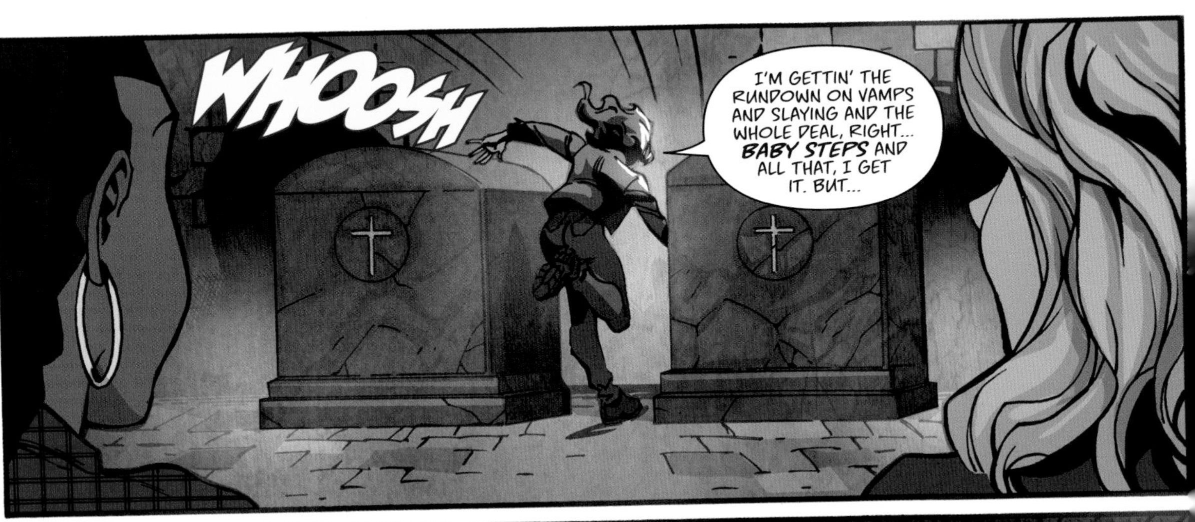
WHOOSH
I'M GETTIN' THE RUNDOWN ON VAMPS AND SLAYING AND THE WHOLE DEAL, RIGHT... BABY STEPS AND ALL THAT, I GET IT. BUT...

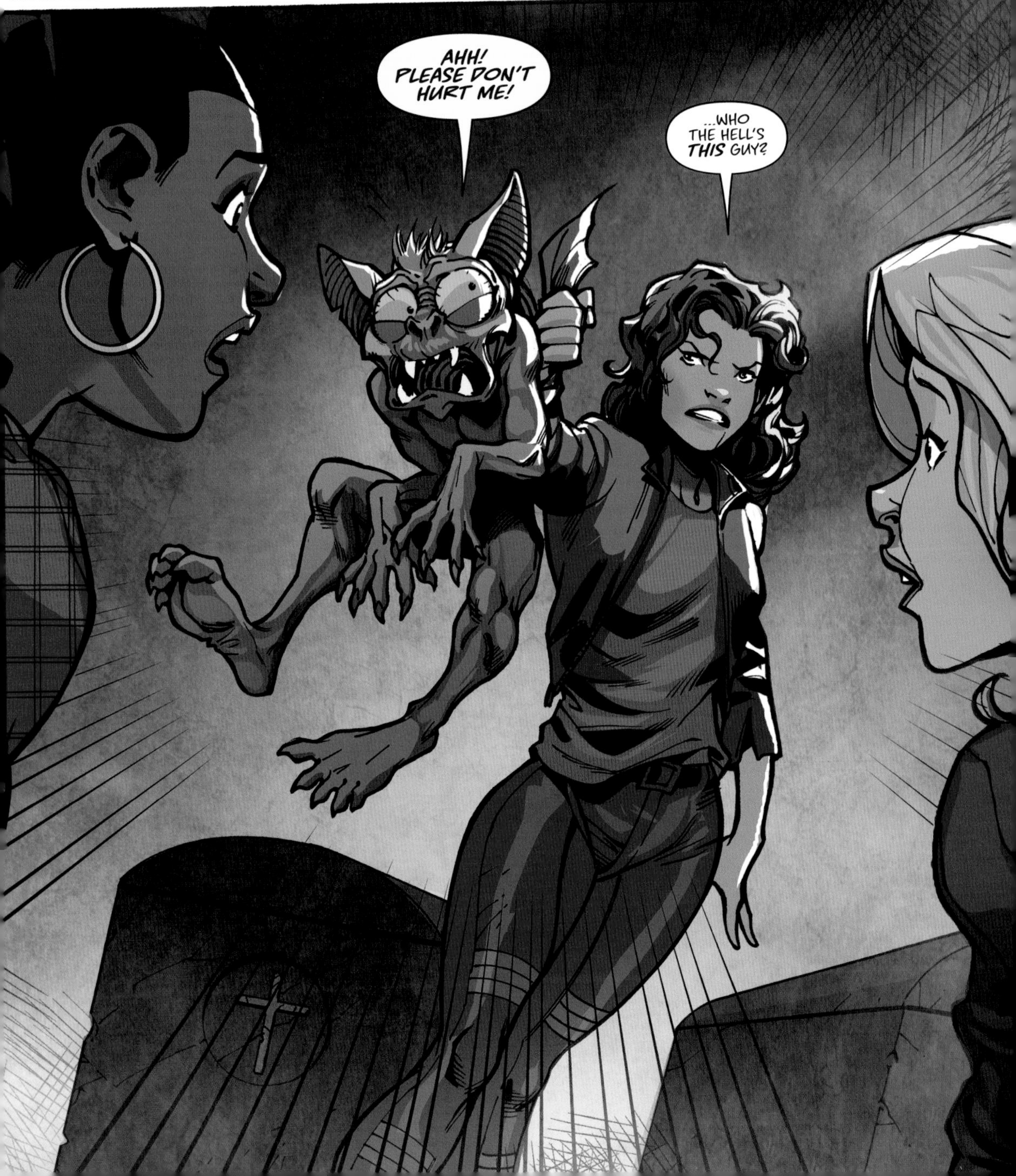
AHH! PLEASE DON'T HURT ME!
...WHO THE HELL'S THIS GUY?

LOVELY BREW.

SO...

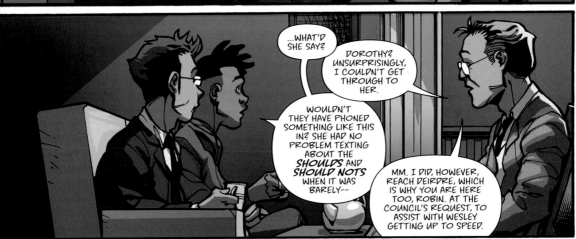

...WHAT'D SHE SAY?

DOROTHY? UNSURPRISINGLY, I COULDN'T GET THROUGH TO HER.

WOULDN'T THEY HAVE PHONED SOMETHING LIKE THIS IN? SHE HAD NO PROBLEM TEXTING ABOUT THE *SHOULDS* AND *SHOULD NOTS* WHEN IT WAS BARELY--

MM. I DID, HOWEVER, REACH DEIRDRE, WHICH IS WHY YOU ARE HERE TOO, ROBIN. AT THE COUNCIL'S REQUEST, TO ASSIST WITH WESLEY GETTING UP TO SPEED.

YOU...ER, PARDON ME, BUT *HE* RECEIVED *TEXT MESSAGES* FROM THE HEAD OF THE COUNCIL?

I SUGGEST YOU SPEAK TO HIM ON THAT MATTER, HE'S SITTING RIGHT NEXT TO YOU, AFTER ALL. AND IN DEFENSE OF MR. WOOD, THE ONLY FOREWARNING I MANAGED TO RECEIVE WAS A LETTER FROM *YOU.*

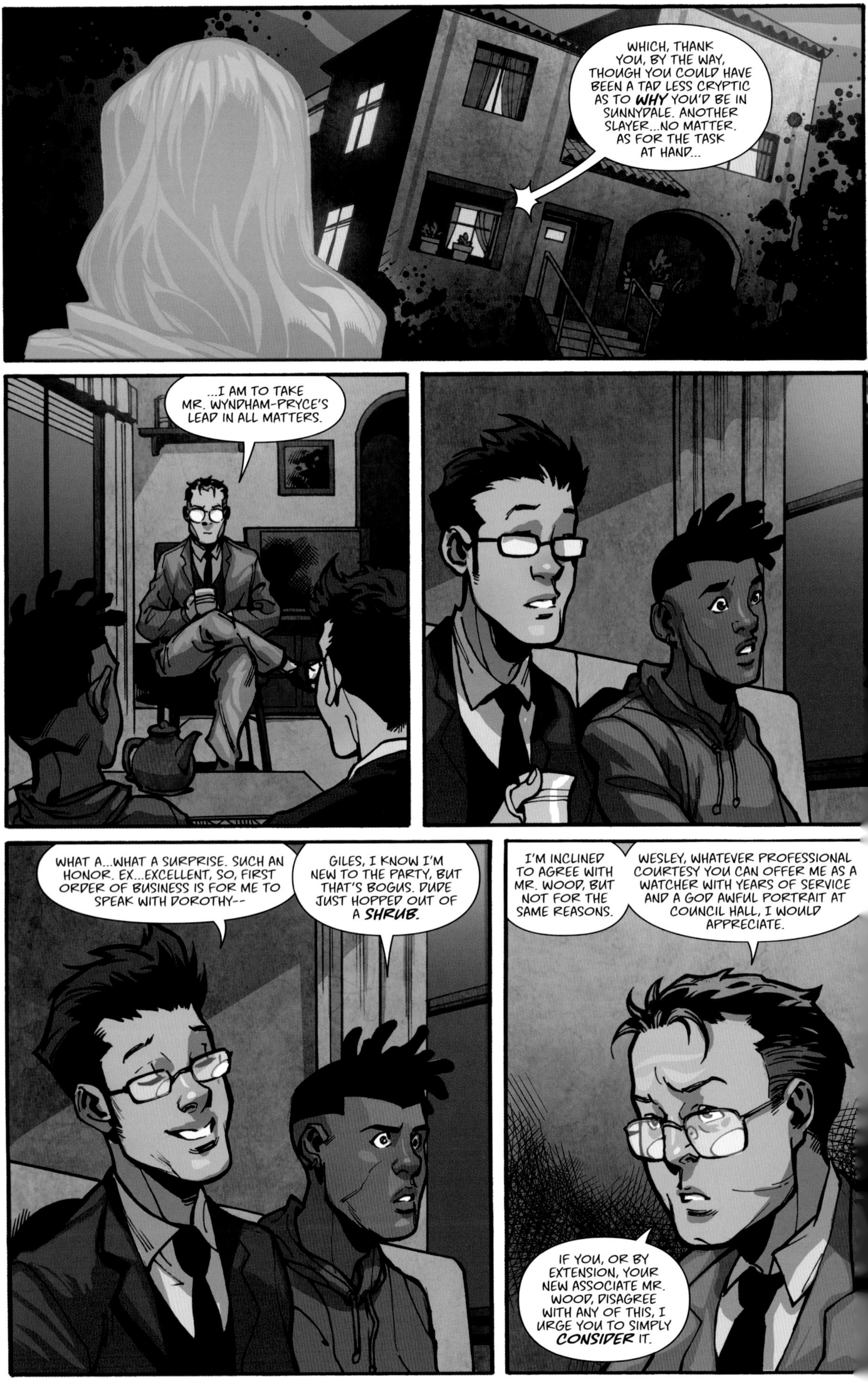
WHICH, THANK YOU, BY THE WAY, THOUGH YOU COULD HAVE BEEN A TAD LESS CRYPTIC AS TO WHY YOU'D BE IN SUNNYDALE. ANOTHER SLAYER...NO MATTER. AS FOR THE TASK AT HAND...
...I AM TO TAKE MR. WYNDHAM-PRYCE'S LEAD IN ALL MATTERS.
WHAT A...WHAT A SURPRISE. SUCH AN HONOR. EX...EXCELLENT, SO, FIRST ORDER OF BUSINESS IS FOR ME TO SPEAK WITH DOROTHY--
GILES, I KNOW I'M NEW TO THE PARTY, BUT THAT'S BOGUS. DUDE JUST HOPPED OUT OF A SHRUB.
I'M INCLINED TO AGREE WITH MR. WOOD, BUT NOT FOR THE SAME REASONS.
WESLEY, WHATEVER PROFESSIONAL COURTESY YOU CAN OFFER ME AS A WATCHER WITH YEARS OF SERVICE AND A GOD AWFUL PORTRAIT AT COUNCIL HALL, I WOULD APPRECIATE.
IF YOU, OR BY EXTENSION, YOUR NEW ASSOCIATE MR. WOOD, DISAGREE WITH ANY OF THIS, I URGE YOU TO SIMPLY CONSIDER IT.

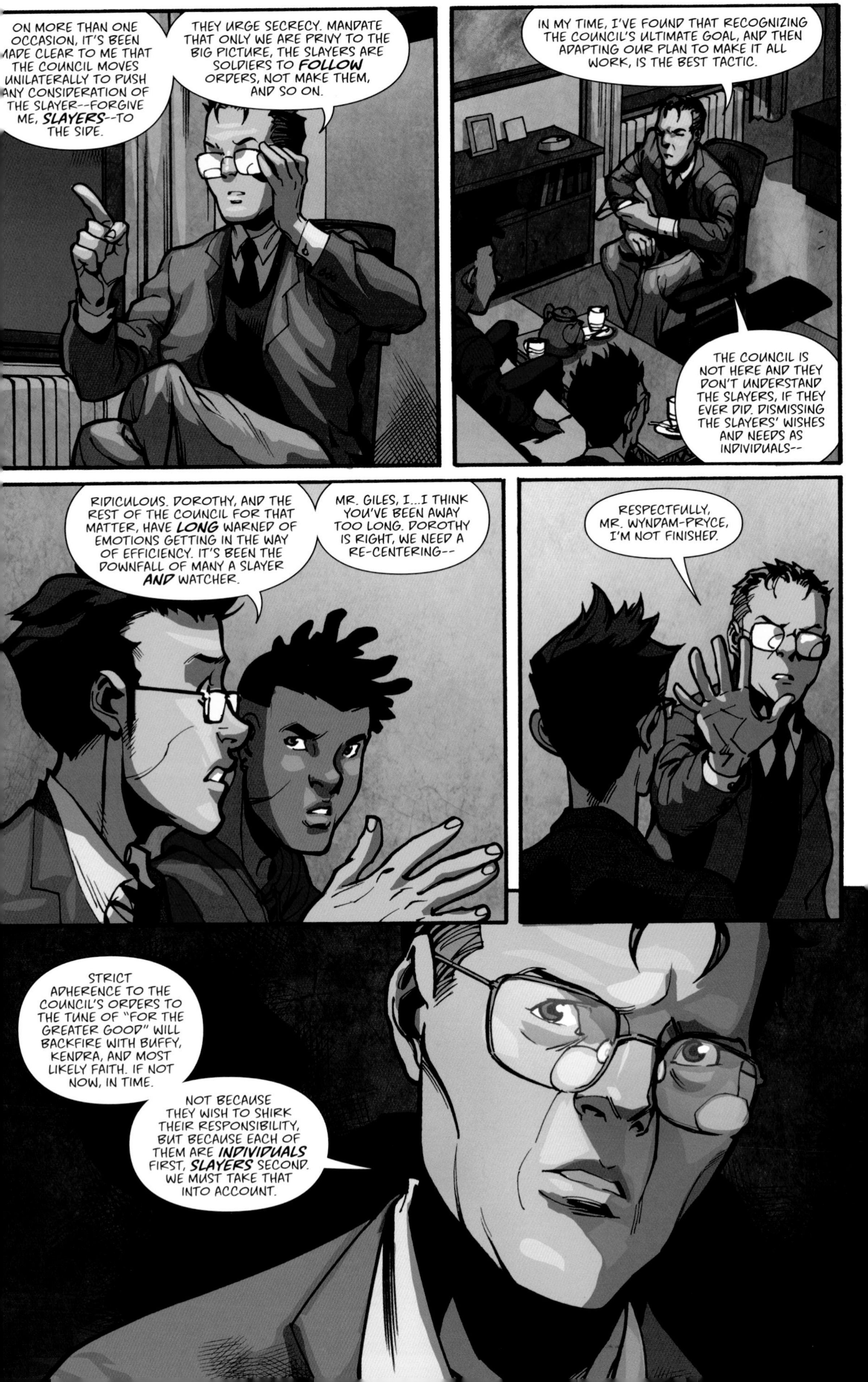
ON MORE THAN ONE OCCASION, IT'S BEEN MADE CLEAR TO ME THAT THE COUNCIL MOVES UNILATERALLY TO PUSH ANY CONSIDERATION OF THE SLAYER--FORGIVE ME, SLAYERS--TO THE SIDE.
THEY URGE SECRECY. MANDATE THAT ONLY WE ARE PRIVY TO THE BIG PICTURE, THE SLAYERS ARE SOLDIERS TO FOLLOW ORDERS, NOT MAKE THEM, AND SO ON.
IN MY TIME, I'VE FOUND THAT RECOGNIZING THE COUNCIL'S ULTIMATE GOAL, AND THEN ADAPTING OUR PLAN TO MAKE IT ALL WORK, IS THE BEST TACTIC.
THE COUNCIL IS NOT HERE AND THEY DON'T UNDERSTAND THE SLAYERS, IF THEY EVER DID. DISMISSING THE SLAYERS' WISHES AND NEEDS AS INDIVIDUALS--
RIDICULOUS. DOROTHY, AND THE REST OF THE COUNCIL FOR THAT MATTER, HAVE LONG WARNED OF EMOTIONS GETTING IN THE WAY OF EFFICIENCY. IT'S BEEN THE DOWNFALL OF MANY A SLAYER AND WATCHER.
MR. GILES, I...I THINK YOU'VE BEEN AWAY TOO LONG. DOROTHY IS RIGHT, WE NEED A RE-CENTERING--
RESPECTFULLY, MR. WYNDAM-PRYCE, I'M NOT FINISHED.
STRICT ADHERENCE TO THE COUNCIL'S ORDERS TO THE TUNE OF "FOR THE GREATER GOOD" WILL BACKFIRE WITH BUFFY, KENDRA, AND MOST LIKELY FAITH. IF NOT NOW, IN TIME.
NOT BECAUSE THEY WISH TO SHIRK THEIR RESPONSIBILITY, BUT BECAUSE EACH OF THEM ARE INDIVIDUALS FIRST, SLAYERS SECOND. WE MUST TAKE THAT INTO ACCOUNT.

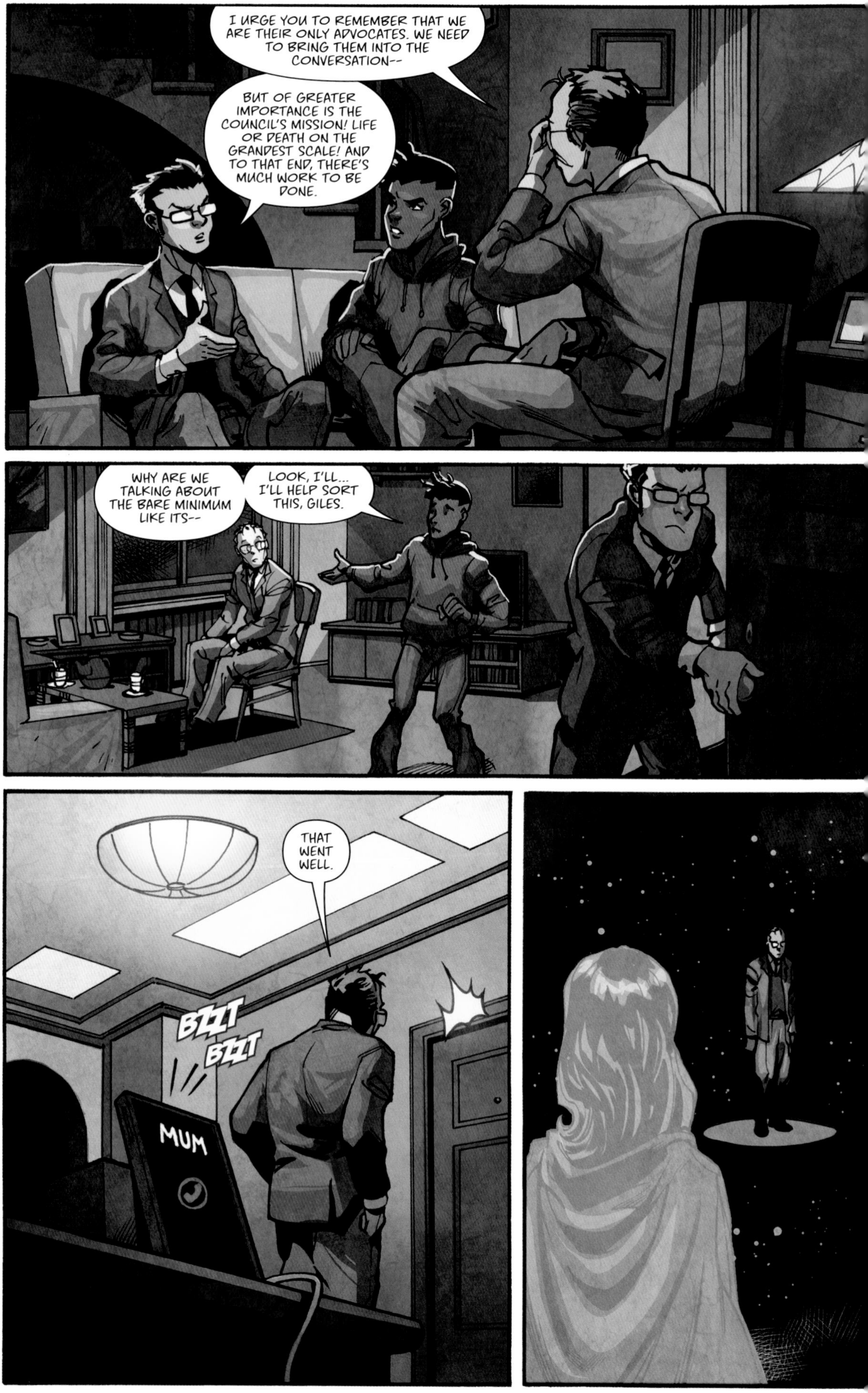
I URGE YOU TO REMEMBER THAT WE ARE THEIR ONLY ADVOCATES. WE NEED TO BRING THEM INTO THE CONVERSATION--
BUT OF GREATER IMPORTANCE IS THE COUNCIL'S MISSION! LIFE OR DEATH ON THE GRANDEST SCALE! AND TO THAT END, THERE'S MUCH WORK TO BE DONE.
WHY ARE WE TALKING ABOUT THE BARE MINIMUM LIKE ITS--
LOOK, I'LL... I'LL HELP SORT THIS, GILES.
THAT WENT WELL.
BZZT
BZZT
MUM

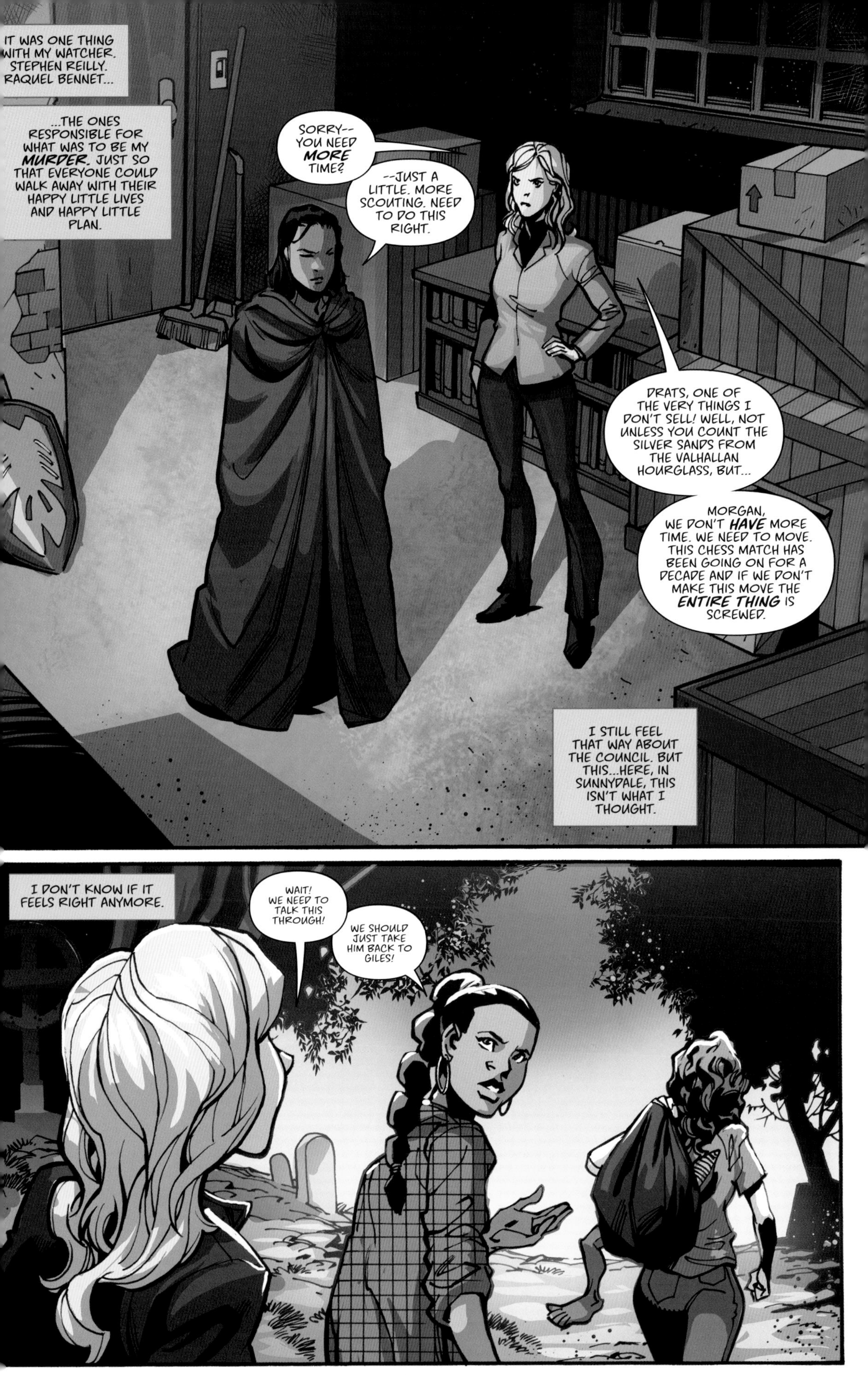
IT WAS ONE THING WITH MY WATCHER. STEPHEN REILLY. RAQUEL BENNET...
...THE ONES RESPONSIBLE FOR WHAT WAS TO BE MY MURDER. JUST SO THAT EVERYONE COULD WALK AWAY WITH THEIR HAPPY LITTLE LIVES AND HAPPY LITTLE PLAN.
SORRY-- YOU NEED MORE TIME?
--JUST A LITTLE. MORE SCOUTING. NEED TO DO THIS RIGHT.
DRATS, ONE OF THE VERY THINGS I DON'T SELL! WELL, NOT UNLESS YOU COUNT THE SILVER SANDS FROM THE VALHALLAN HOURGLASS, BUT...
MORGAN, WE DON'T HAVE MORE TIME. WE NEED TO MOVE. THIS CHESS MATCH HAS BEEN GOING ON FOR A DECADE AND IF WE DON'T MAKE THIS MOVE THE ENTIRE THING IS SCREWED.
I STILL FEEL THAT WAY ABOUT THE COUNCIL. BUT THIS...HERE, IN SUNNYDALE, THIS ISN'T WHAT I THOUGHT.
I DON'T KNOW IF IT FEELS RIGHT ANYMORE.
WAIT! WE NEED TO TALK THIS THROUGH!
WE SHOULD JUST TAKE HIM BACK TO GILES!

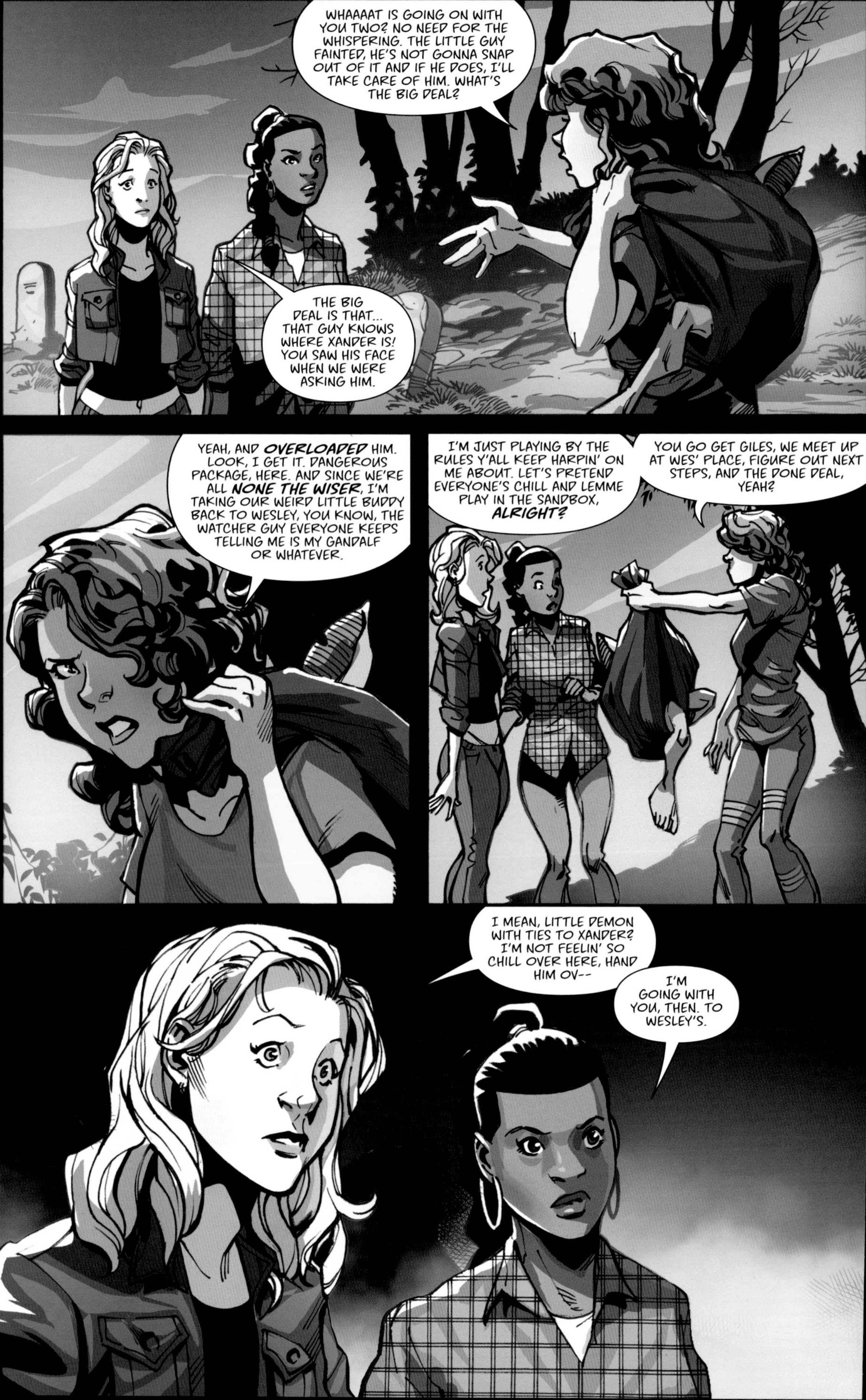
WHAAAAT IS GOING ON WITH YOU TWO? NO NEED FOR THE WHISPERING. THE LITTLE GUY FAINTED, HE'S NOT GONNA SNAP OUT OF IT AND IF HE DOES, I'LL TAKE CARE OF HIM. WHAT'S THE BIG DEAL?
THE BIG DEAL IS THAT... THAT GUY KNOWS WHERE XANDER IS! YOU SAW HIS FACE WHEN WE WERE ASKING HIM.
YEAH, AND OVERLOADED HIM. LOOK, I GET IT. DANGEROUS PACKAGE, HERE. AND SINCE WE'RE ALL NONE THE WISER, I'M TAKING OUR WEIRD LITTLE BUDDY BACK TO WESLEY, YOU KNOW, THE WATCHER GUY EVERYONE KEEPS TELLING ME IS MY GANDALF OR WHATEVER.
I'M JUST PLAYING BY THE RULES Y'ALL KEEP HARPIN' ON ME ABOUT. LET'S PRETEND EVERYONE'S CHILL AND LEMME PLAY IN THE SANDBOX, ALRIGHT?
YOU GO GET GILES, WE MEET UP AT WES' PLACE, FIGURE OUT NEXT STEPS, AND THE DONE DEAL, YEAH?
I MEAN, LITTLE DEMON WITH TIES TO XANDER? I'M NOT FEELIN' SO CHILL OVER HERE, HAND HIM OV--
I'M GOING WITH YOU, THEN. TO WESLEY'S.

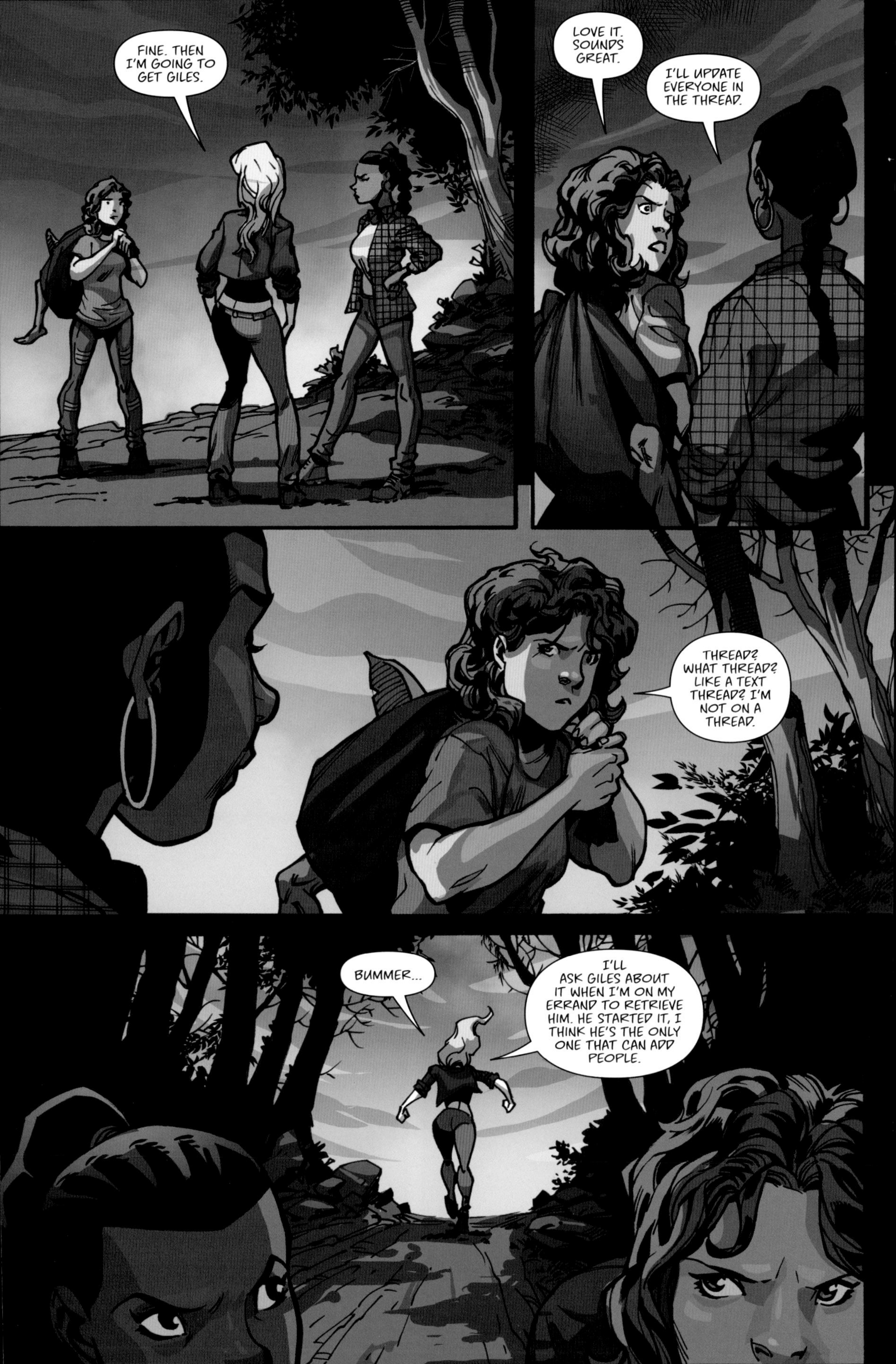

FINE. THEN I'M GOING TO GET GILES.
LOVE IT. SOUNDS GREAT.
I'LL UPDATE EVERYONE IN THE THREAD.
THREAD? WHAT THREAD? LIKE A TEXT THREAD? I'M NOT ON A THREAD.
BUMMER...
I'LL ASK GILES ABOUT IT WHEN I'M ON MY ERRAND TO RETRIEVE HIM. HE STARTED IT, I THINK HE'S THE ONLY ONE THAT CAN ADD PEOPLE.

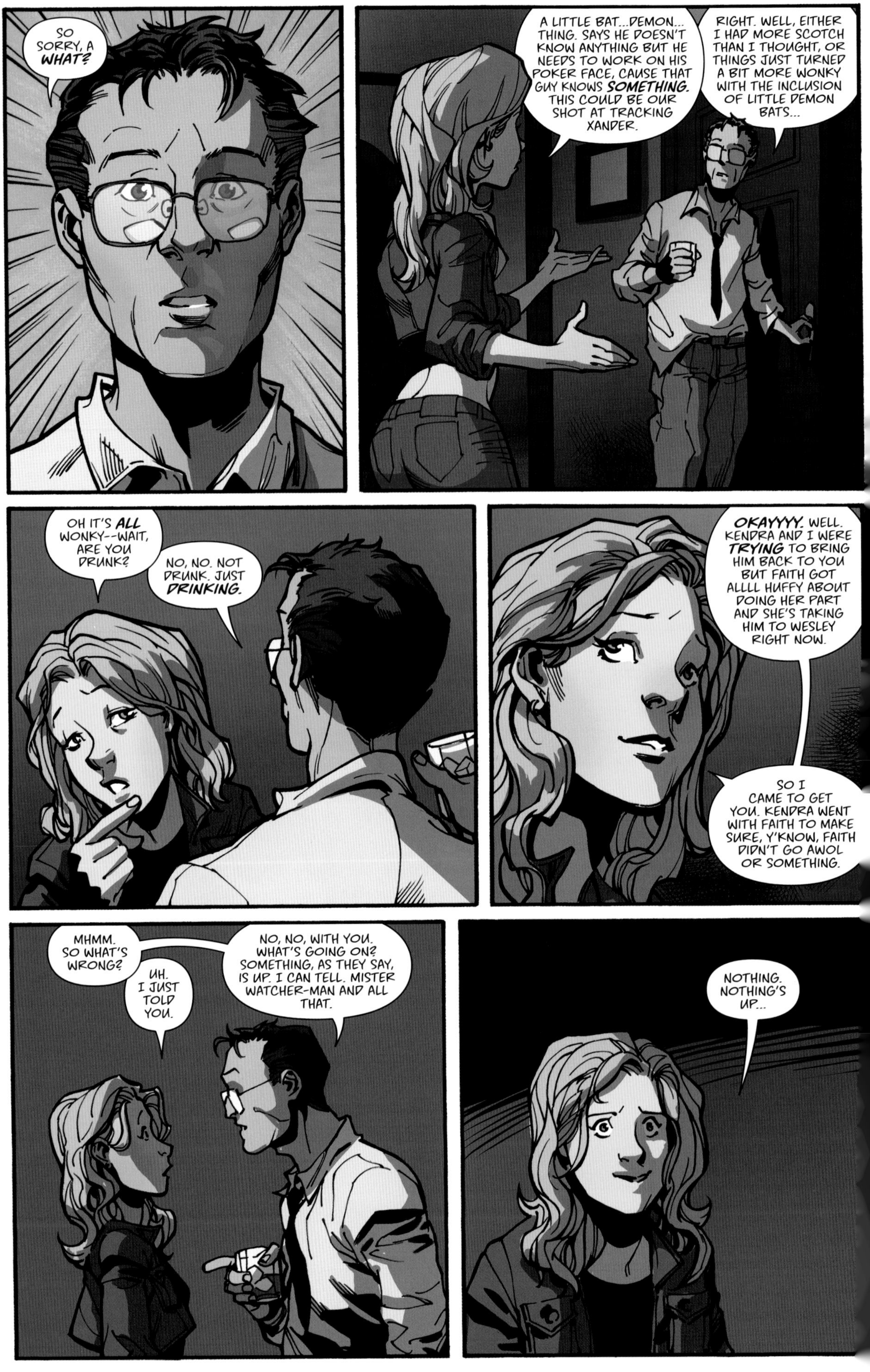

SO SORRY, A WHAT?
A LITTLE BAT...DEMON... THING. SAYS HE DOESN'T KNOW ANYTHING BUT HE NEEDS TO WORK ON HIS POKER FACE, CAUSE THAT GUY KNOWS SOMETHING. THIS COULD BE OUR SHOT AT TRACKING XANDER.
RIGHT. WELL, EITHER I HAD MORE SCOTCH THAN I THOUGHT, OR THINGS JUST TURNED A BIT MORE WONKY WITH THE INCLUSION OF LITTLE DEMON BATS...
OH IT'S ALL WONKY--WAIT, ARE YOU DRUNK?
NO, NO. NOT DRUNK. JUST DRINKING.
OKAYYYY. WELL. KENDRA AND I WERE TRYING TO BRING HIM BACK TO YOU BUT FAITH GOT ALLLL HUFFY ABOUT DOING HER PART AND SHE'S TAKING HIM TO WESLEY RIGHT NOW.
SO I CAME TO GET YOU. KENDRA WENT WITH FAITH TO MAKE SURE, Y'KNOW, FAITH DIDN'T GO AWOL OR SOMETHING.
MHMM. SO WHAT'S WRONG?
UH. I JUST TOLD YOU.
NO, NO, WITH YOU. WHAT'S GOING ON? SOMETHING, AS THEY SAY, IS UP. I CAN TELL. MISTER WATCHER-MAN AND ALL THAT.
NOTHING. NOTHING'S UP...

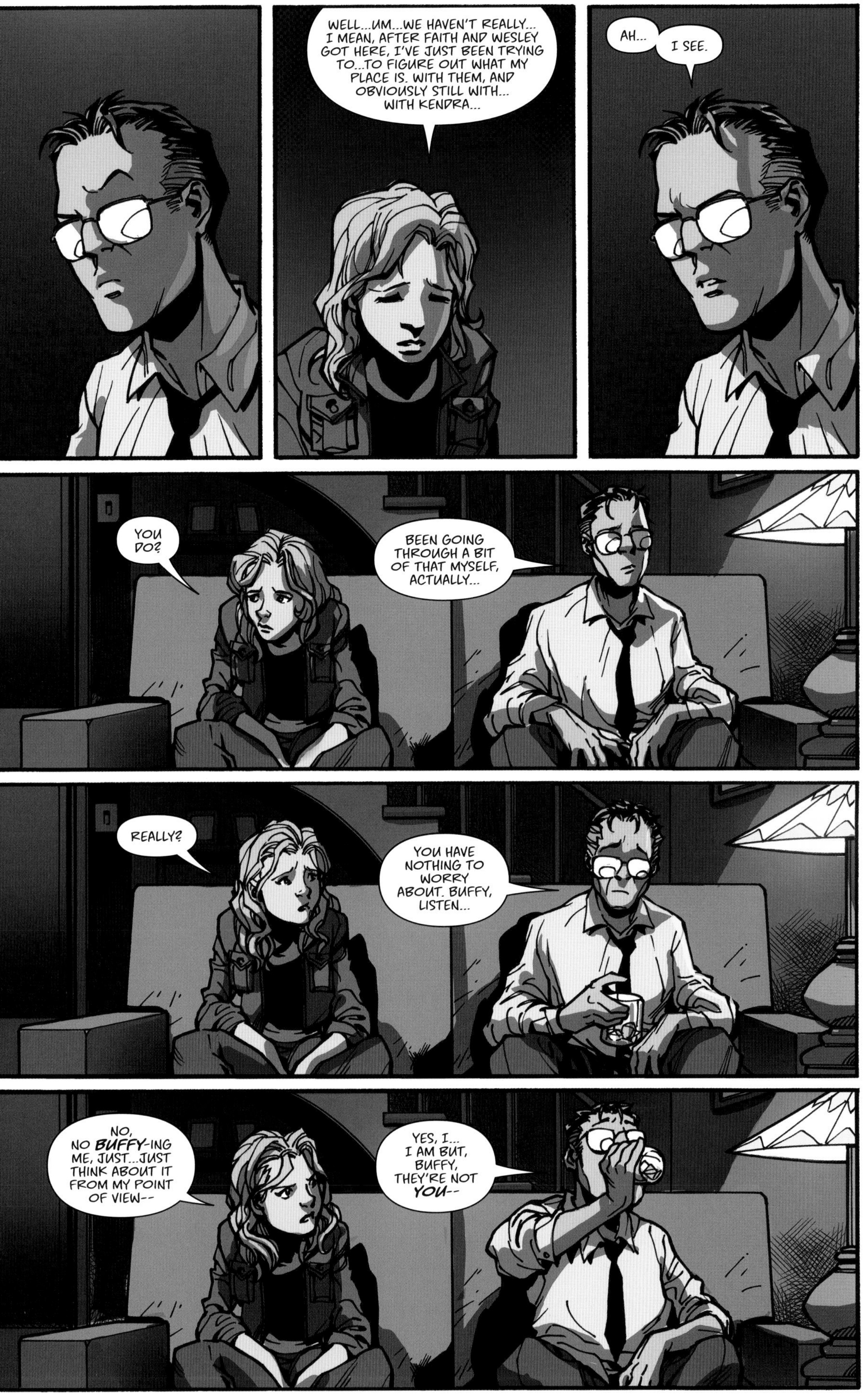
WELL...UM...WE HAVEN'T REALLY... I MEAN, AFTER FAITH AND WESLEY GOT HERE, I'VE JUST BEEN TRYING TO...TO FIGURE OUT WHAT MY PLACE IS. WITH THEM, AND OBVIOUSLY STILL WITH... WITH KENDRA...
AH...
I SEE.
BEEN GOING THROUGH A BIT OF THAT MYSELF, ACTUALLY...
YOU DO?
YOU HAVE NOTHING TO WORRY ABOUT. BUFFY, LISTEN...
REALLY?
YES, I... I AM BUT, BUFFY, THEY'RE NOT *YOU*--
NO, NO ***BUFFY***-ING ME, JUST...JUST THINK ABOUT IT FROM MY POINT OF VIEW--

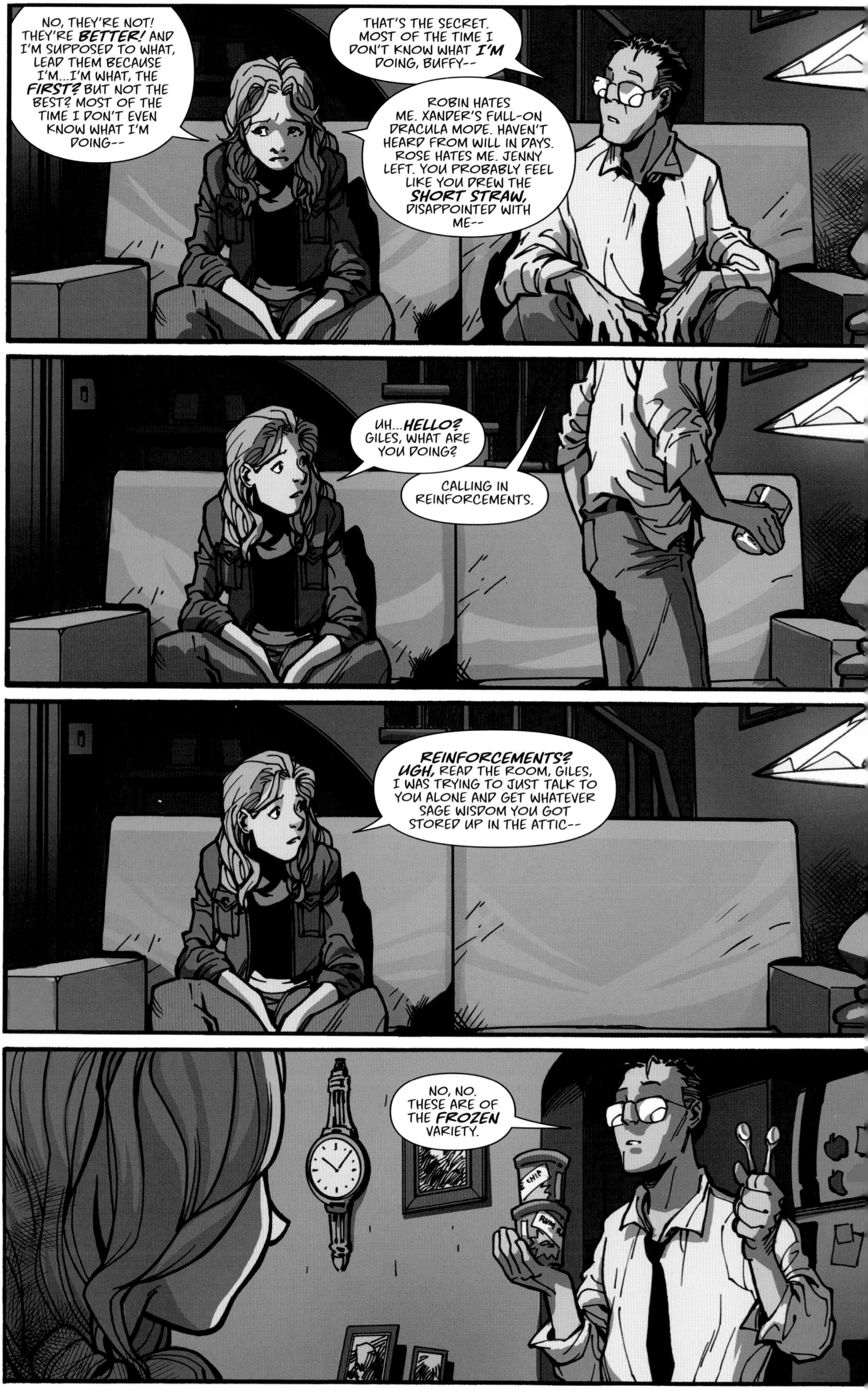
NO, THEY'RE NOT! THEY'RE BETTER! AND I'M SUPPOSED TO WHAT, LEAD THEM BECAUSE I'M...I'M WHAT, THE FIRST? BUT NOT THE BEST? MOST OF THE TIME I DON'T EVEN KNOW WHAT I'M DOING--
THAT'S THE SECRET. MOST OF THE TIME I DON'T KNOW WHAT I'M DOING, BUFFY--
ROBIN HATES ME. XANDER'S FULL-ON DRACULA MODE. HAVEN'T HEARD FROM WILL IN DAYS. ROSE HATES ME. JENNY LEFT. YOU PROBABLY FEEL LIKE YOU DREW THE SHORT STRAW, DISAPPOINTED WITH ME--
UH...HELLO? GILES, WHAT ARE YOU DOING?
CALLING IN REINFORCEMENTS.
REINFORCEMENTS? UGH, READ THE ROOM, GILES, I WAS TRYING TO JUST TALK TO YOU ALONE AND GET WHATEVER SAGE WISDOM YOU GOT STORED UP IN THE ATTIC--
NO, NO. THESE ARE OF THE FROZEN VARIETY.

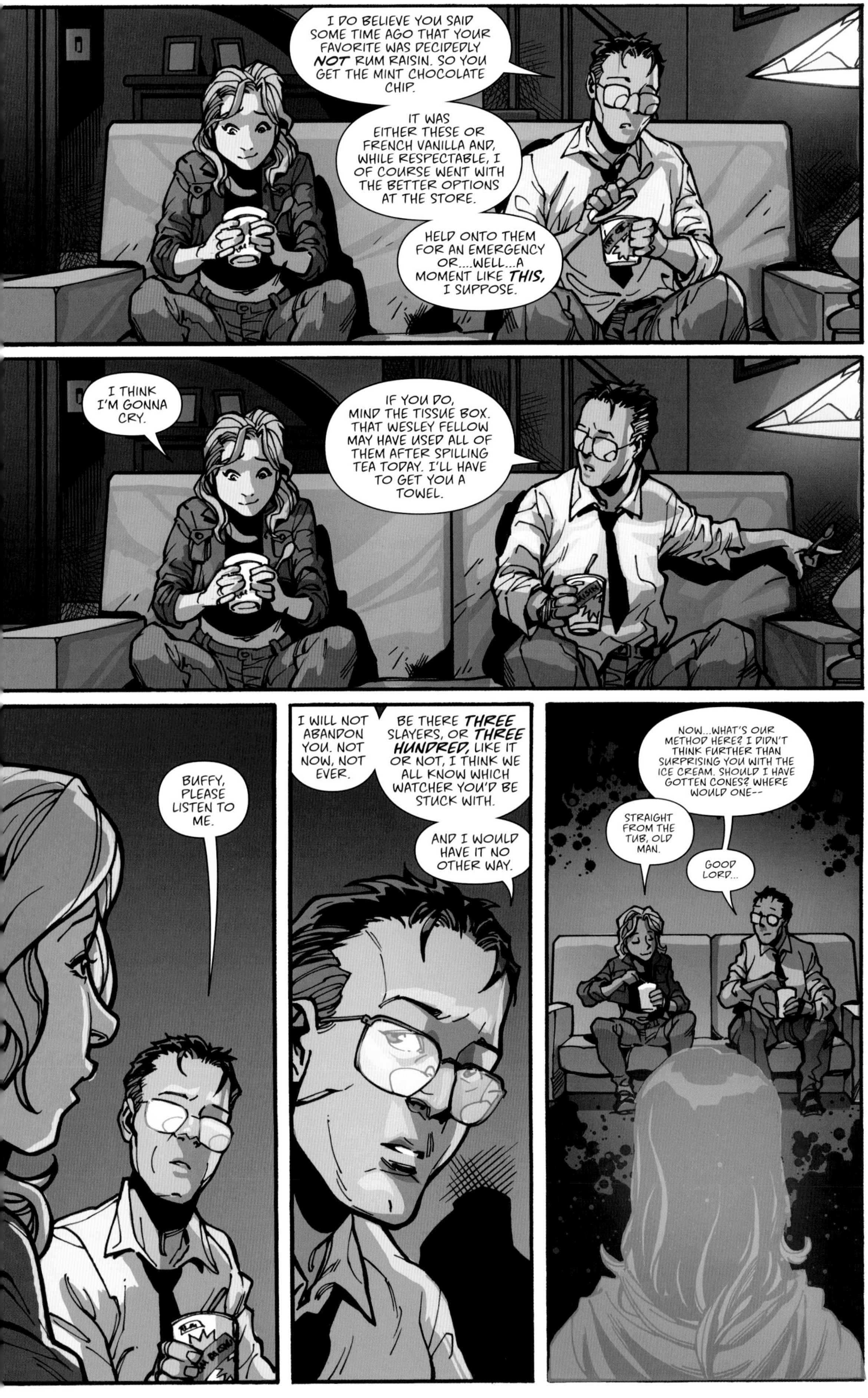
I DO BELIEVE YOU SAID SOME TIME AGO THAT YOUR FAVORITE WAS DECIDEDLY NOT RUM RAISIN. SO YOU GET THE MINT CHOCOLATE CHIP.
IT WAS EITHER THESE OR FRENCH VANILLA AND, WHILE RESPECTABLE, I OF COURSE WENT WITH THE BETTER OPTIONS AT THE STORE.
HELD ONTO THEM FOR AN EMERGENCY OR....WELL...A MOMENT LIKE THIS, I SUPPOSE.
I THINK I'M GONNA CRY.
IF YOU DO, MIND THE TISSUE BOX. THAT WESLEY FELLOW MAY HAVE USED ALL OF THEM AFTER SPILLING TEA TODAY. I'LL HAVE TO GET YOU A TOWEL.
BUFFY, PLEASE LISTEN TO ME.
I WILL NOT ABANDON YOU. NOT NOW, NOT EVER.
BE THERE THREE SLAYERS, OR THREE HUNDRED, LIKE IT OR NOT, I THINK WE ALL KNOW WHICH WATCHER YOU'D BE STUCK WITH.
AND I WOULD HAVE IT NO OTHER WAY.
NOW...WHAT'S OUR METHOD HERE? I DIDN'T THINK FURTHER THAN SURPRISING YOU WITH THE ICE CREAM. SHOULD I HAVE GOTTEN CONES? WHERE WOULD ONE--
STRAIGHT FROM THE TUB, OLD MAN.
GOOD LORD...

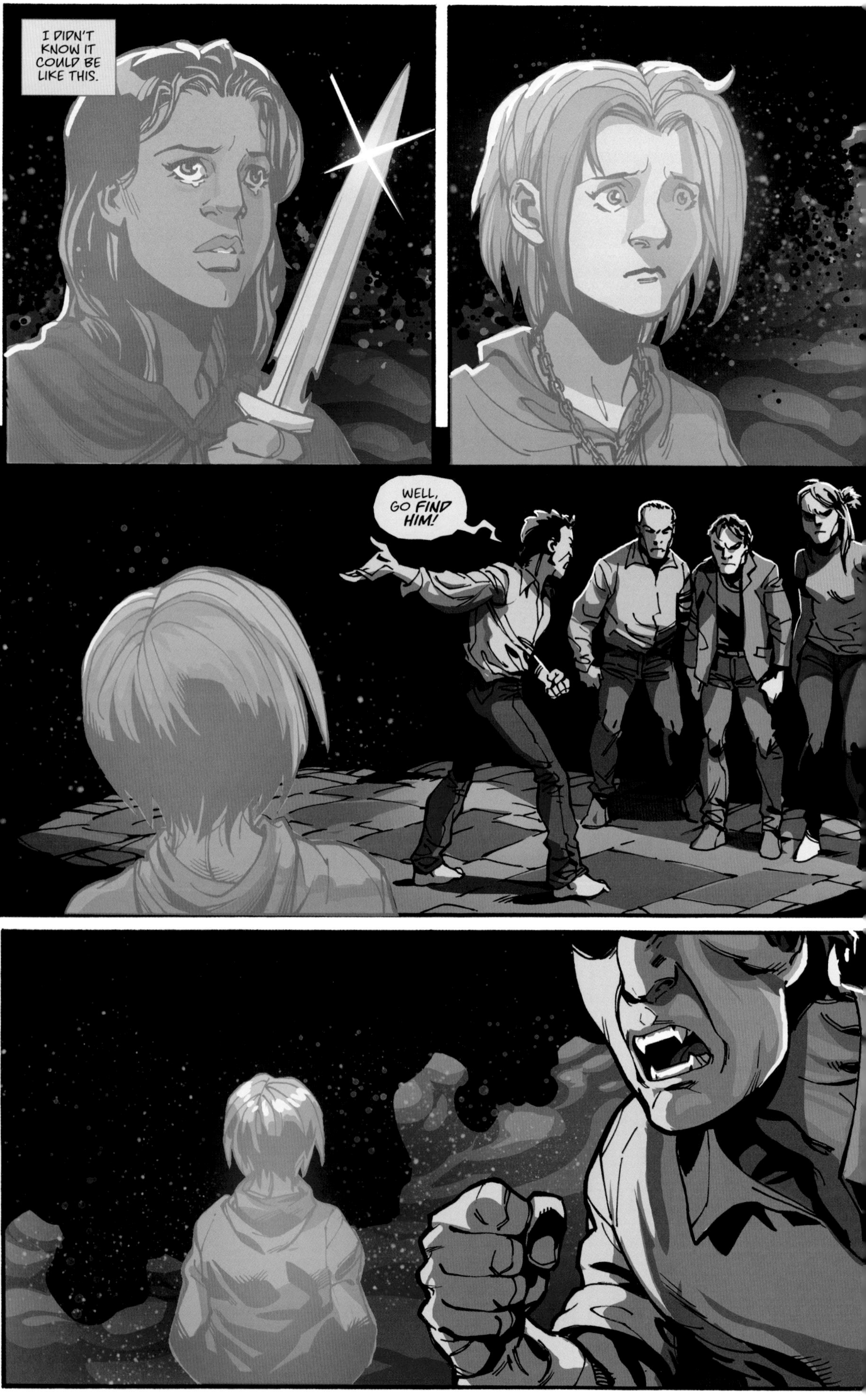
I DIDN'T KNOW IT COULD BE LIKE THIS.
WELL, GO FIND HIM!

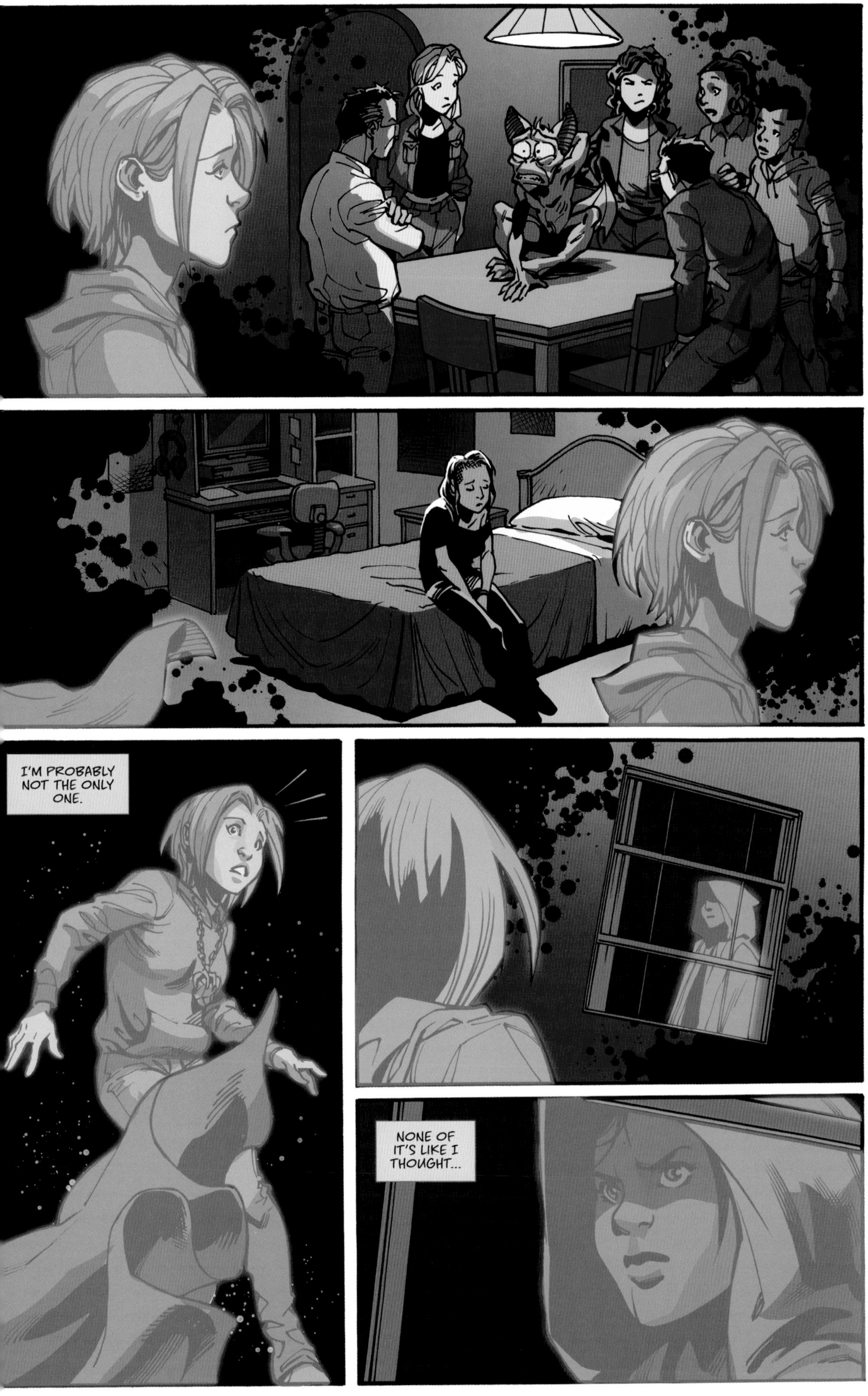
I'M PROBABLY NOT THE ONLY ONE.
NONE OF IT'S LIKE I THOUGHT...

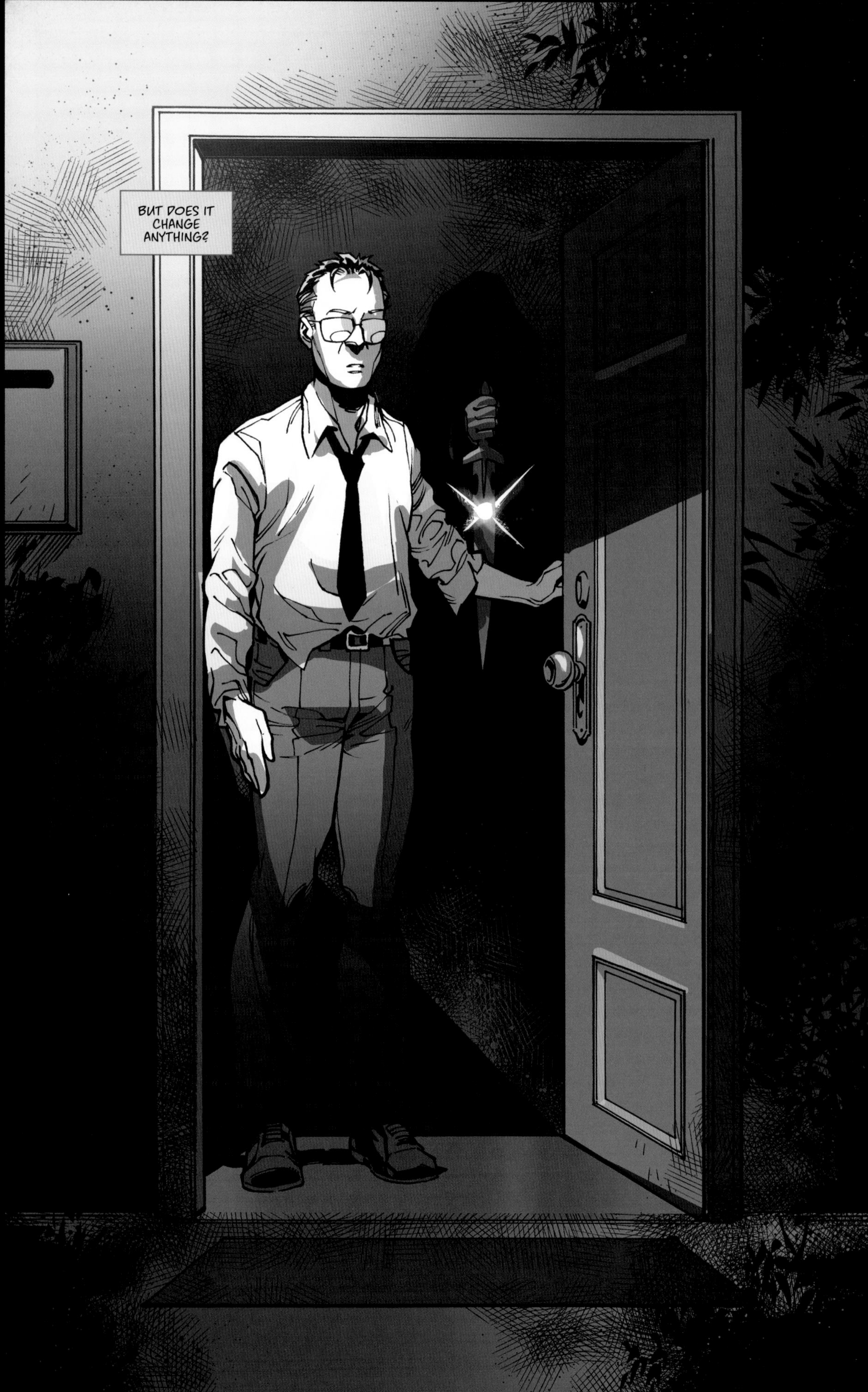
BUT DOES IT CHANGE ANYTHING?

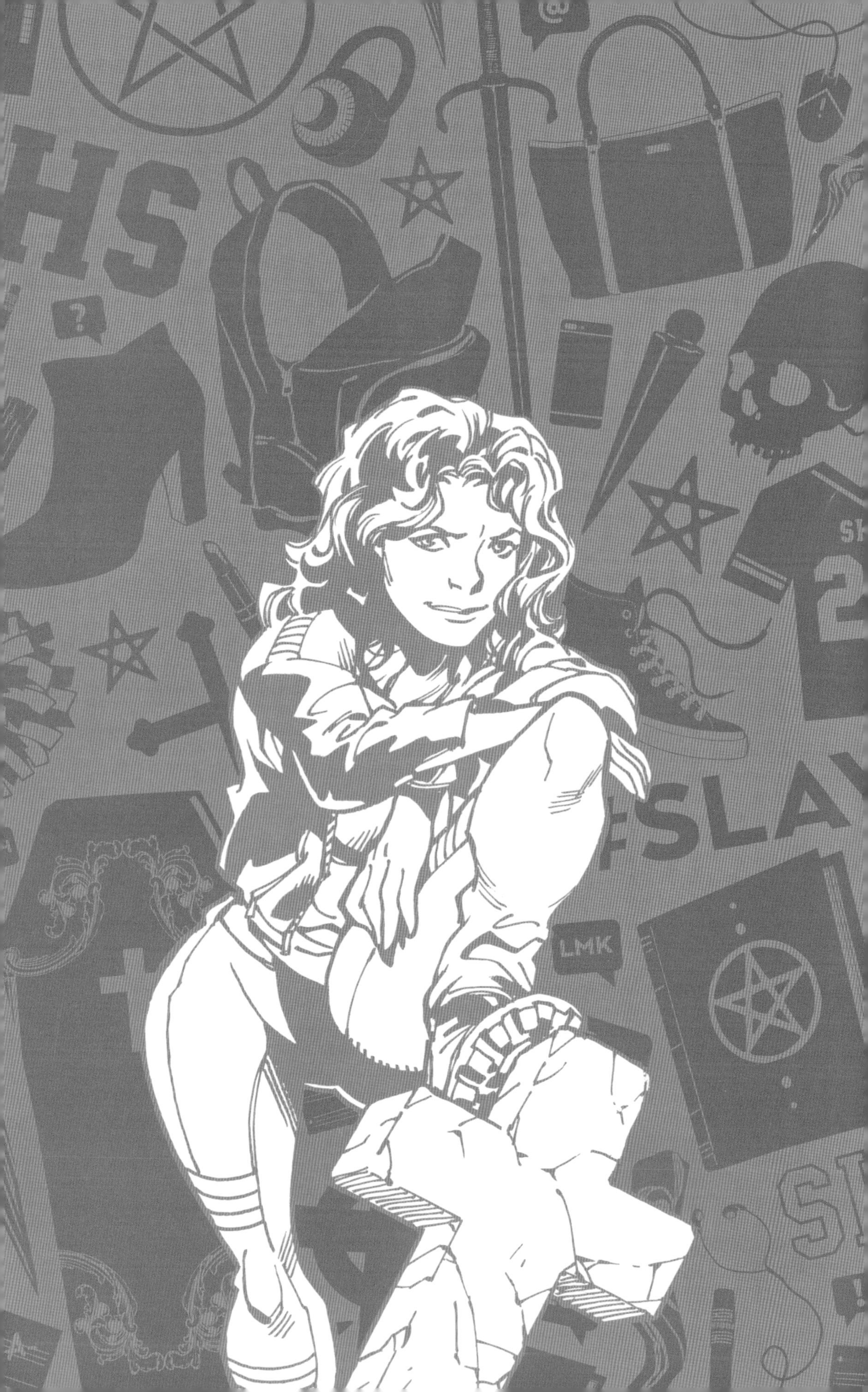
HS
FSLAY
LMK

FAITH

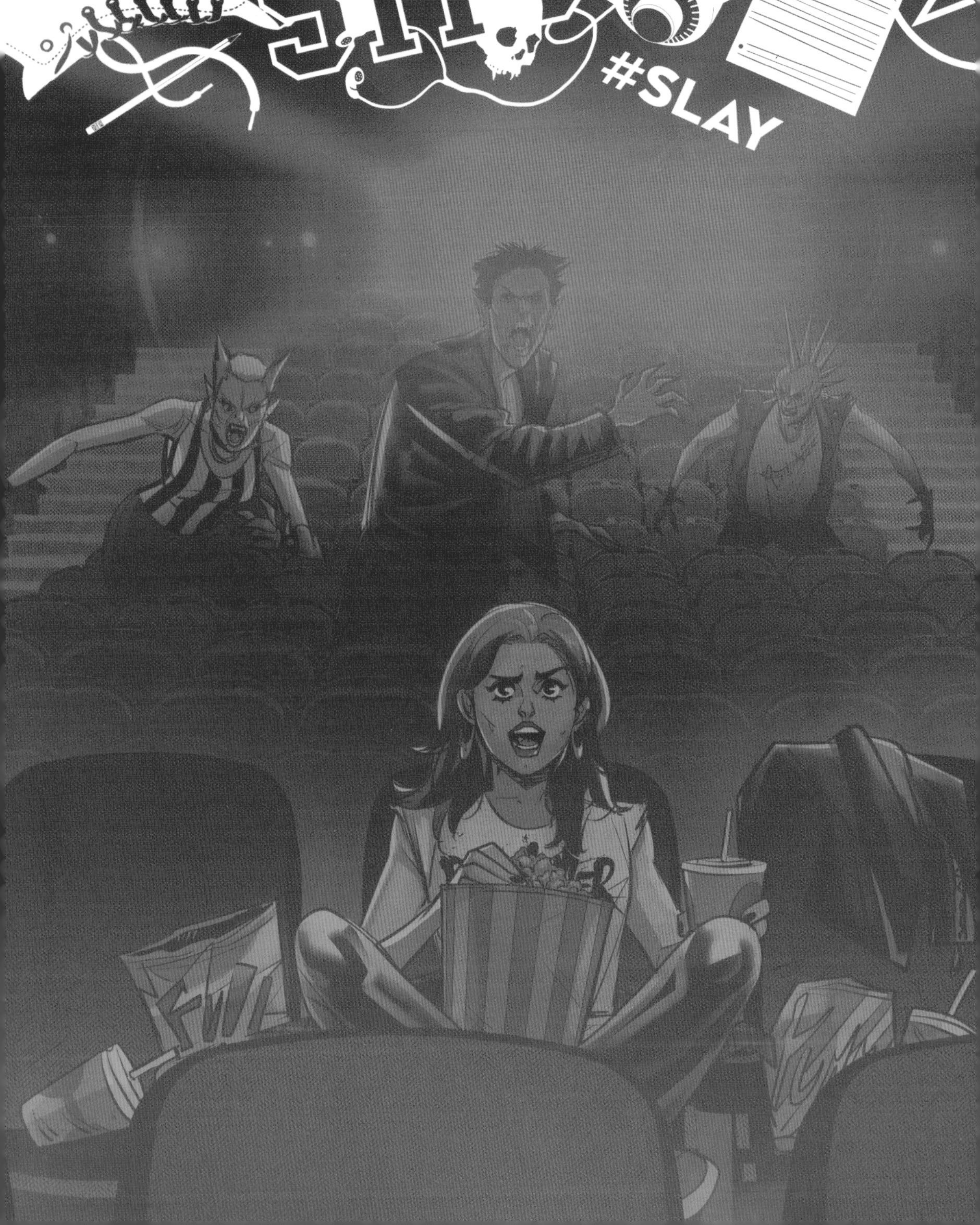
S.H.S
SMH
#SLAY

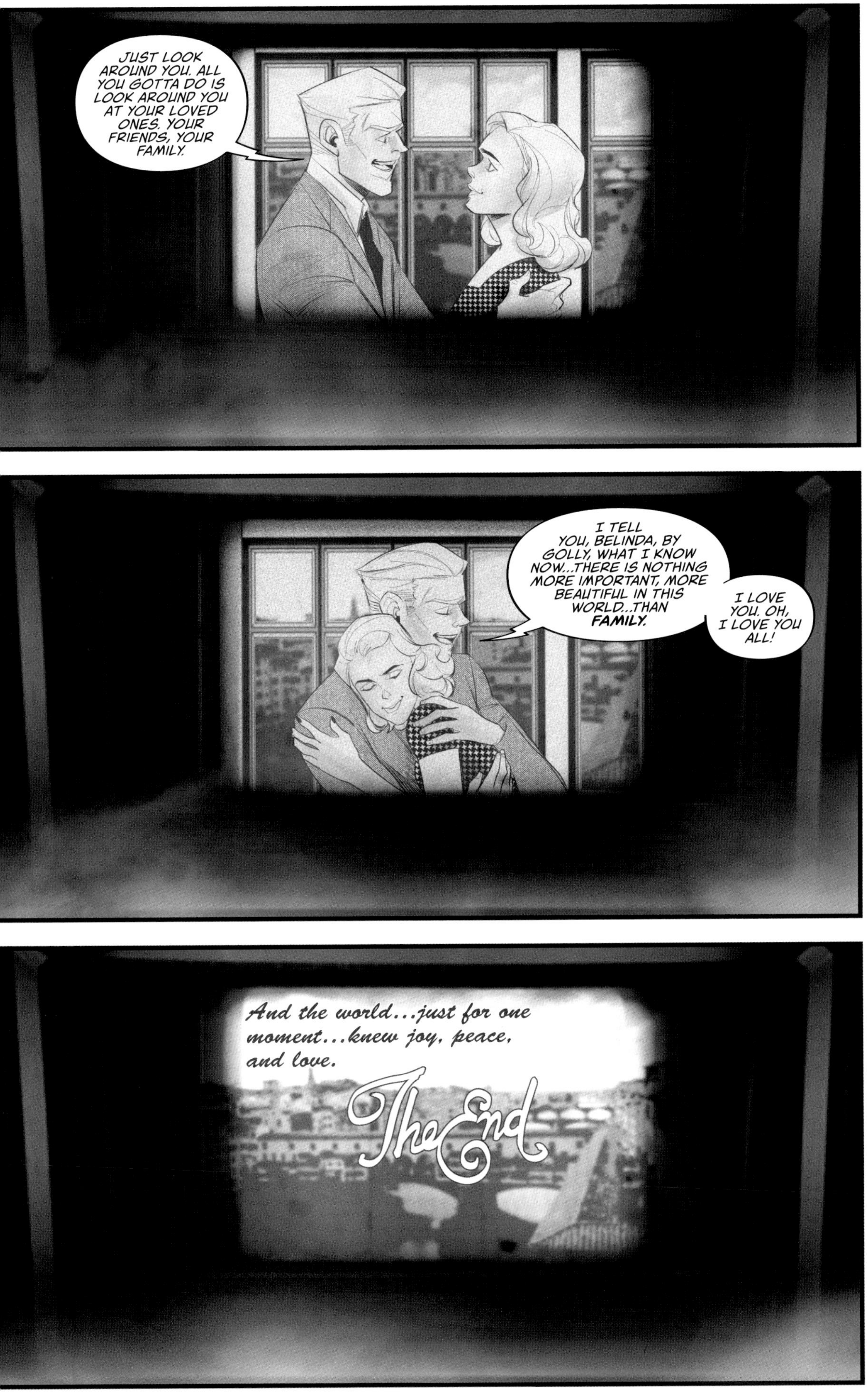
JUST LOOK AROUND YOU. ALL YOU GOTTA DO IS LOOK AROUND YOU AT YOUR LOVED ONES. YOUR FRIENDS, YOUR FAMILY.
I TELL YOU, BELINDA, BY GOLLY, WHAT I KNOW NOW...THERE IS NOTHING MORE IMPORTANT, MORE BEAUTIFUL IN THIS WORLD...THAN **FAMILY.**
I LOVE YOU. OH, I LOVE YOU ALL!
And the world...just for one moment...knew joy, peace, and love.
The End

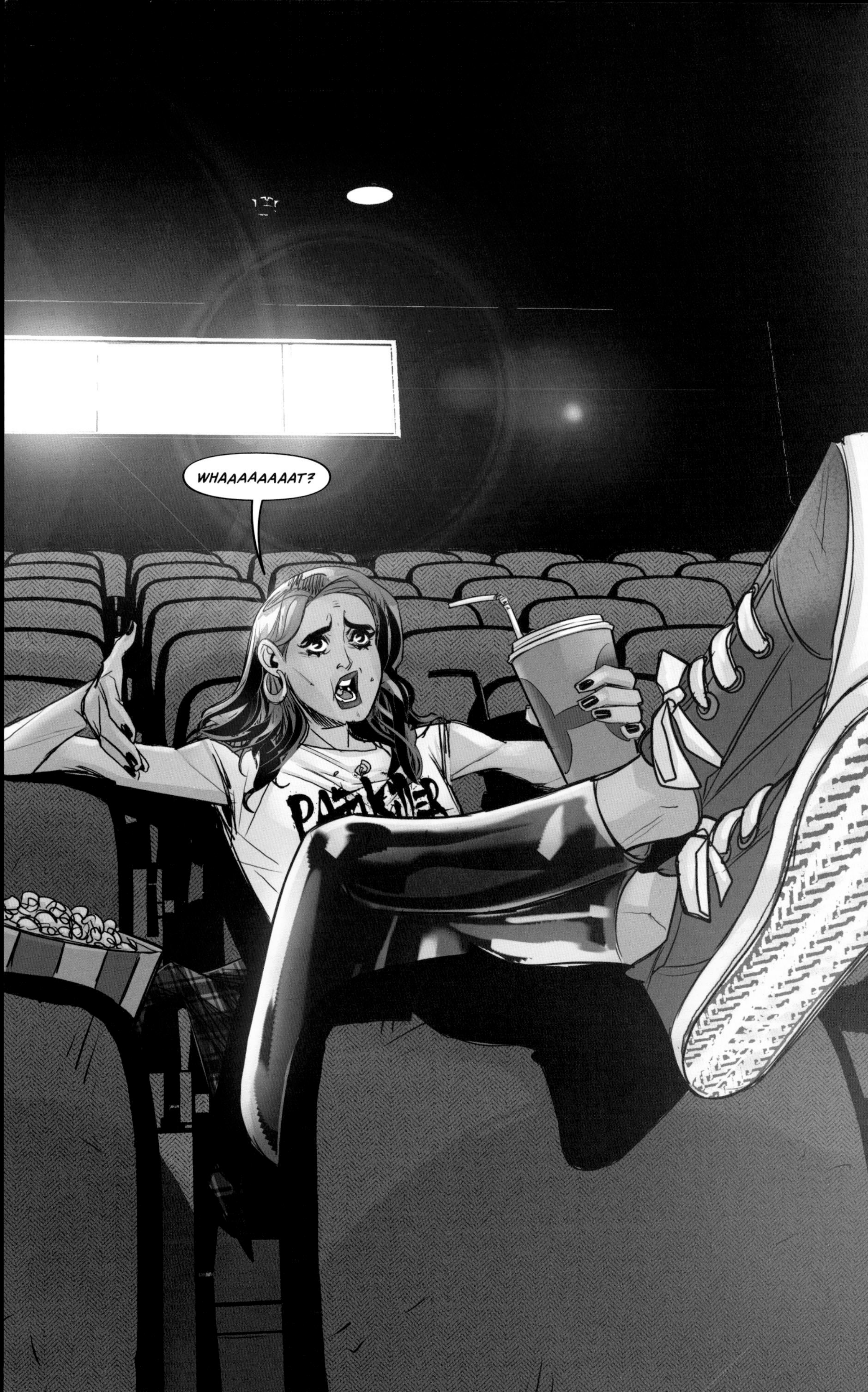
WHAAAAAAAAT?

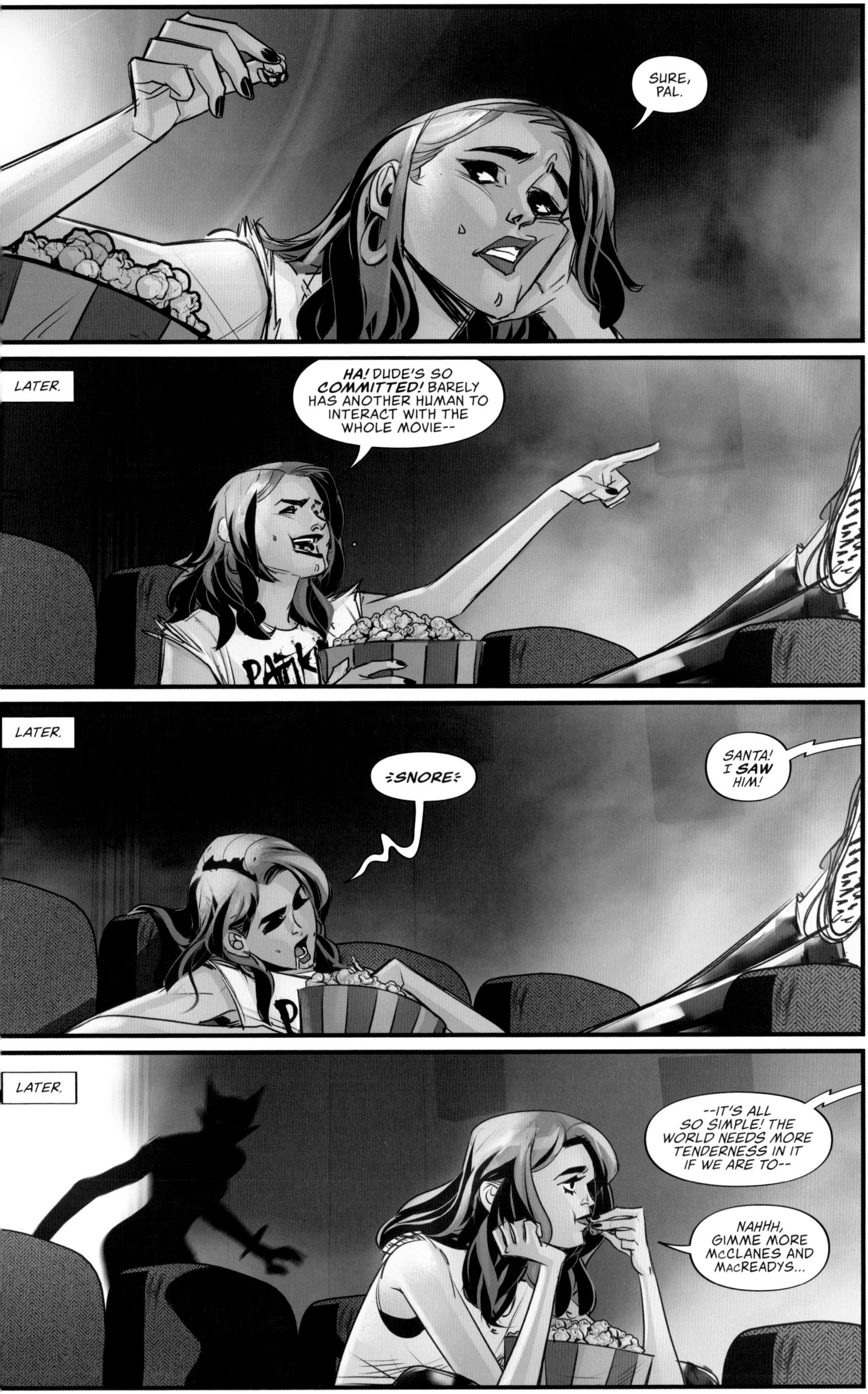
SURE, PAL.
LATER.
HA! DUDE'S SO COMMITTED! BARELY HAS ANOTHER HUMAN TO INTERACT WITH THE WHOLE MOVIE--
LATER.
SANTA! I SAW HIM!
SNORE
LATER.
--IT'S ALL SO SIMPLE! THE WORLD NEEDS MORE TENDERNESS IN IT IF WE ARE TO--
NAHHH, GIMME MORE McCLANES AND MacREADYS...

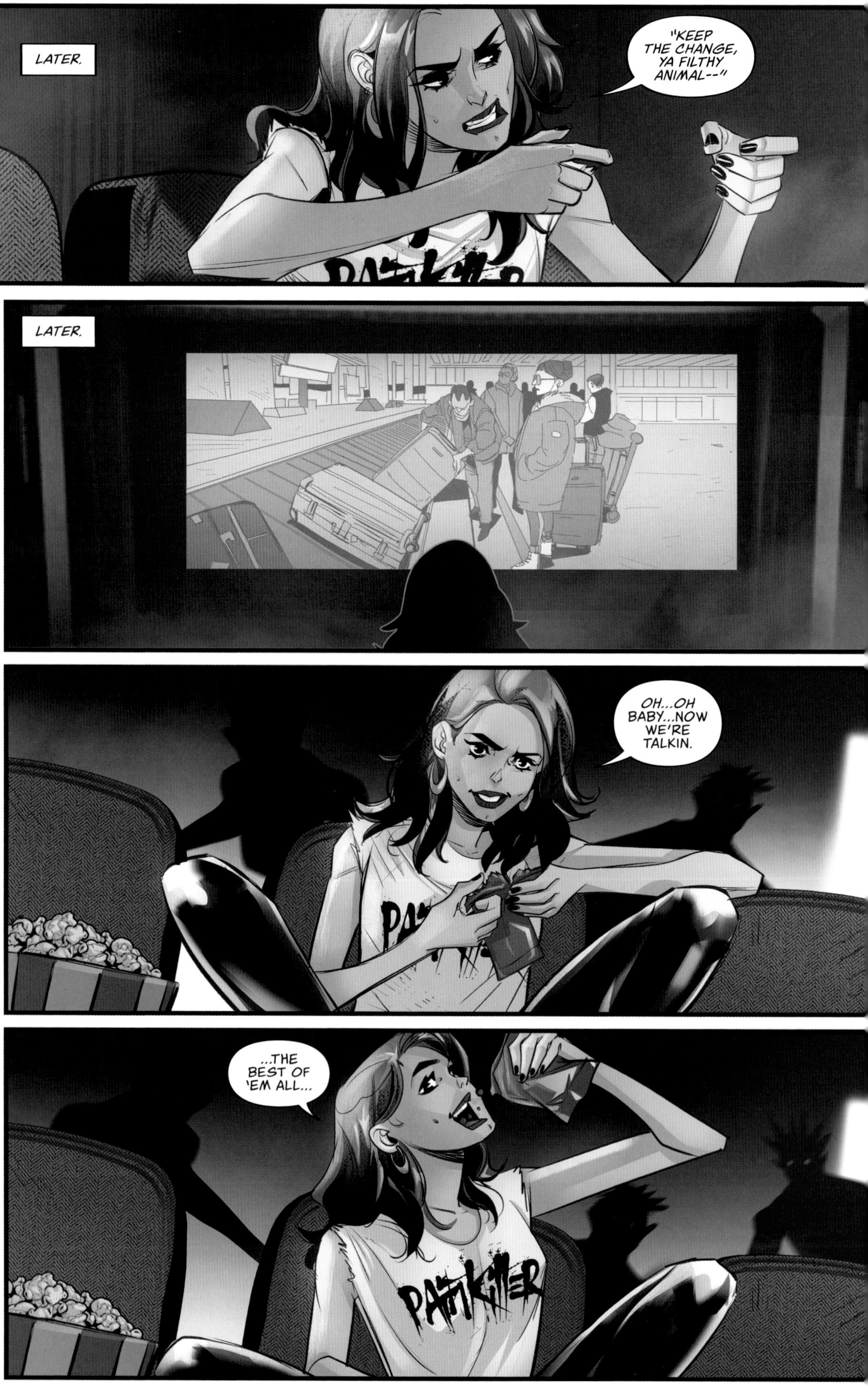
LATER.
"KEEP THE CHANGE, YA FILTHY ANIMAL--"
LATER.
OH...OH BABY...NOW WE'RE TALKIN.
...THE BEST OF 'EM ALL...

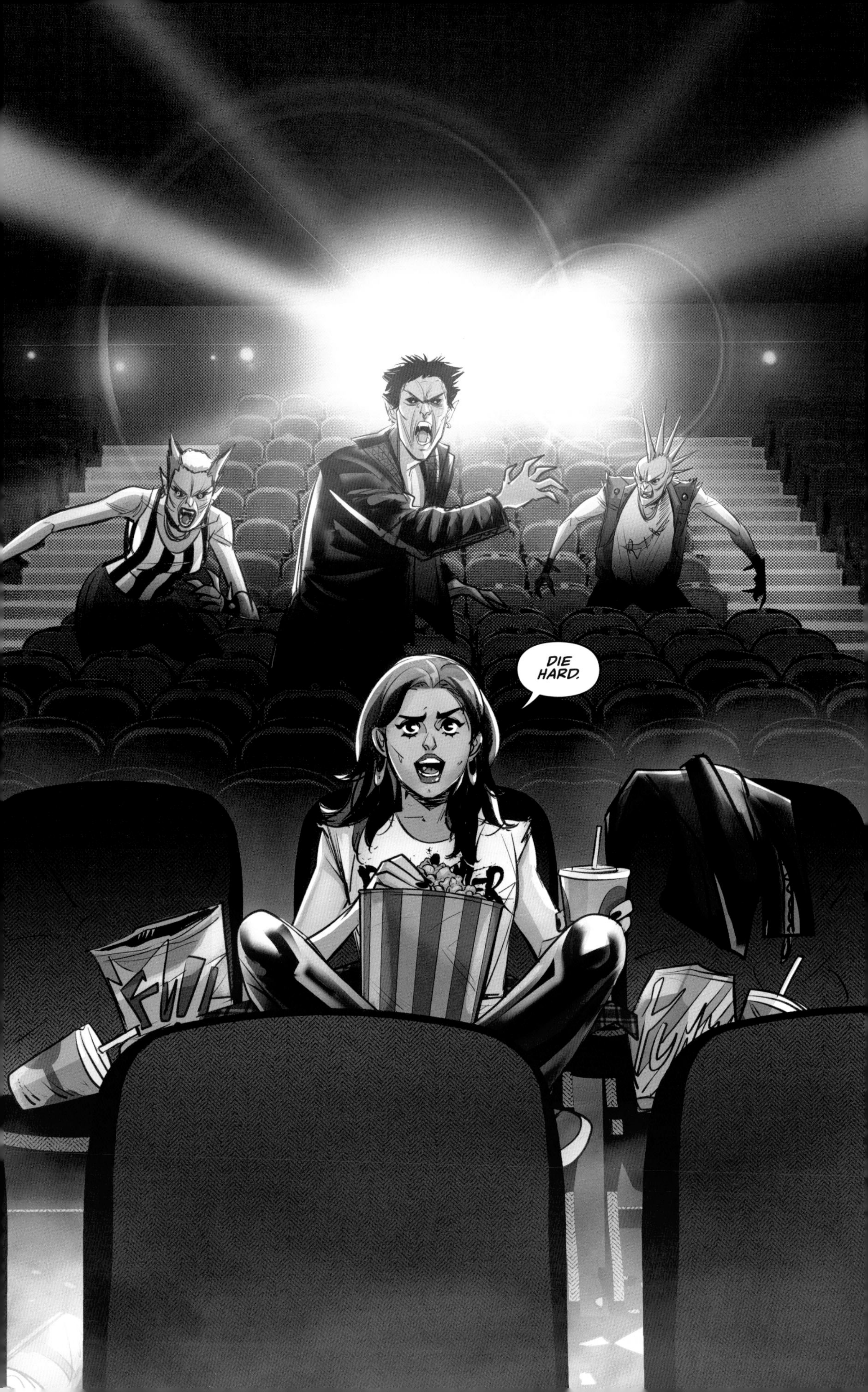
DIE HARD.

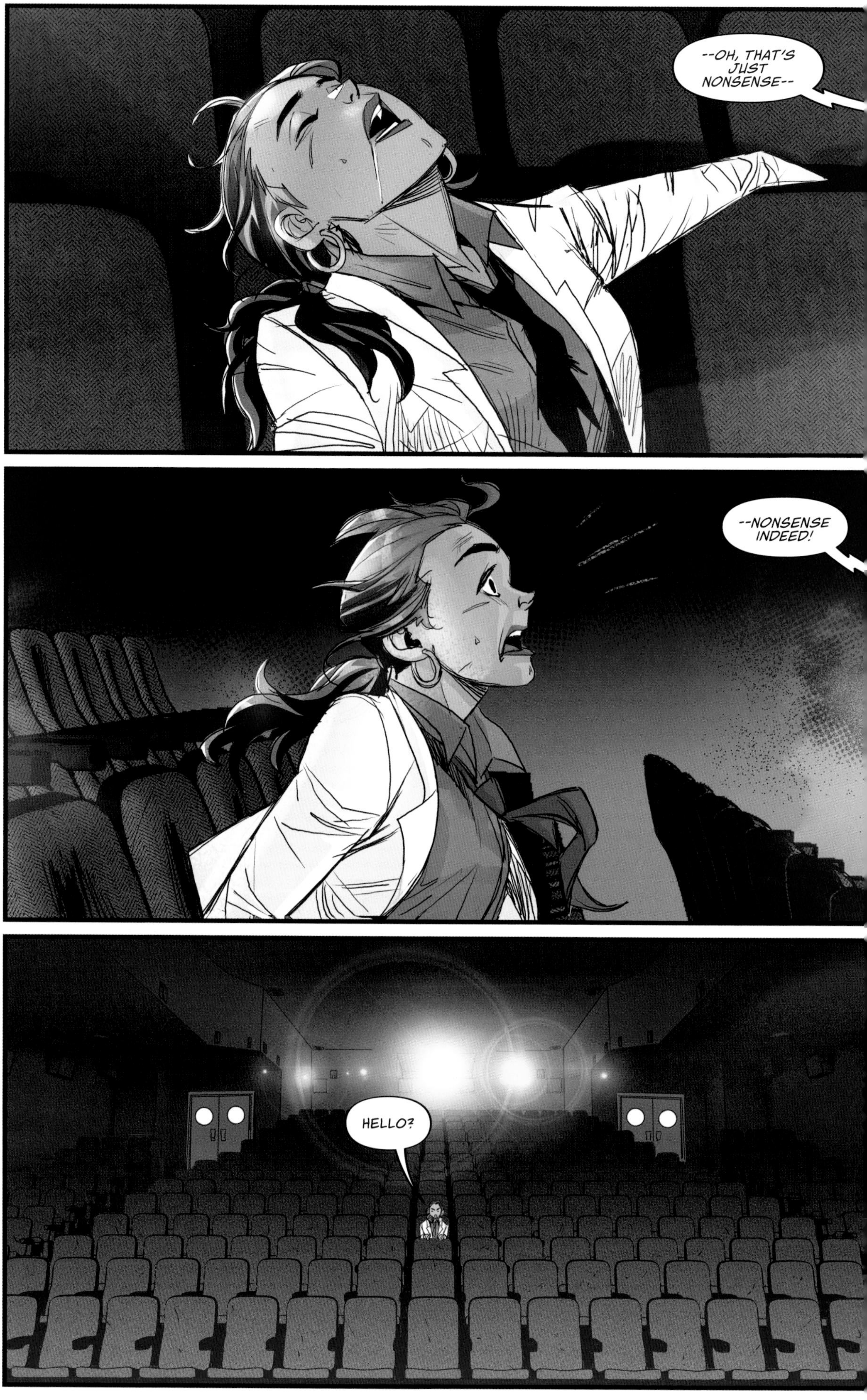
--OH, THAT'S JUST NONSENSE--
--NONSENSE INDEED!
HELLO?

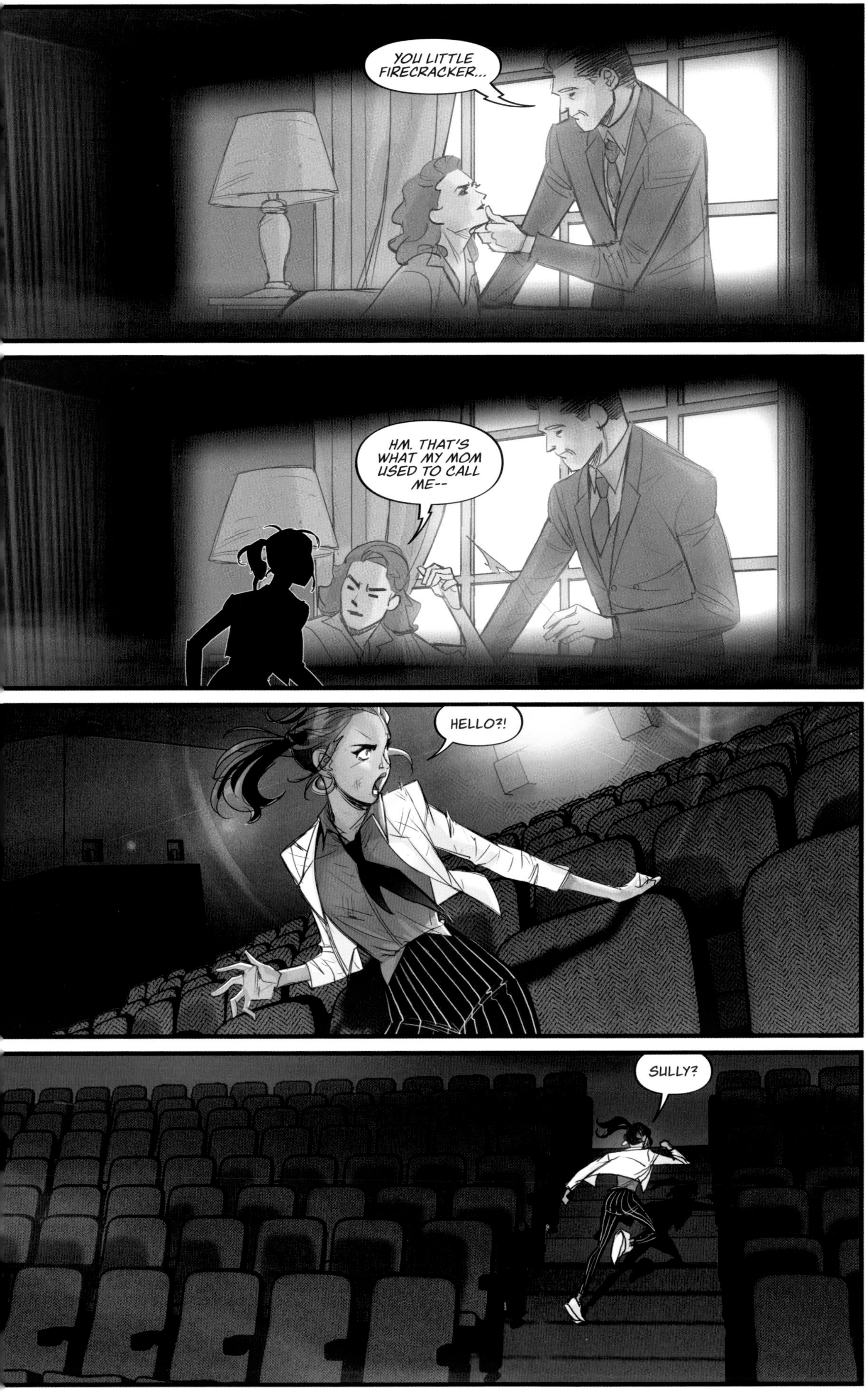
YOU LITTLE FIRECRACKER...
HM. THAT'S WHAT MY MOM USED TO CALL ME--
HELLO?!
SULLY?

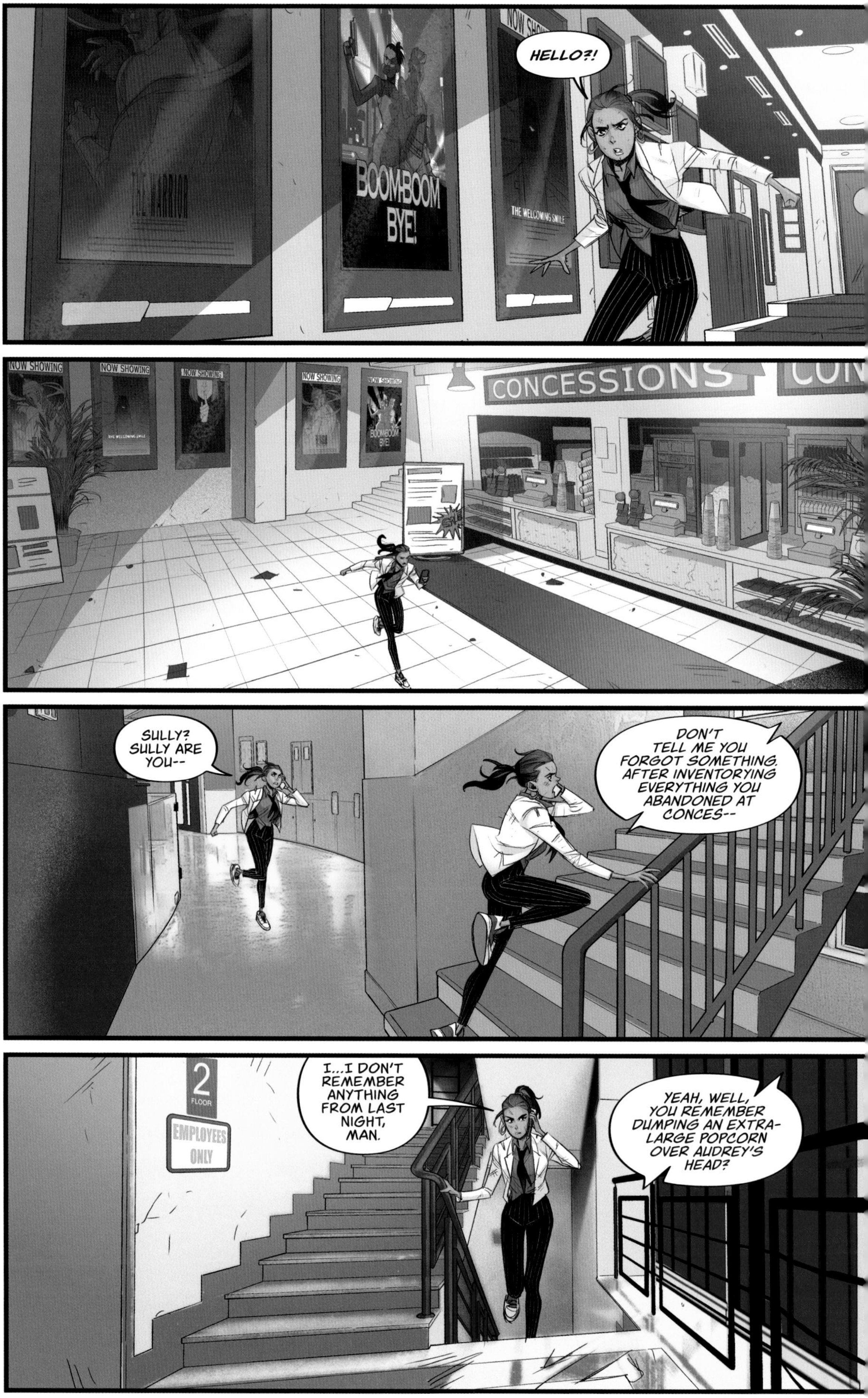
HELLO?!
THE WARRIOR
BOOM-BOOM BYE!
THE WELCOMING SMILE
NOW SHOWING
CONCESSIONS
SULLY? SULLY ARE YOU--
DON'T TELL ME YOU FORGOT SOMETHING. AFTER INVENTORYING EVERYTHING YOU ABANDONED AT CONCES--
2 FLOOR
EMPLOYEES ONLY
I...I DON'T REMEMBER ANYTHING FROM LAST NIGHT, MAN.
YEAH, WELL, YOU REMEMBER DUMPING AN EXTRA-LARGE POPCORN OVER AUDREY'S HEAD?

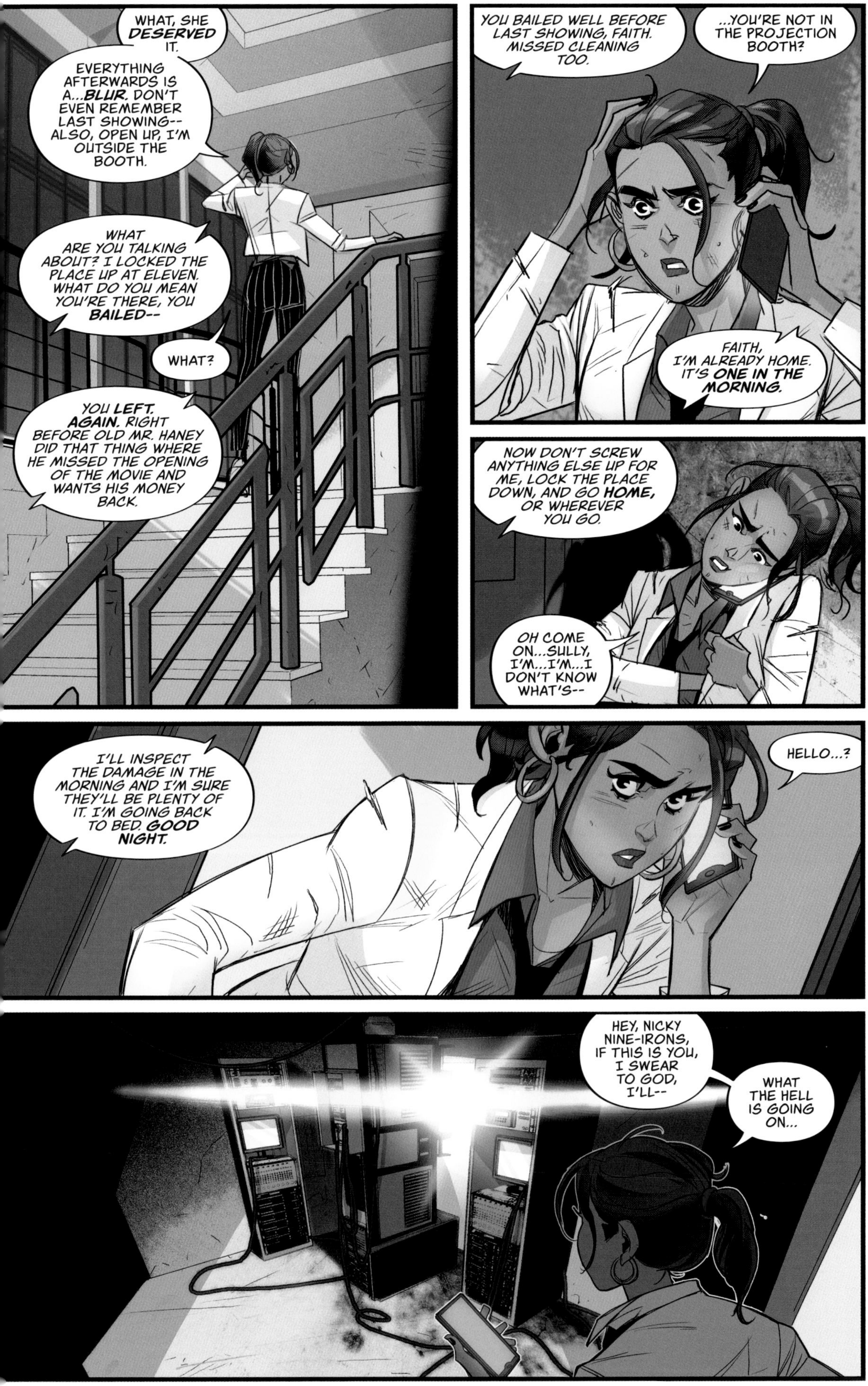
WHAT, SHE DESERVED IT.
EVERYTHING AFTERWARDS IS A...BLUR. DON'T EVEN REMEMBER LAST SHOWING-- ALSO, OPEN UP, I'M OUTSIDE THE BOOTH.
WHAT ARE YOU TALKING ABOUT? I LOCKED THE PLACE UP AT ELEVEN. WHAT DO YOU MEAN YOU'RE THERE, YOU BAILED--
WHAT?
YOU LEFT. AGAIN. RIGHT BEFORE OLD MR. HANEY DID THAT THING WHERE HE MISSED THE OPENING OF THE MOVIE AND WANTS HIS MONEY BACK.
YOU BAILED WELL BEFORE LAST SHOWING, FAITH. MISSED CLEANING TOO.
...YOU'RE NOT IN THE PROJECTION BOOTH?
FAITH, I'M ALREADY HOME. IT'S ONE IN THE MORNING.
NOW DON'T SCREW ANYTHING ELSE UP FOR ME, LOCK THE PLACE DOWN, AND GO HOME, OR WHEREVER YOU GO.
OH COME ON...SULLY, I'M...I'M...I DON'T KNOW WHAT'S--
I'LL INSPECT THE DAMAGE IN THE MORNING AND I'M SURE THEY'LL BE PLENTY OF IT. I'M GOING BACK TO BED. GOOD NIGHT.
HELLO...?
HEY, NICKY NINE-IRONS, IF THIS IS YOU, I SWEAR TO GOD, I'LL--
WHAT THE HELL IS GOING ON...

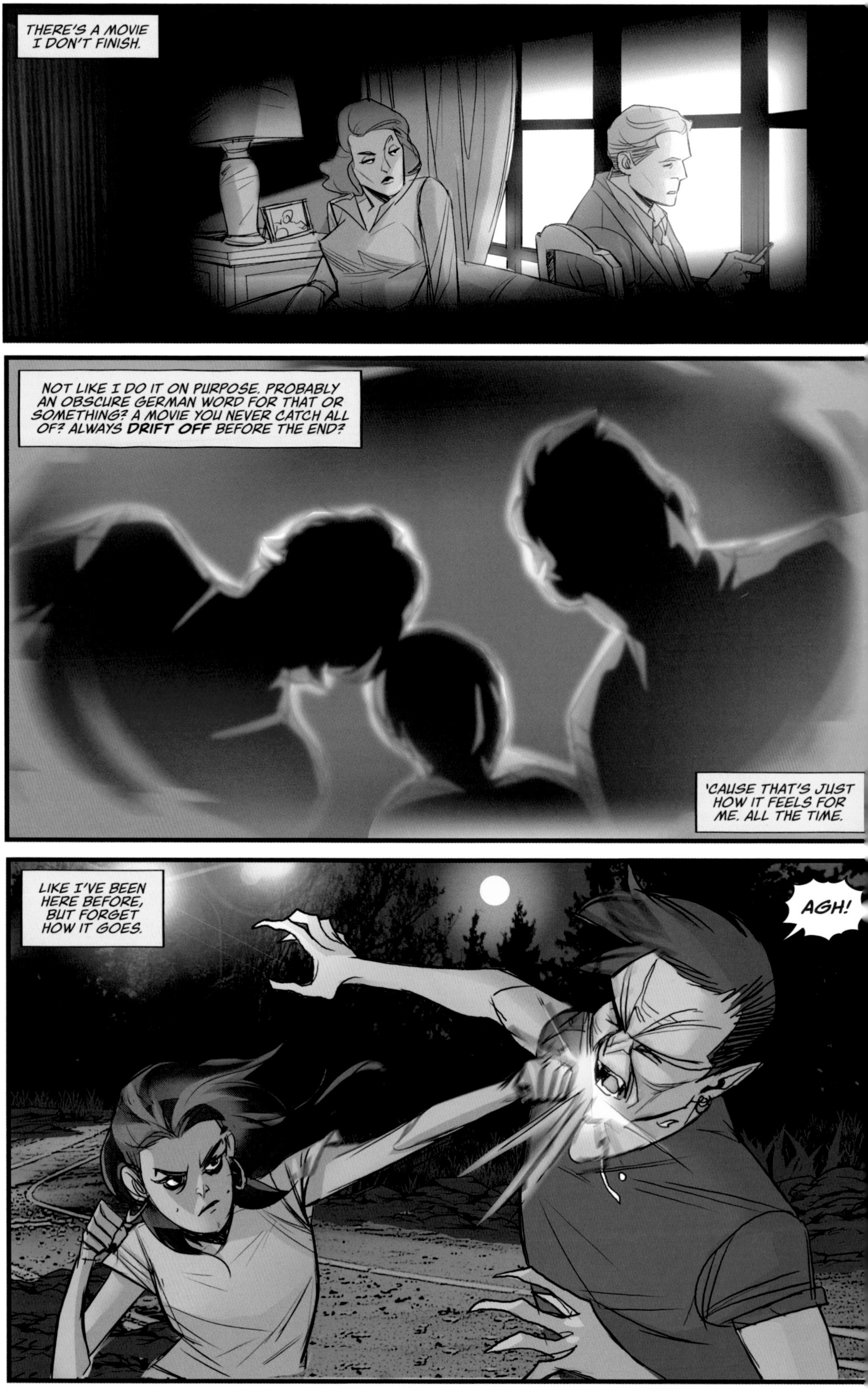
THERE'S A MOVIE I DON'T FINISH.
NOT LIKE I DO IT ON PURPOSE. PROBABLY AN OBSCURE GERMAN WORD FOR THAT OR SOMETHING? A MOVIE YOU NEVER CATCH ALL OF? ALWAYS DRIFT OFF BEFORE THE END?
'CAUSE THAT'S JUST HOW IT FEELS FOR ME. ALL THE TIME.
LIKE I'VE BEEN HERE BEFORE, BUT FORGET HOW IT GOES.
AGH!

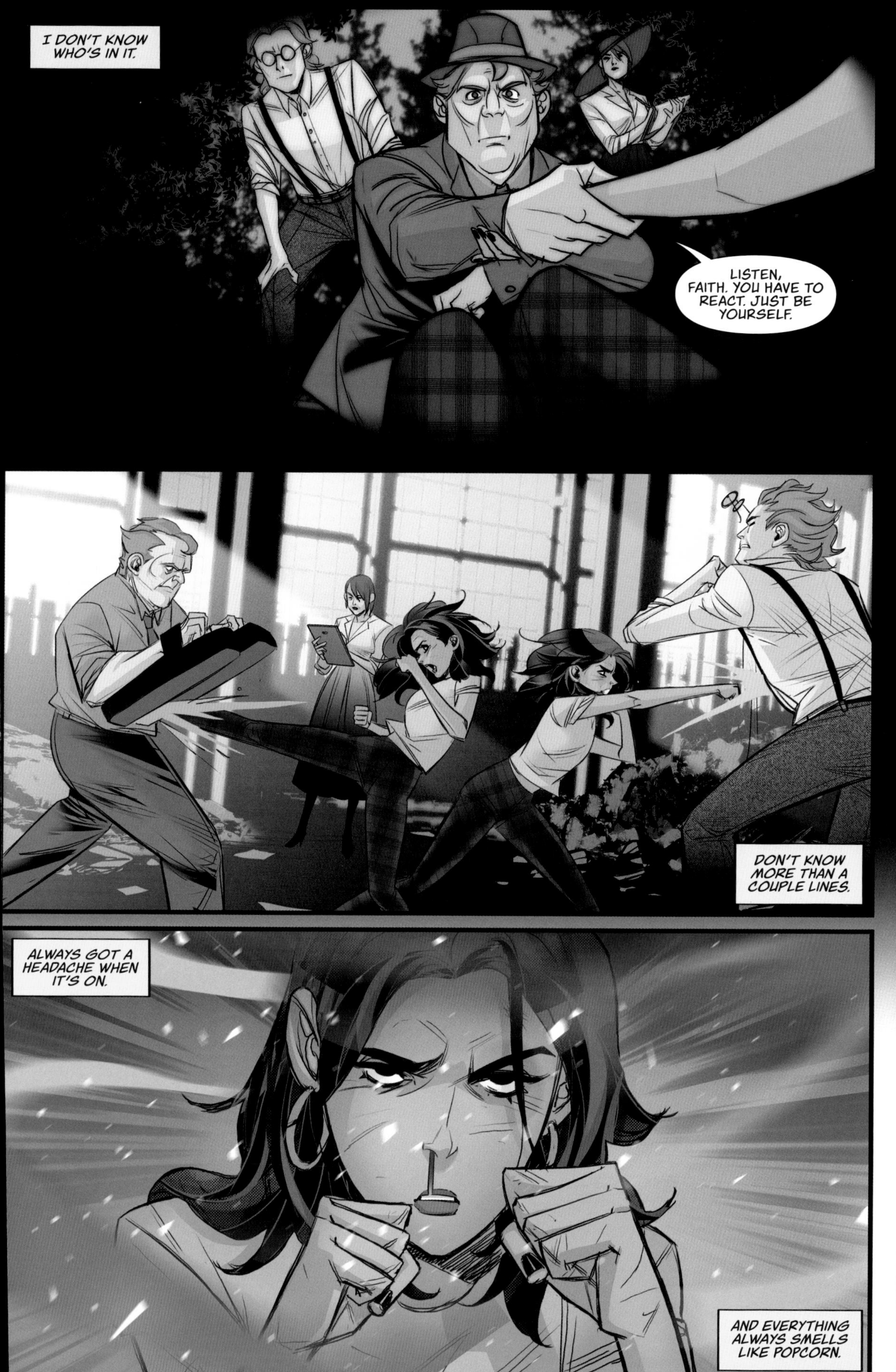
I DON'T KNOW WHO'S IN IT.
LISTEN, FAITH. YOU HAVE TO REACT. JUST BE YOURSELF.
DON'T KNOW MORE THAN A COUPLE LINES.
ALWAYS GOT A HEADACHE WHEN IT'S ON.
AND EVERYTHING ALWAYS SMELLS LIKE POPCORN.

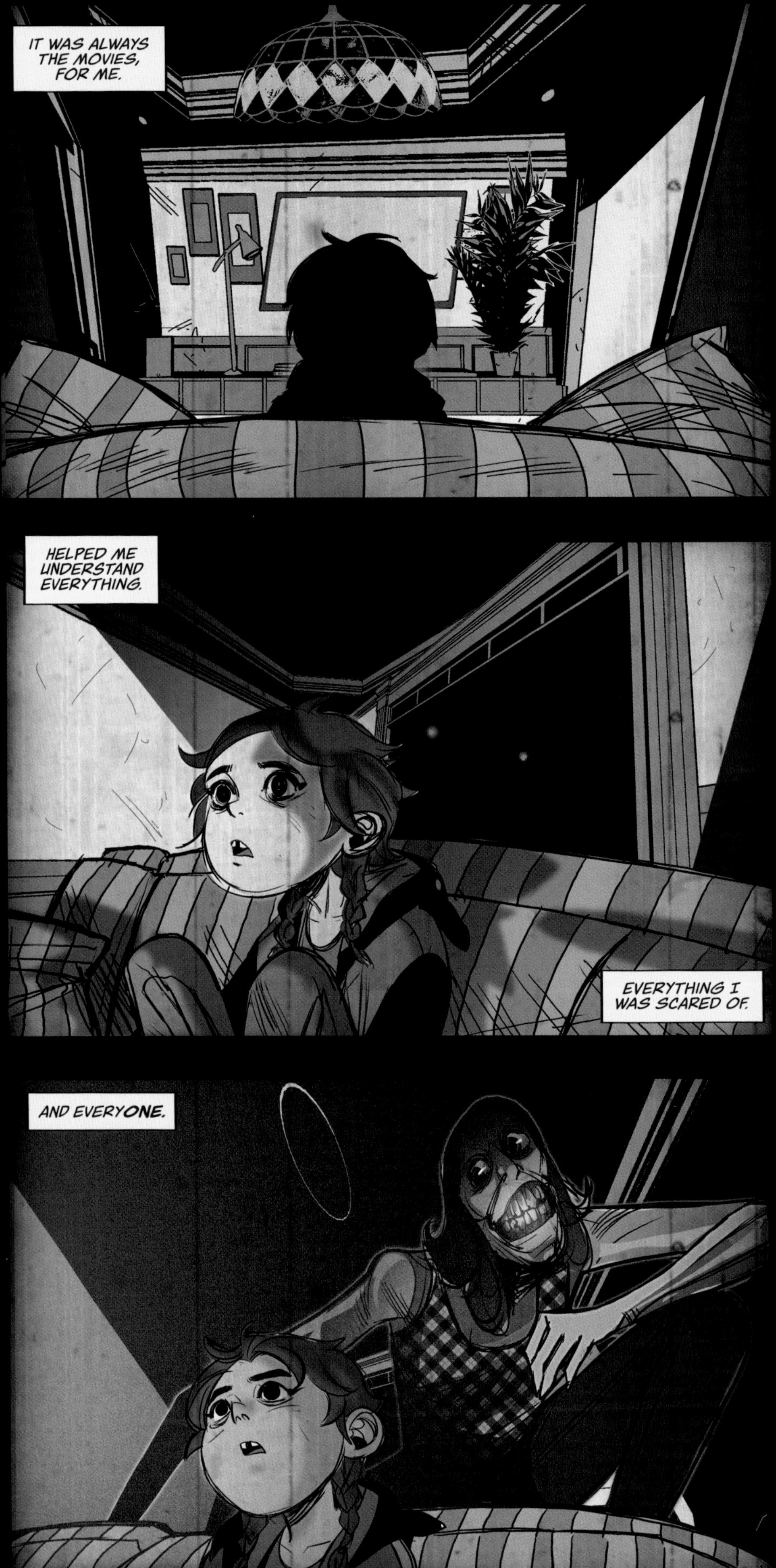
IT WAS ALWAYS THE MOVIES, FOR ME.
HELPED ME UNDERSTAND EVERYTHING.
EVERYTHING I WAS SCARED OF.
AND EVERYONE.

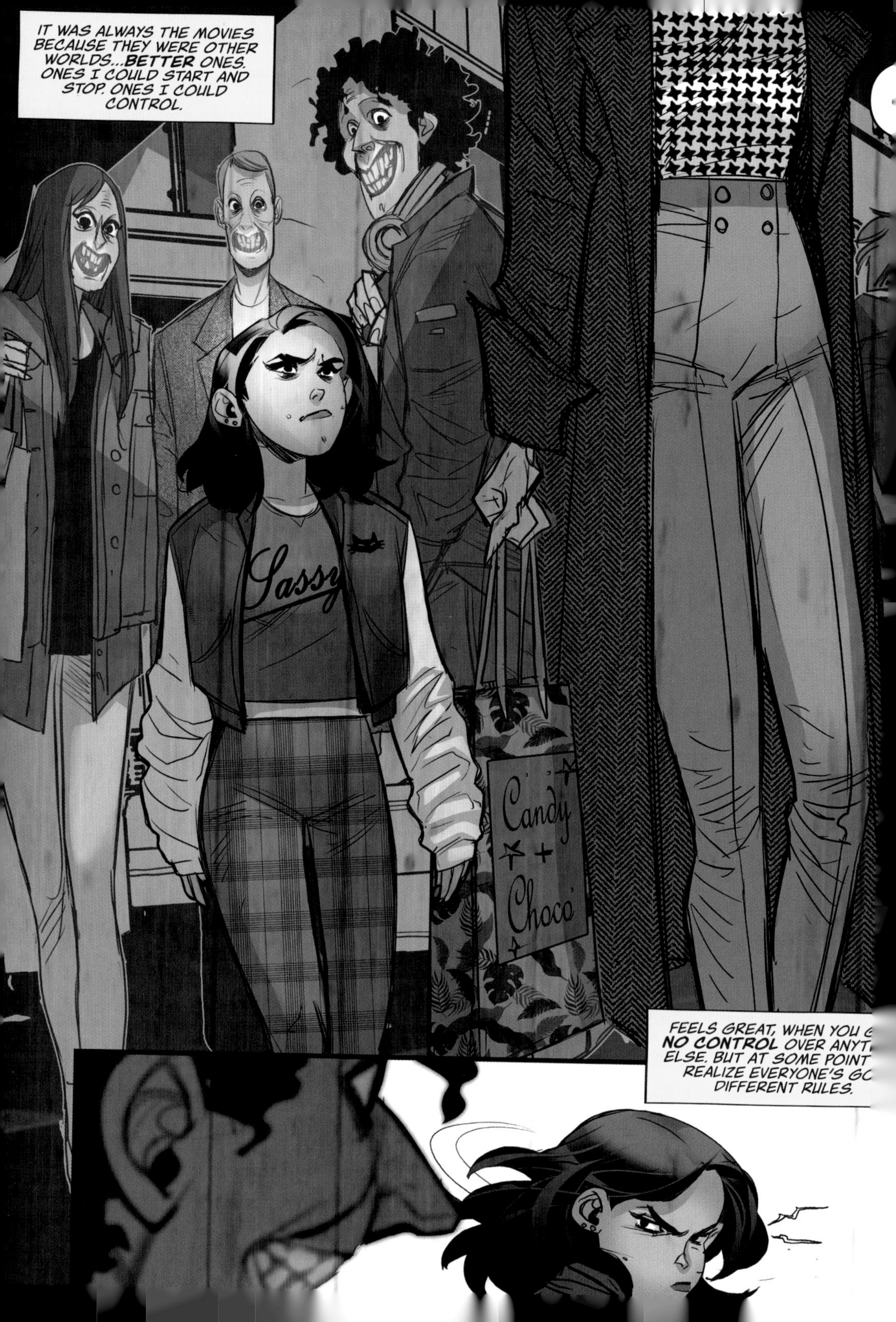
IT WAS ALWAYS THE MOVIES BECAUSE THEY WERE OTHER WORLDS...**BETTER** ONES. ONES I COULD START AND STOP. ONES I COULD CONTROL.
Sassy
Candy + Choco
FEELS GREAT, WHEN YOU
NO CONTROL OVER
ELSE. BUT AT SOME
REALIZE EVERYONE'S
DIFFERENT RULES.

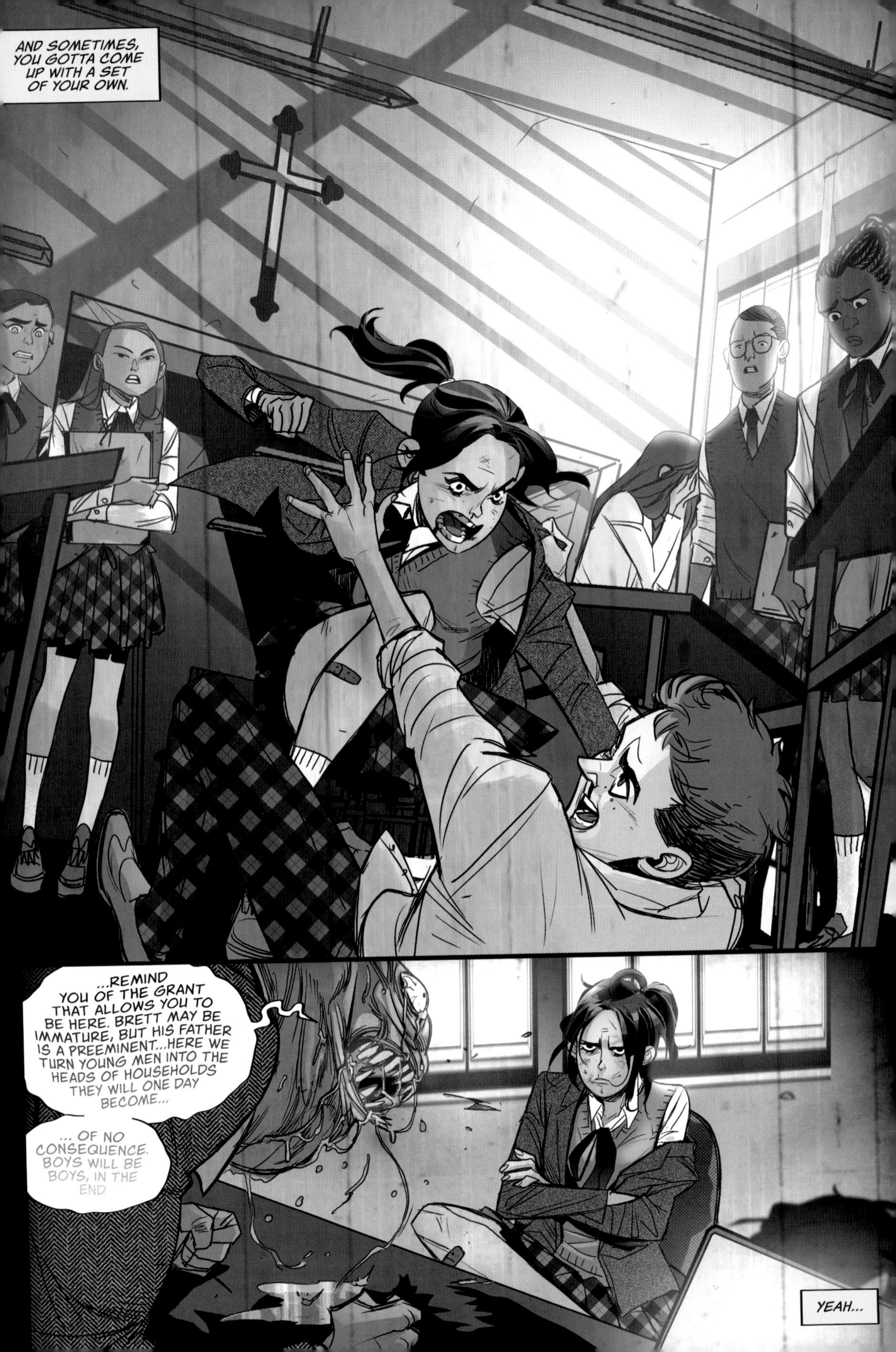
AND SOMETIMES, YOU GOTTA COME UP WITH A SET OF YOUR OWN.
...REMIND YOU OF THE GRANT THAT ALLOWS YOU TO BE HERE. BRETT MAY BE IMMATURE, BUT HIS FATHER IS A PREEMINENT... HERE WE TURN YOUNG MEN INTO THE HEADS OF HOUSEHOLDS THEY WILL ONE DAY BECOME...
... OF NO CONSEQUENCE. BOYS WILL BE BOYS, IN THE END.
YEAH...

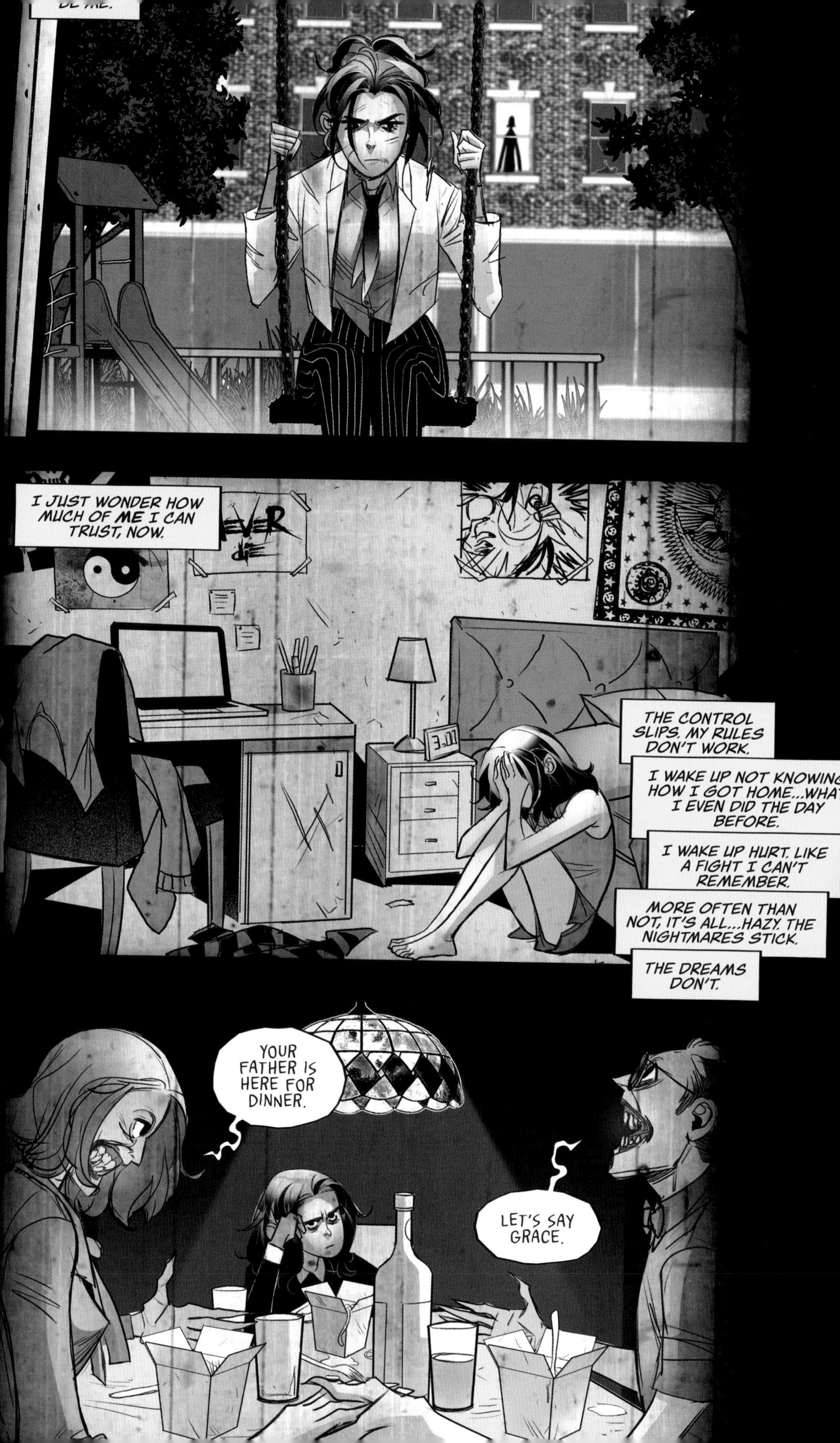
I JUST WONDER HOW MUCH OF ME I CAN TRUST, NOW.
THE CONTROL SLIPS. MY RULES DON'T WORK.
I WAKE UP NOT KNOWING HOW I GOT HOME...WHAT I EVEN DID THE DAY BEFORE.
I WAKE UP HURT. LIKE A FIGHT I CAN'T REMEMBER.
MORE OFTEN THAN NOT, IT'S ALL...HAZY. THE NIGHTMARES STICK.
THE DREAMS DON'T.
YOUR FATHER IS HERE FOR DINNER.
LET'S SAY GRACE.

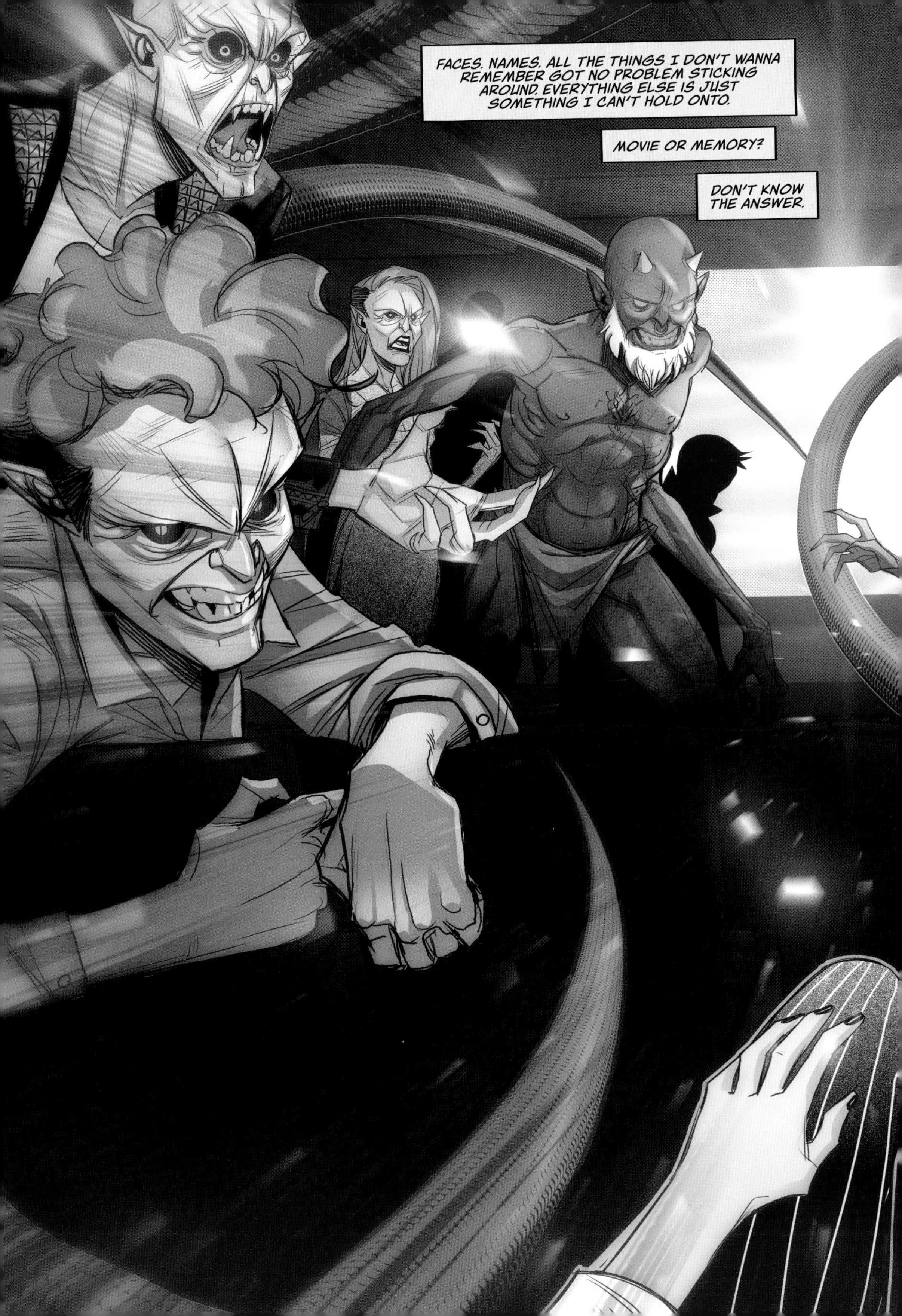
FACES. NAMES. ALL THE THINGS I DON'T WANNA REMEMBER GOT NO PROBLEM STICKING AROUND. EVERYTHING ELSE IS JUST SOMETHING I CAN'T HOLD ONTO.
MOVIE OR MEMORY?
DON'T KNOW THE ANSWER.

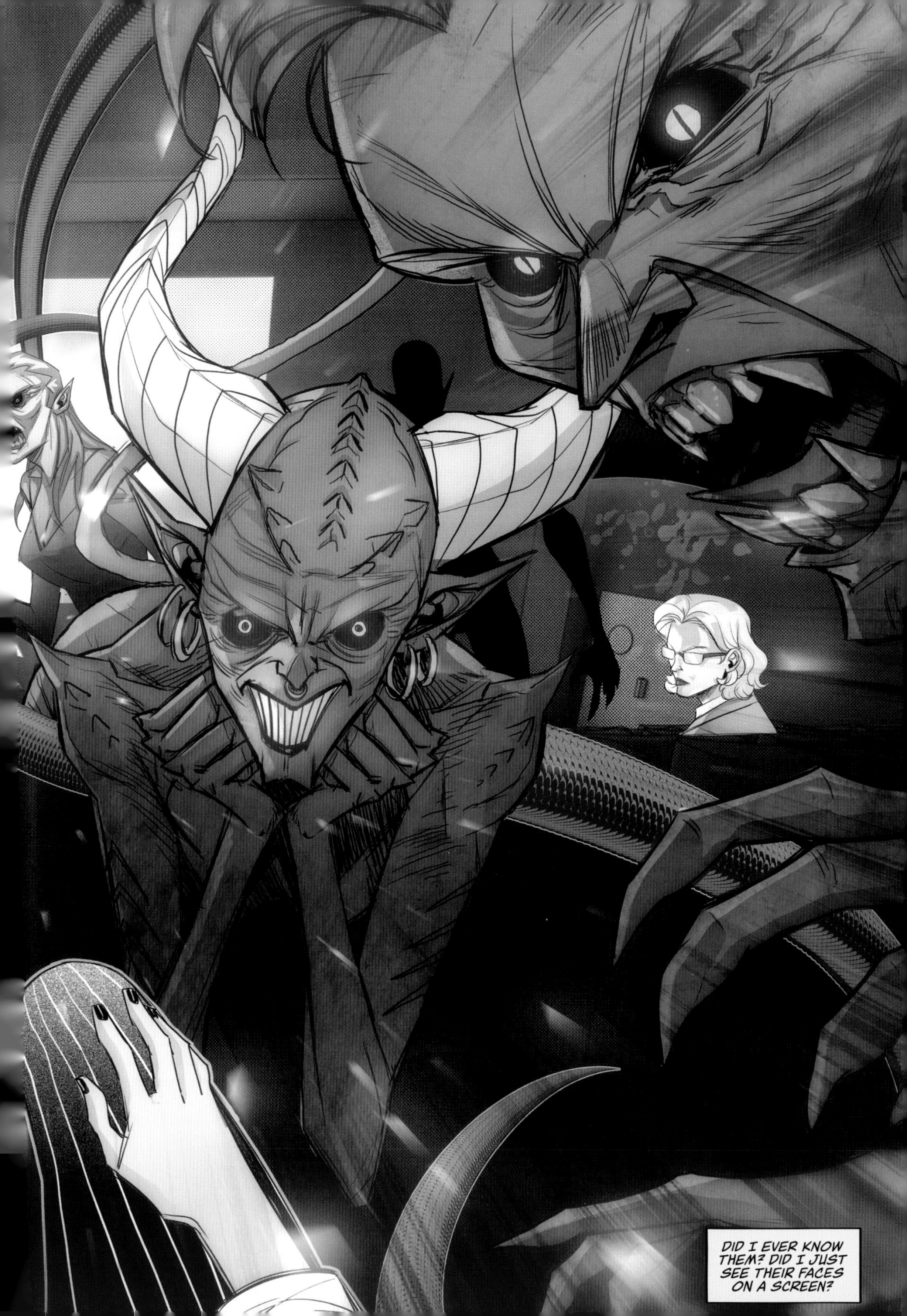
DID I EVER KNOW THEM? DID I JUST SEE THEIR FACES ON A SCREEN?

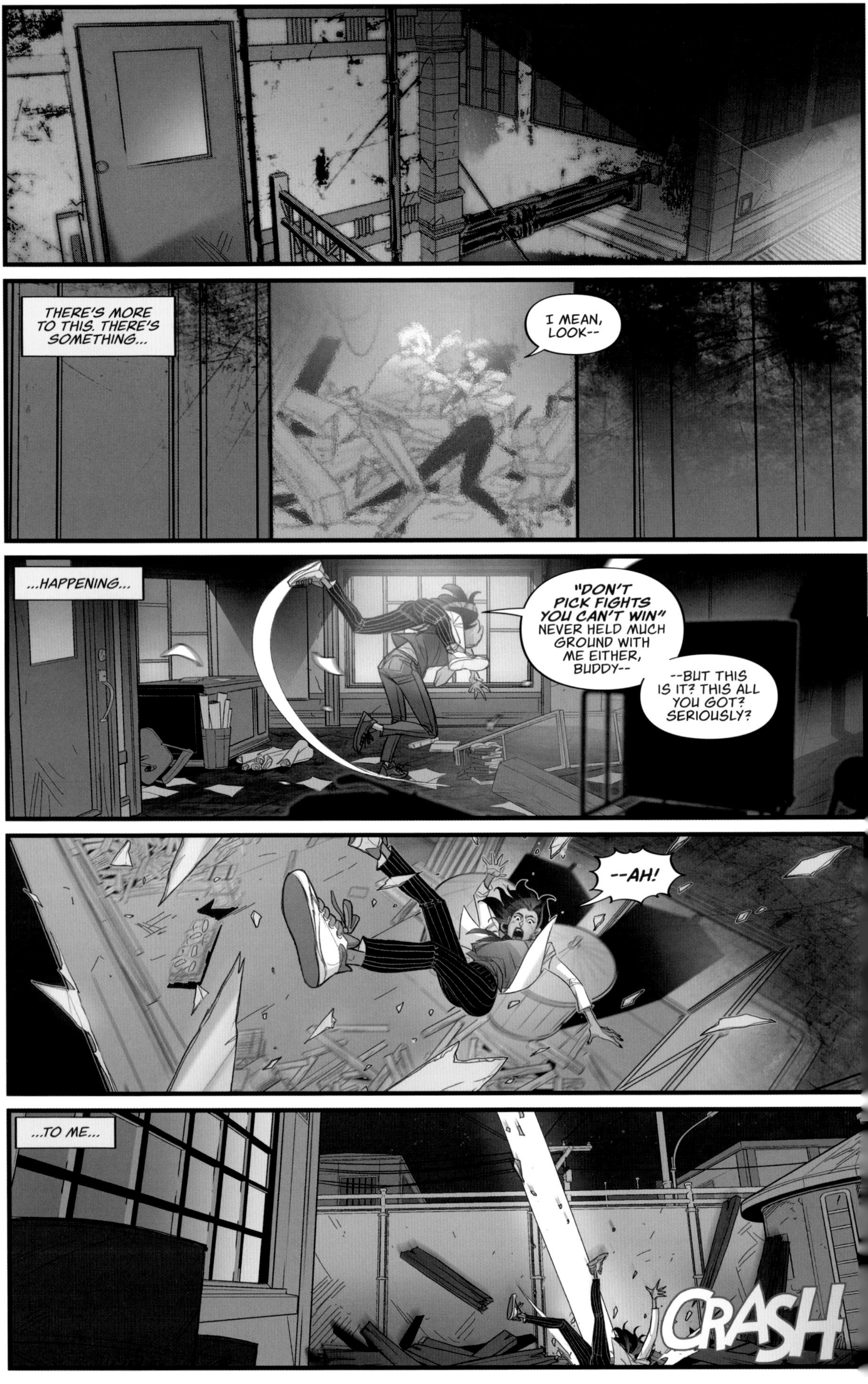
THERE'S MORE TO THIS. THERE'S SOMETHING...
I MEAN, LOOK--
...HAPPENING...
"DON'T PICK FIGHTS YOU CAN'T WIN" NEVER HELD MUCH GROUND WITH ME EITHER, BUDDY--
--BUT THIS IS IT? THIS ALL YOU GOT? SERIOUSLY?
--AH!
...TO ME...
CRASH

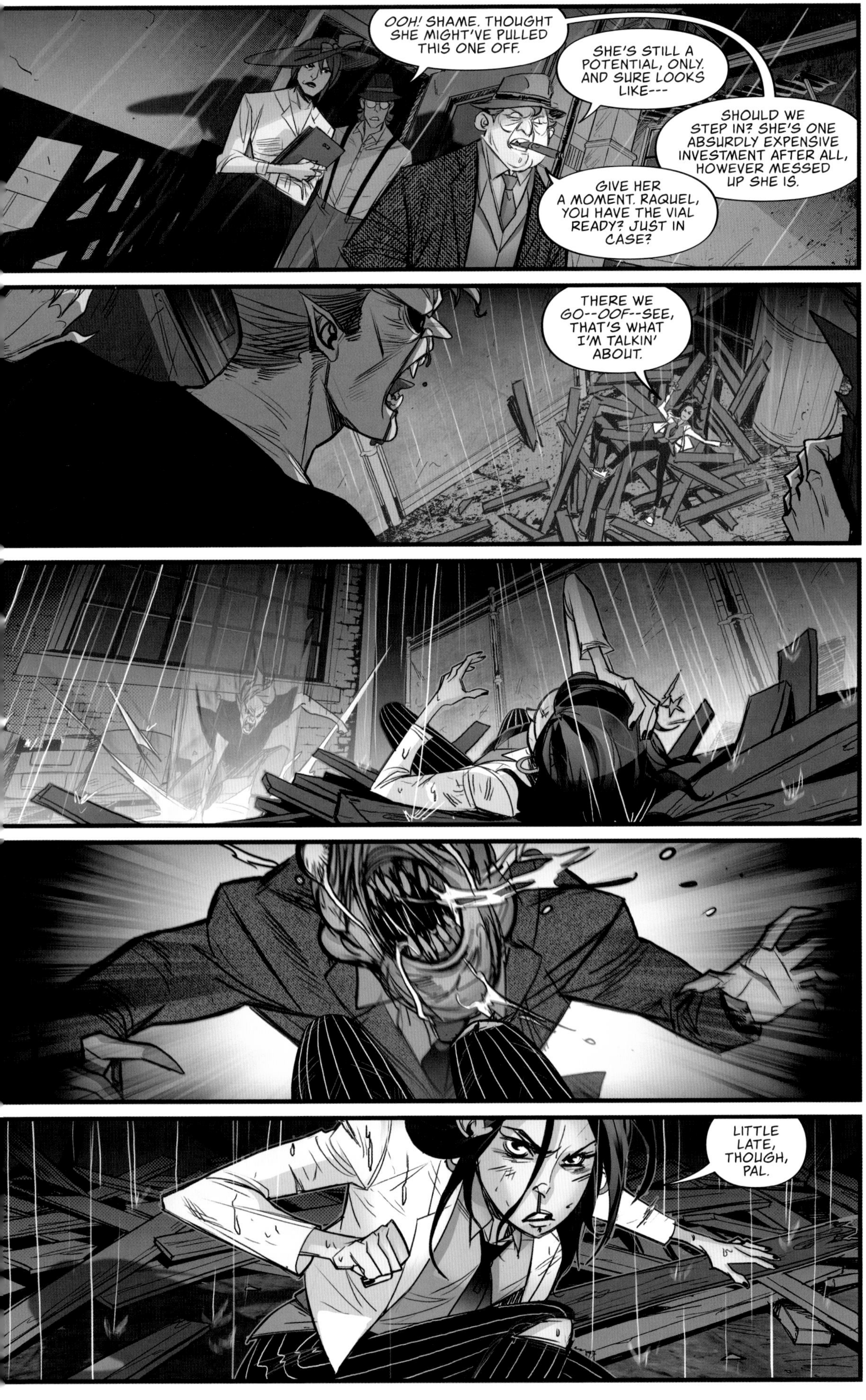
OOH! SHAME. THOUGHT SHE MIGHT'VE PULLED THIS ONE OFF.
SHE'S STILL A POTENTIAL, ONLY. AND SURE LOOKS LIKE---
SHOULD WE STEP IN? SHE'S ONE ABSURDLY EXPENSIVE INVESTMENT AFTER ALL, HOWEVER MESSED UP SHE IS.
GIVE HER A MOMENT. RAQUEL, YOU HAVE THE VIAL READY? JUST IN CASE?
THERE WE GO--OOF--SEE, THAT'S WHAT I'M TALKIN' ABOUT.
LITTLE LATE, THOUGH, PAL.

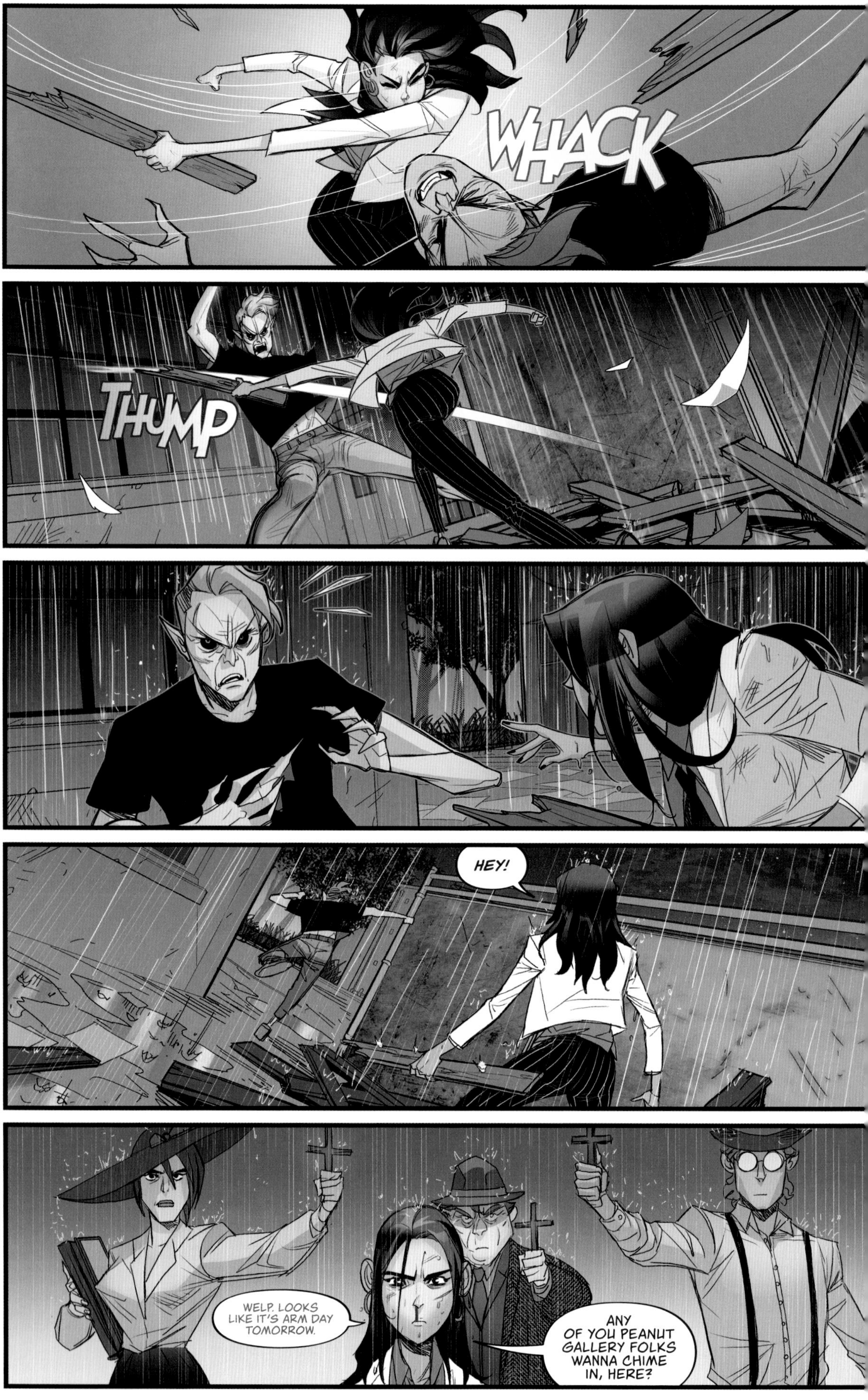
WHACK
THUMP
HEY!
WELP. LOOKS LIKE IT'S ARM DAY TOMORROW.
ANY OF YOU PEANUT GALLERY FOLKS WANNA CHIME IN, HERE?

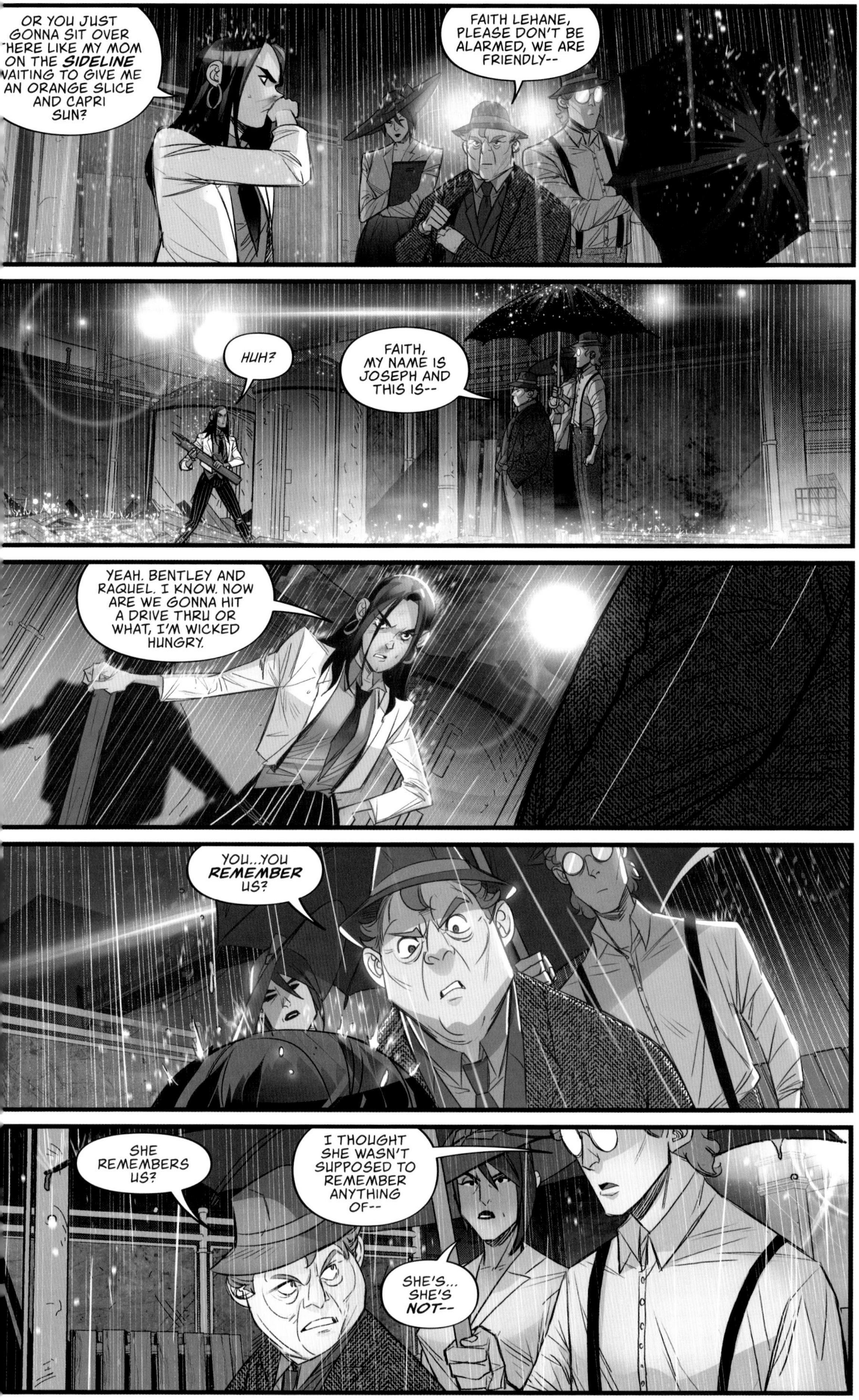
OR YOU JUST GONNA SIT OVER HERE LIKE MY MOM ON THE **SIDELINE** VAITING TO GIVE ME AN ORANGE SLICE AND CAPRI SUN?
FAITH LEHANE, PLEASE DON'T BE ALARMED, WE ARE FRIENDLY--
HUH?
FAITH, MY NAME IS JOSEPH AND THIS IS--
YEAH. BENTLEY AND RAQUEL. I KNOW. NOW ARE WE GONNA HIT A DRIVE THRU OR WHAT, I'M WICKED HUNGRY.
YOU...YOU ***REMEMBER*** US?
SHE REMEMBERS US?
I THOUGHT SHE WASN'T SUPPOSED TO REMEMBER ANYTHING OF--
SHE'S... SHE'S ***NOT--***

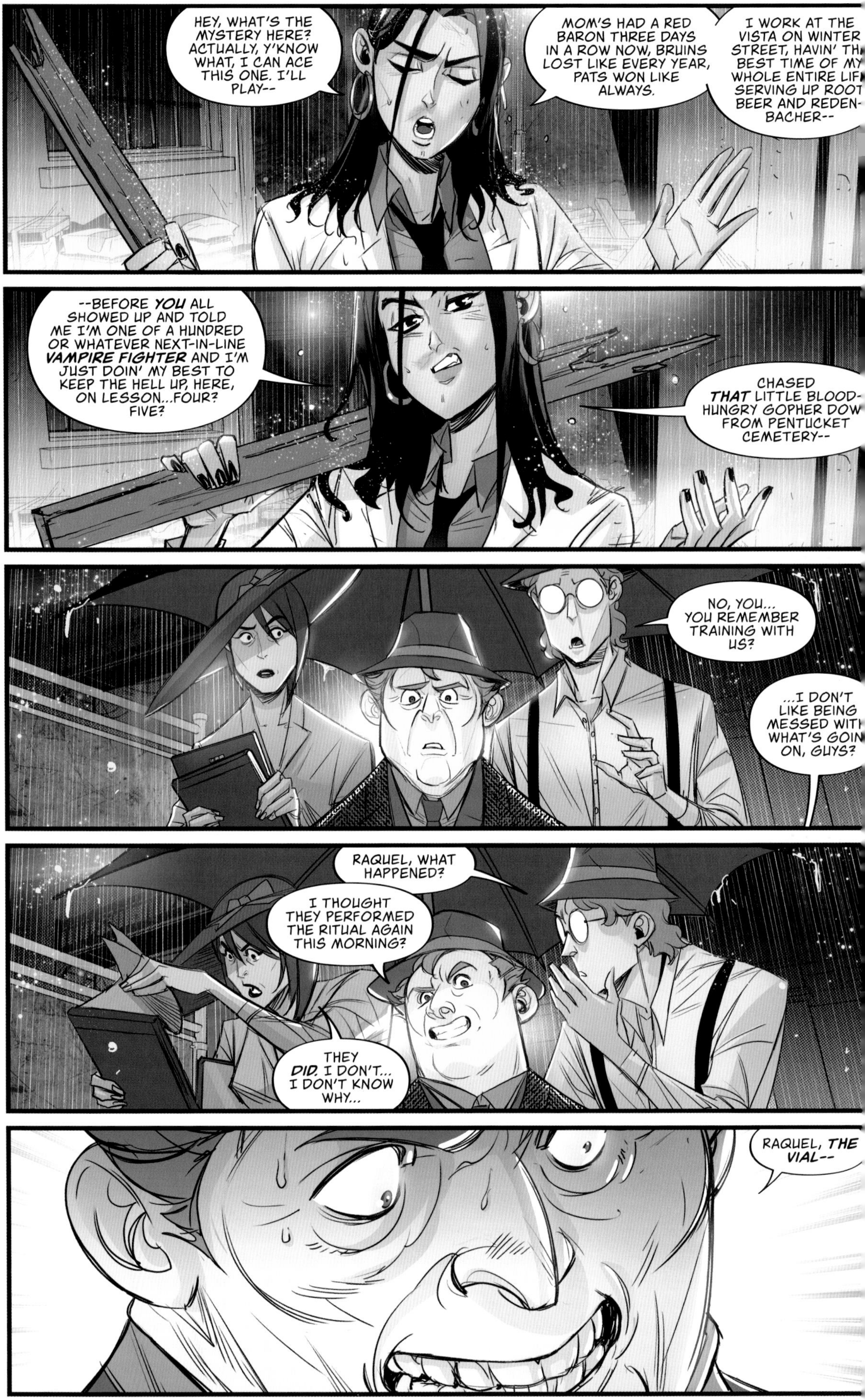
HEY, WHAT'S THE MYSTERY HERE? ACTUALLY, Y'KNOW WHAT, I CAN ACE THIS ONE. I'LL PLAY--
MOM'S HAD A RED BARON THREE DAYS IN A ROW NOW, BRUINS LOST LIKE EVERY YEAR, PATS WON LIKE ALWAYS.
I WORK AT THE VISTA ON WINTER STREET, HAVIN' TH BEST TIME OF MY WHOLE ENTIRE LIF SERVING UP ROOT BEER AND REDEN-BACHER--
--BEFORE YOU ALL SHOWED UP AND TOLD ME I'M ONE OF A HUNDRED OR WHATEVER NEXT-IN-LINE VAMPIRE FIGHTER AND I'M JUST DOIN' MY BEST TO KEEP THE HELL UP, HERE, ON LESSON...FOUR? FIVE?
CHASED THAT LITTLE BLOOD-HUNGRY GOPHER DOW FROM PENTUCKET CEMETERY--
NO, YOU... YOU REMEMBER TRAINING WITH US?
...I DON'T LIKE BEING MESSED WIT WHAT'S GOIN ON, GUYS?
RAQUEL, WHAT HAPPENED?
I THOUGHT THEY PERFORMED THE RITUAL AGAIN THIS MORNING?
THEY DID. I DON'T... I DON'T KNOW WHY...
RAQUEL, THE VIAL--

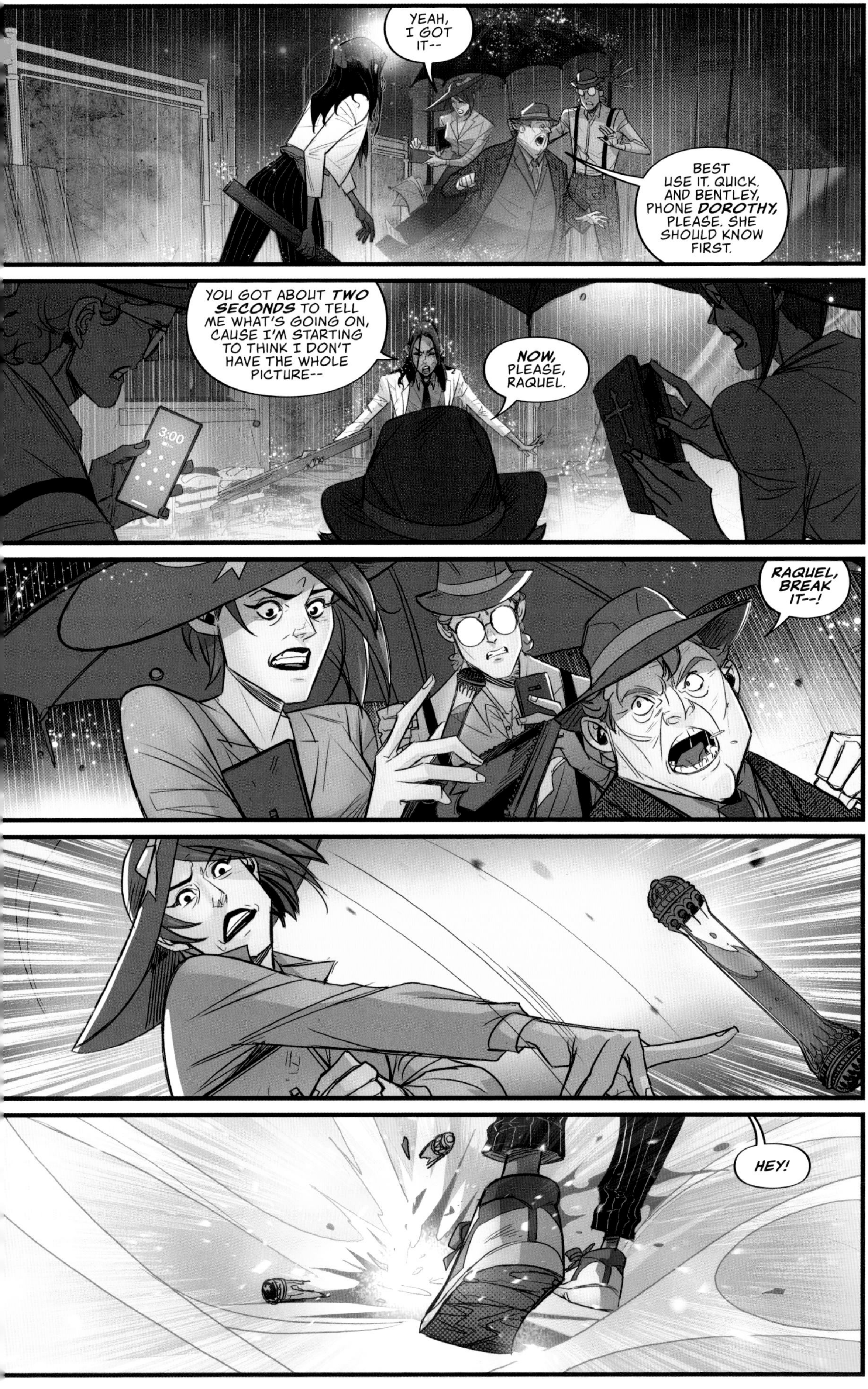
YEAH, I GOT IT--
BEST USE IT. QUICK. AND BENTLEY, PHONE DOROTHY, PLEASE. SHE SHOULD KNOW FIRST.
YOU GOT ABOUT TWO SECONDS TO TELL ME WHAT'S GOING ON, CAUSE I'M STARTING TO THINK I DON'T HAVE THE WHOLE PICTURE--
NOW, PLEASE, RAQUEL.
3:00
RAQUEL, BREAK IT--!
HEY!

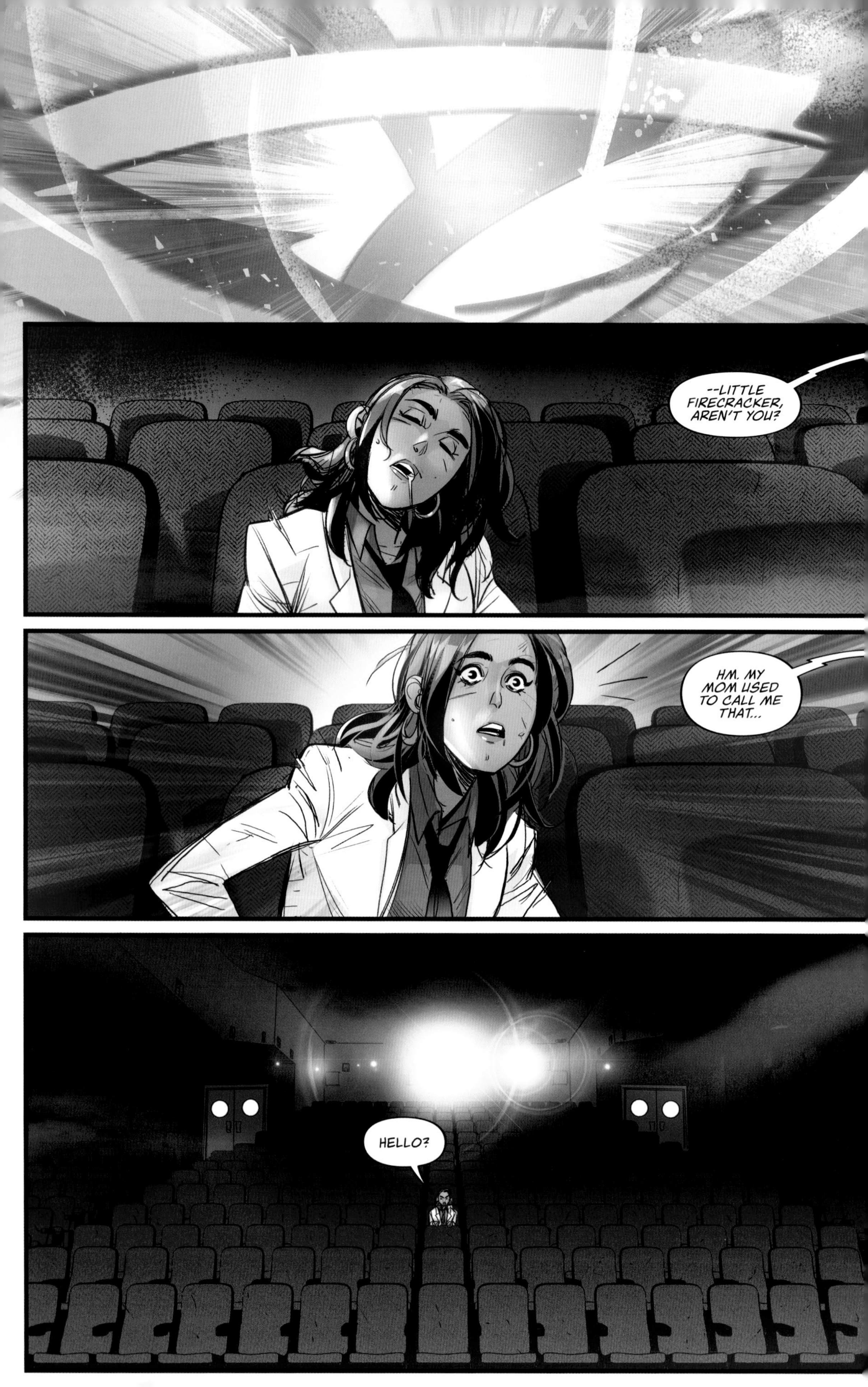
--LITTLE FIRECRACKER, AREN'T YOU?
HM. MY MOM USED TO CALL ME THAT...
HELLO?

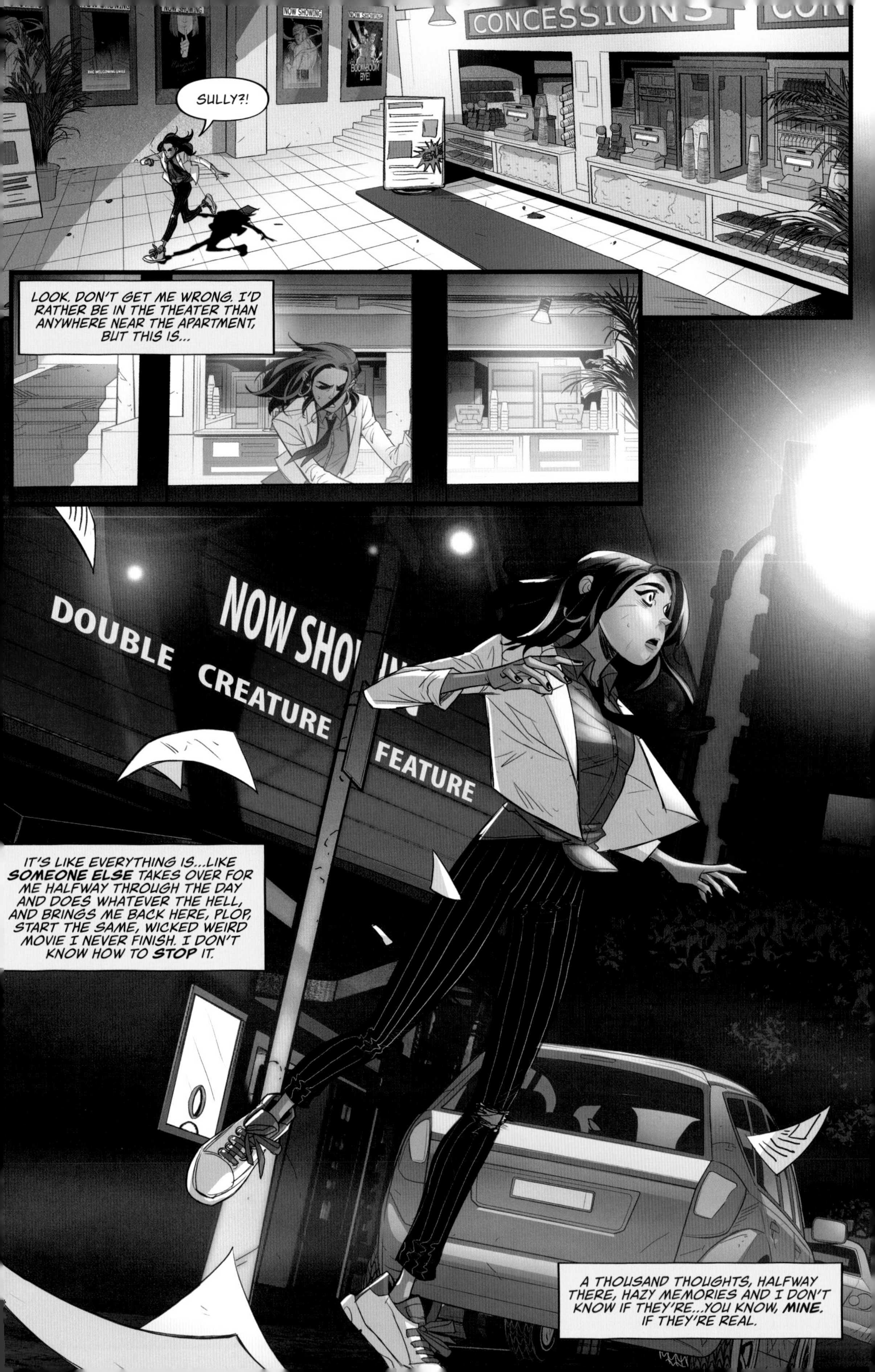
CONCESSIONS
NOW SHOWING
BOOMBOOM BYE!
SULLY?!
LOOK. DON'T GET ME WRONG. I'D RATHER BE IN THE THEATER THAN ANYWHERE NEAR THE APARTMENT, BUT THIS IS...
NOW SHOWING
DOUBLE CREATURE FEATURE
IT'S LIKE EVERYTHING IS...LIKE **SOMEONE ELSE** TAKES OVER FOR ME HALFWAY THROUGH THE DAY AND DOES WHATEVER THE HELL, AND BRINGS ME BACK HERE, PLOP, START THE SAME, WICKED WEIRD MOVIE I NEVER FINISH. I DON'T KNOW HOW TO **STOP** IT.
A THOUSAND THOUGHTS, HALFWAY THERE, HAZY MEMORIES AND I DON'T KNOW IF THEY'RE...YOU KNOW, **MINE.** IF THEY'RE REAL.

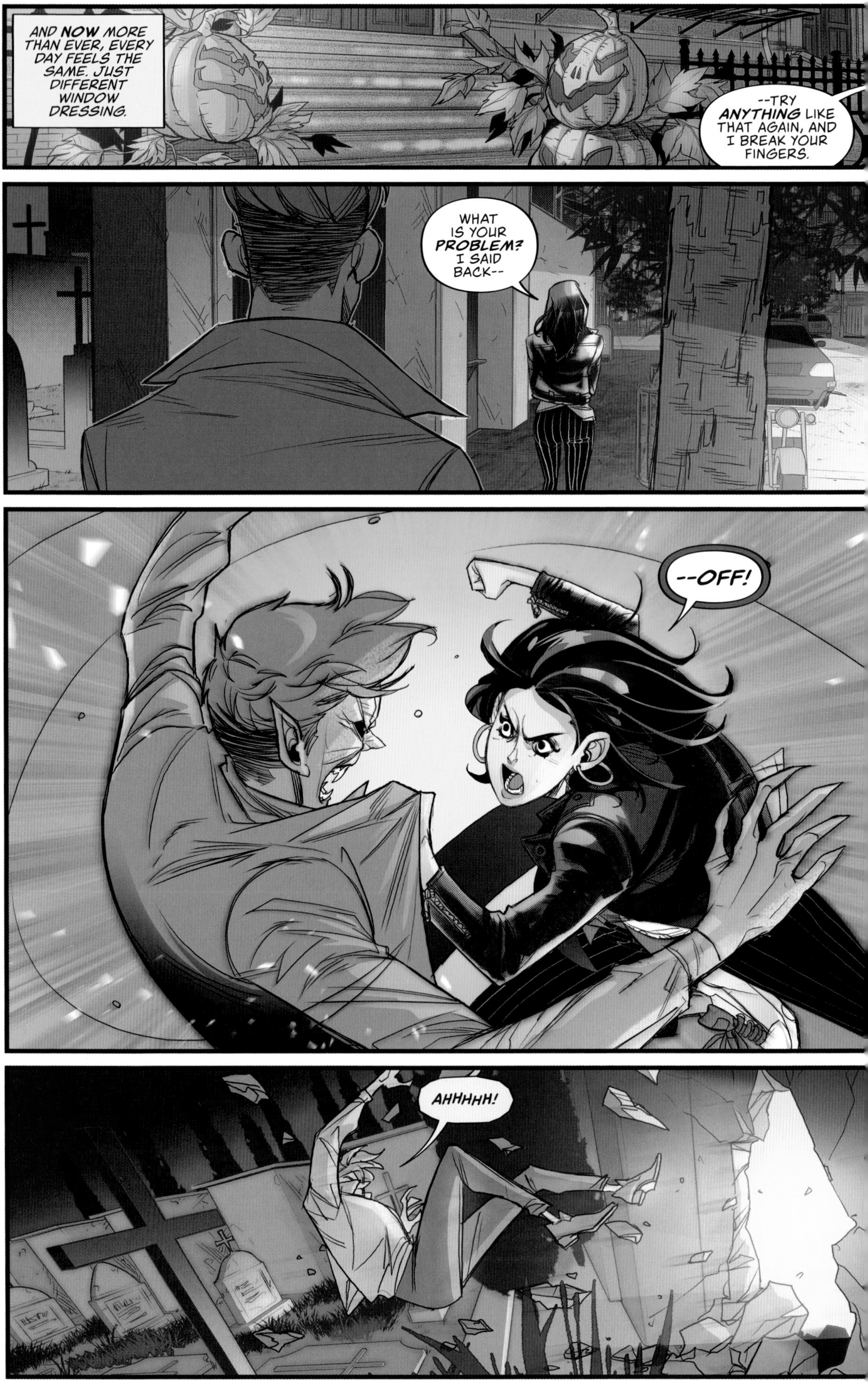
AND NOW MORE THAN EVER, EVERY DAY FEELS THE SAME. JUST DIFFERENT WINDOW DRESSING.
--TRY ANYTHING LIKE THAT AGAIN, AND I BREAK YOUR FINGERS.
WHAT IS YOUR PROBLEM? I SAID BACK--
--OFF!
AHHHHH!

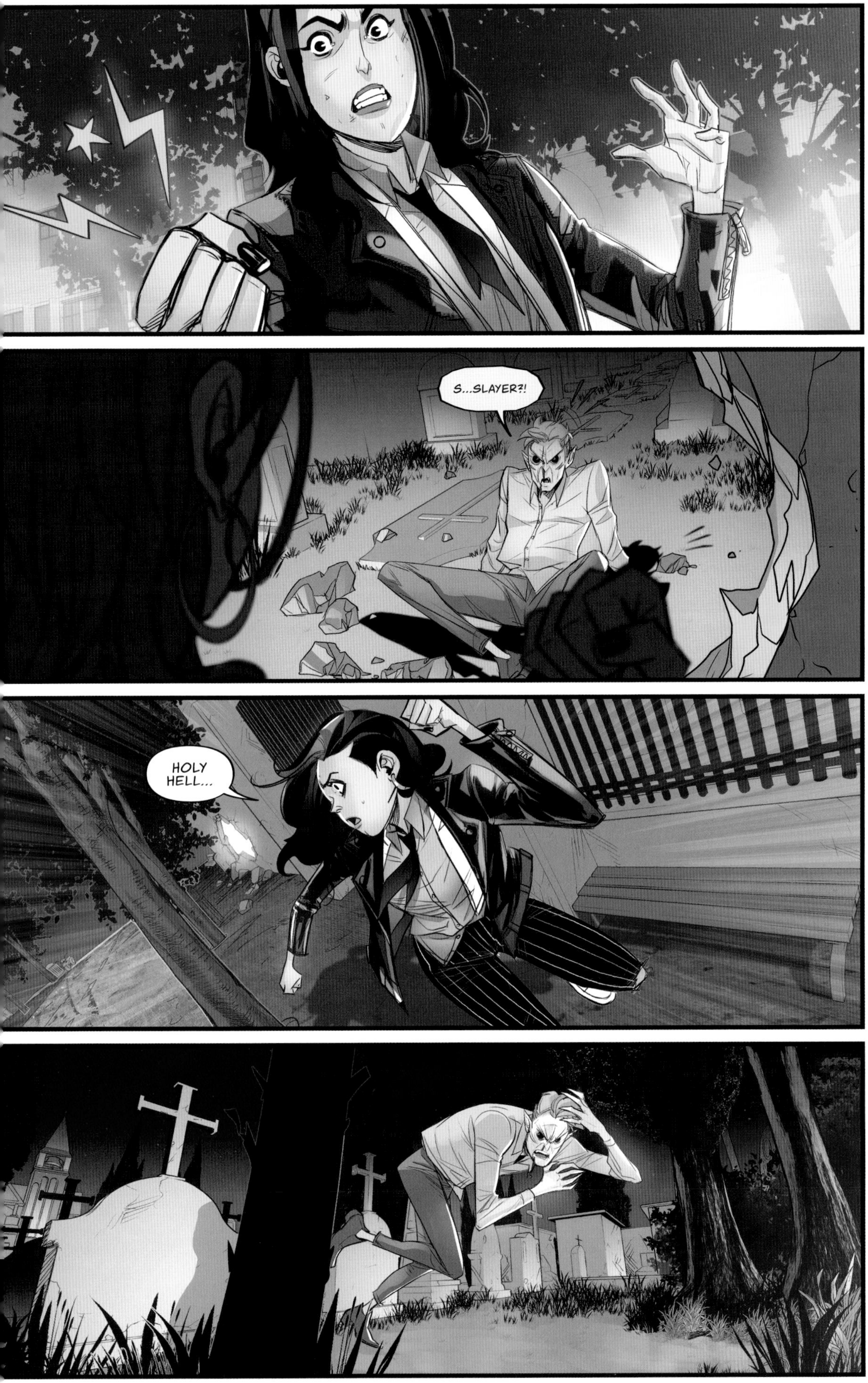
S...SLAYER?!
HOLY HELL...

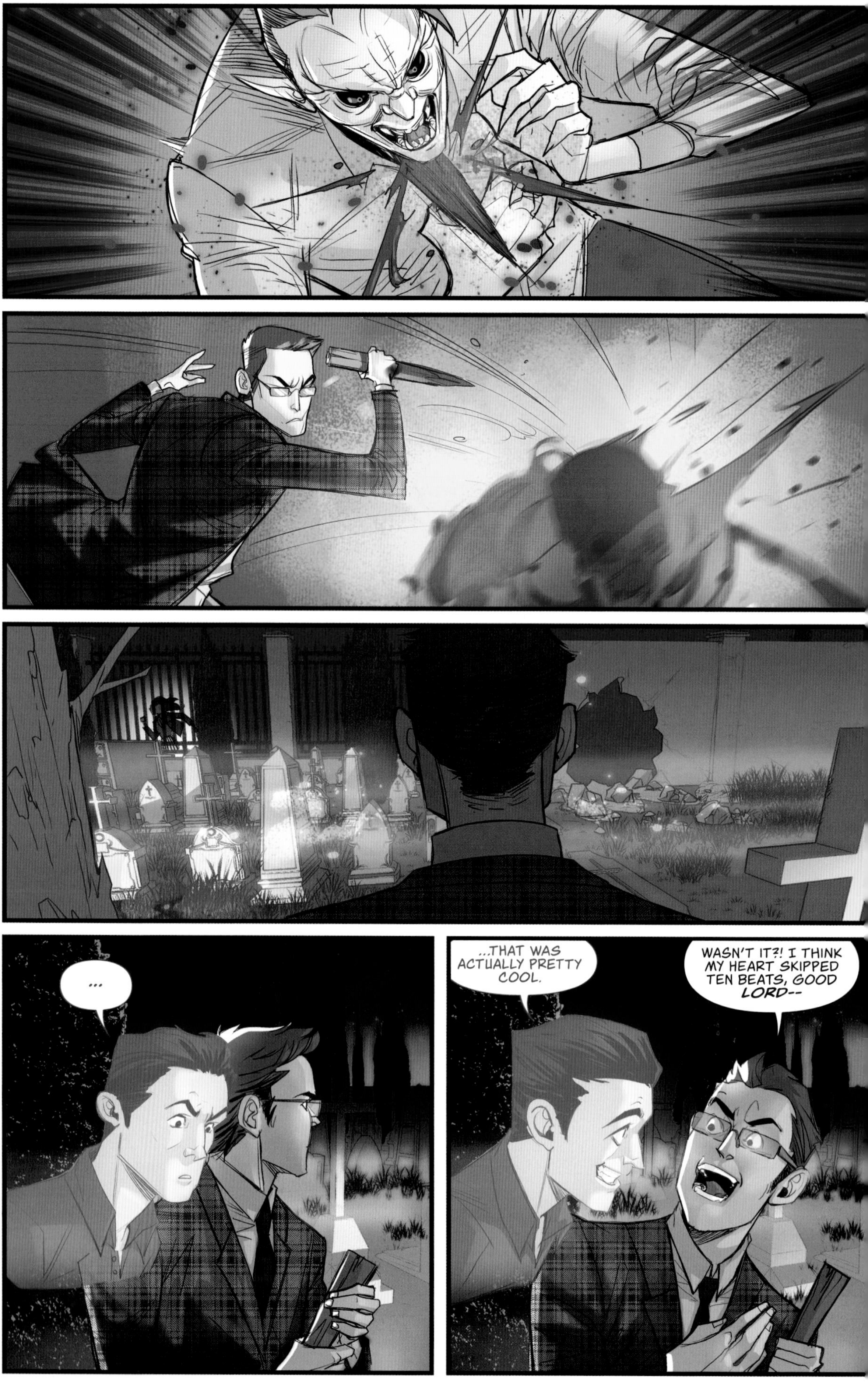
...
...THAT WAS ACTUALLY PRETTY COOL.
WASN'T IT?! I THINK MY HEART SKIPPED TEN BEATS, GOOD LORD--

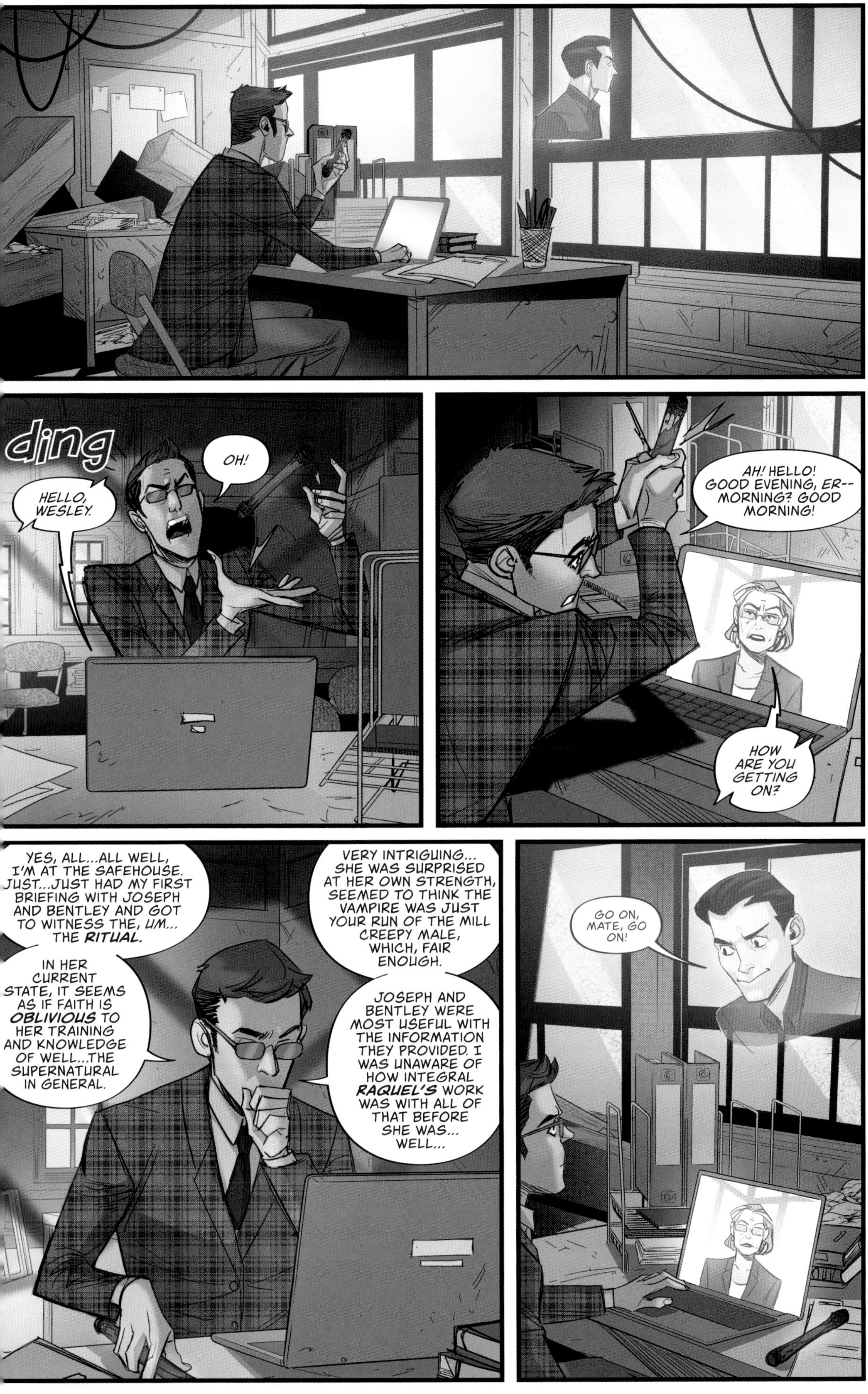

ding
HELLO, WESLEY.
OH!
AH! HELLO! GOOD EVENING, ER-- MORNING? GOOD MORNING!
HOW ARE YOU GETTING ON?
YES, ALL...ALL WELL, I'M AT THE SAFEHOUSE. JUST...JUST HAD MY FIRST BRIEFING WITH JOSEPH AND BENTLEY AND GOT TO WITNESS THE, UM... THE RITUAL.
IN HER CURRENT STATE, IT SEEMS AS IF FAITH IS OBLIVIOUS TO HER TRAINING AND KNOWLEDGE OF WELL...THE SUPERNATURAL IN GENERAL.
VERY INTRIGUING... SHE WAS SURPRISED AT HER OWN STRENGTH, SEEMED TO THINK THE VAMPIRE WAS JUST YOUR RUN OF THE MILL CREEPY MALE, WHICH, FAIR ENOUGH.
JOSEPH AND BENTLEY WERE MOST USEFUL WITH THE INFORMATION THEY PROVIDED. I WAS UNAWARE OF HOW INTEGRAL RAQUEL'S WORK WAS WITH ALL OF THAT BEFORE SHE WAS... WELL...
GO ON, MATE, GO ON!

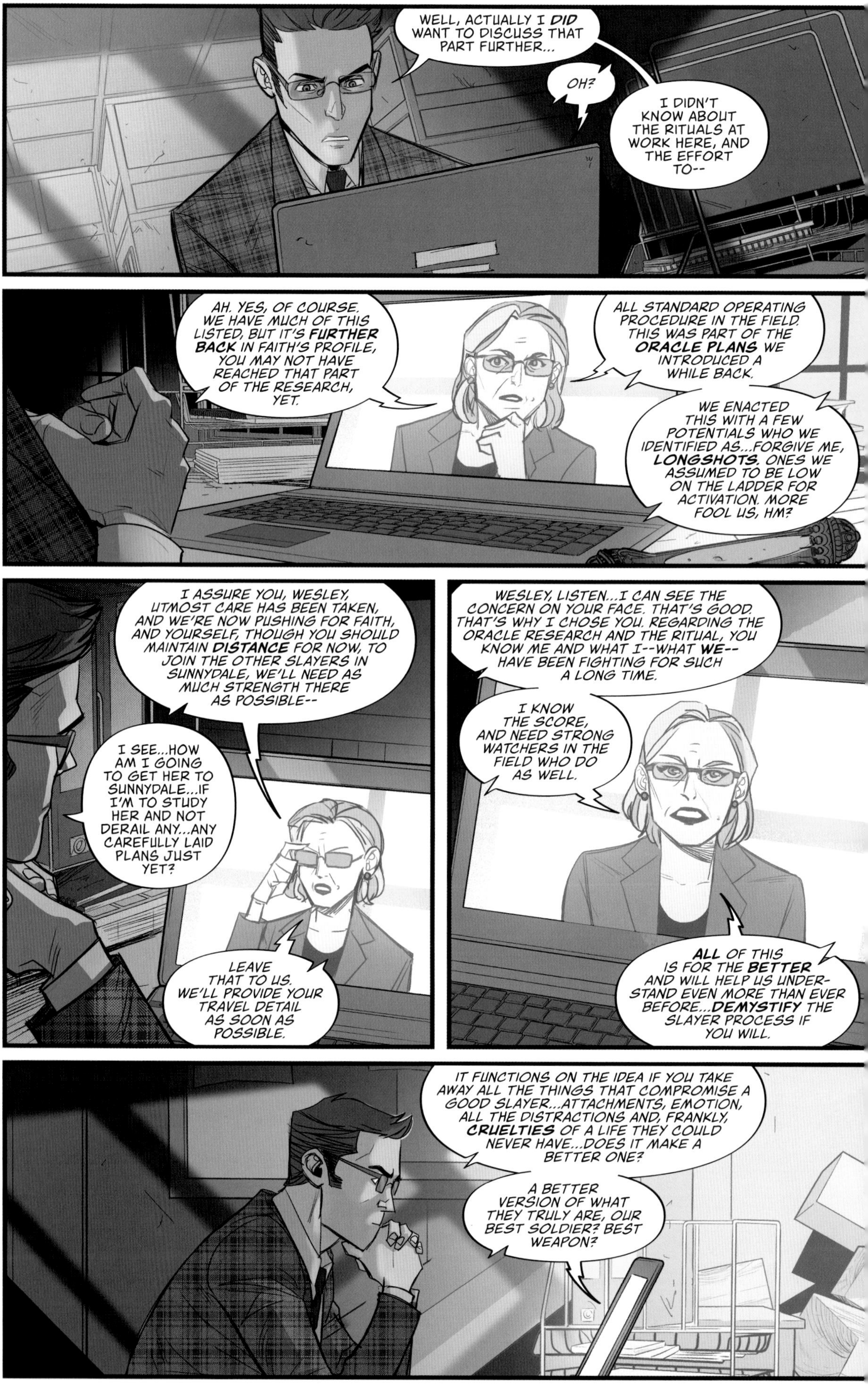
WELL, ACTUALLY I DID WANT TO DISCUSS THAT PART FURTHER...
OH?
I DIDN'T KNOW ABOUT THE RITUALS AT WORK HERE, AND THE EFFORT TO--
AH. YES, OF COURSE. WE HAVE MUCH OF THIS LISTED, BUT IT'S FURTHER BACK IN FAITH'S PROFILE, YOU MAY NOT HAVE REACHED THAT PART OF THE RESEARCH, YET.
ALL STANDARD OPERATING PROCEDURE IN THE FIELD. THIS WAS PART OF THE ORACLE PLANS WE INTRODUCED A WHILE BACK.
WE ENACTED THIS WITH A FEW POTENTIALS WHO WE IDENTIFIED AS...FORGIVE ME, LONGSHOTS. ONES WE ASSUMED TO BE LOW ON THE LADDER FOR ACTIVATION. MORE FOOL US, HM?
I ASSURE YOU, WESLEY, UTMOST CARE HAS BEEN TAKEN, AND WE'RE NOW PUSHING FOR FAITH, AND YOURSELF, THOUGH YOU SHOULD MAINTAIN DISTANCE FOR NOW, TO JOIN THE OTHER SLAYERS IN SUNNYDALE, WE'LL NEED AS MUCH STRENGTH THERE AS POSSIBLE--
I SEE...HOW AM I GOING TO GET HER TO SUNNYDALE...IF I'M TO STUDY HER AND NOT DERAIL ANY...ANY CAREFULLY LAID PLANS JUST YET?
LEAVE THAT TO US. WE'LL PROVIDE YOUR TRAVEL DETAIL AS SOON AS POSSIBLE.
WESLEY, LISTEN...I CAN SEE THE CONCERN ON YOUR FACE. THAT'S GOOD. THAT'S WHY I CHOSE YOU. REGARDING THE ORACLE RESEARCH AND THE RITUAL, YOU KNOW ME AND WHAT I--WHAT WE--HAVE BEEN FIGHTING FOR SUCH A LONG TIME.
I KNOW THE SCORE, AND NEED STRONG WATCHERS IN THE FIELD WHO DO AS WELL.
ALL OF THIS IS FOR THE BETTER AND WILL HELP US UNDERSTAND EVEN MORE THAN EVER BEFORE...DEMYSTIFY THE SLAYER PROCESS IF YOU WILL.
IT FUNCTIONS ON THE IDEA IF YOU TAKE AWAY ALL THE THINGS THAT COMPROMISE A GOOD SLAYER...ATTACHMENTS, EMOTION, ALL THE DISTRACTIONS AND, FRANKLY, CRUELTIES OF A LIFE THEY COULD NEVER HAVE...DOES IT MAKE A BETTER ONE?
A BETTER VERSION OF WHAT THEY TRULY ARE, OUR BEST SOLDIER? BEST WEAPON?

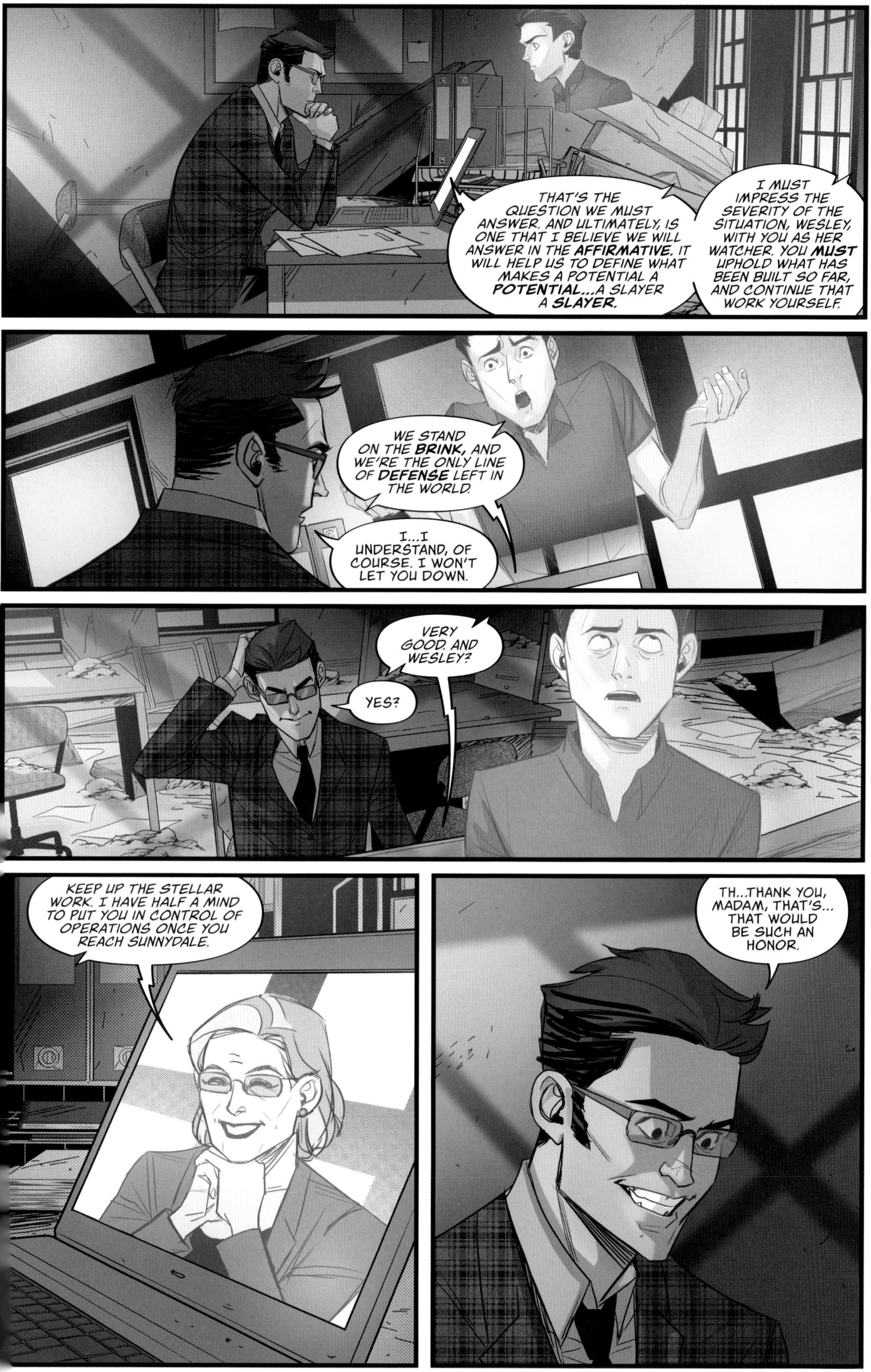
THAT'S THE QUESTION WE MUST ANSWER. AND ULTIMATELY, IS ONE THAT I BELIEVE WE WILL ANSWER IN THE AFFIRMATIVE. IT WILL HELP US TO DEFINE WHAT MAKES A POTENTIAL A POTENTIAL...A SLAYER A SLAYER.
I MUST IMPRESS THE SEVERITY OF THE SITUATION, WESLEY, WITH YOU AS HER WATCHER. YOU MUST UPHOLD WHAT HAS BEEN BUILT SO FAR, AND CONTINUE THAT WORK YOURSELF.
WE STAND ON THE BRINK, AND WE'RE THE ONLY LINE OF DEFENSE LEFT IN THE WORLD.
I...I UNDERSTAND, OF COURSE. I WON'T LET YOU DOWN.
VERY GOOD. AND WESLEY?
YES?
KEEP UP THE STELLAR WORK. I HAVE HALF A MIND TO PUT YOU IN CONTROL OF OPERATIONS ONCE YOU REACH SUNNYDALE.
TH...THANK YOU, MADAM, THAT'S... THAT WOULD BE SUCH AN HONOR.

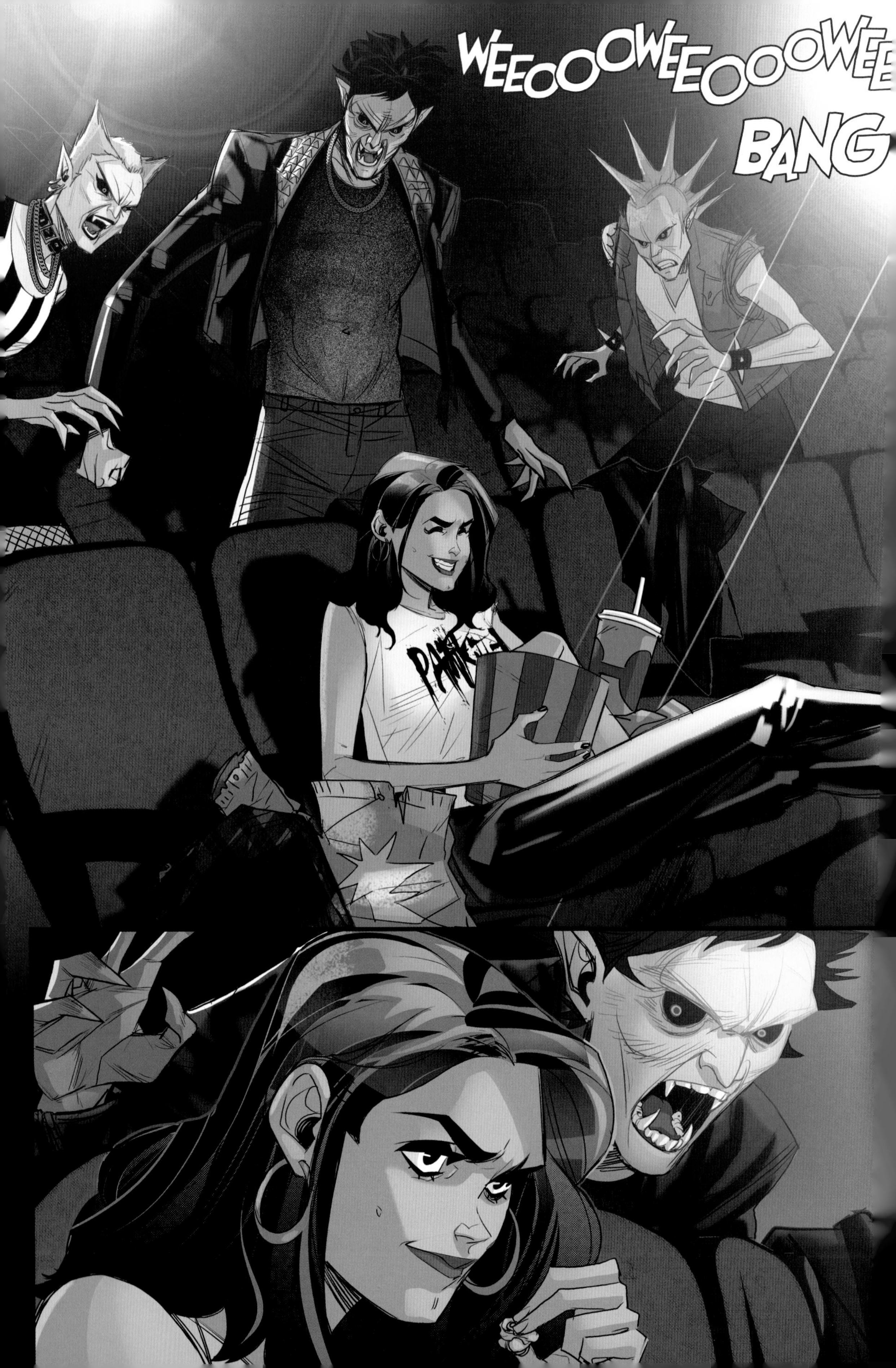
WEEOOOWEEOOOWEE
BANG

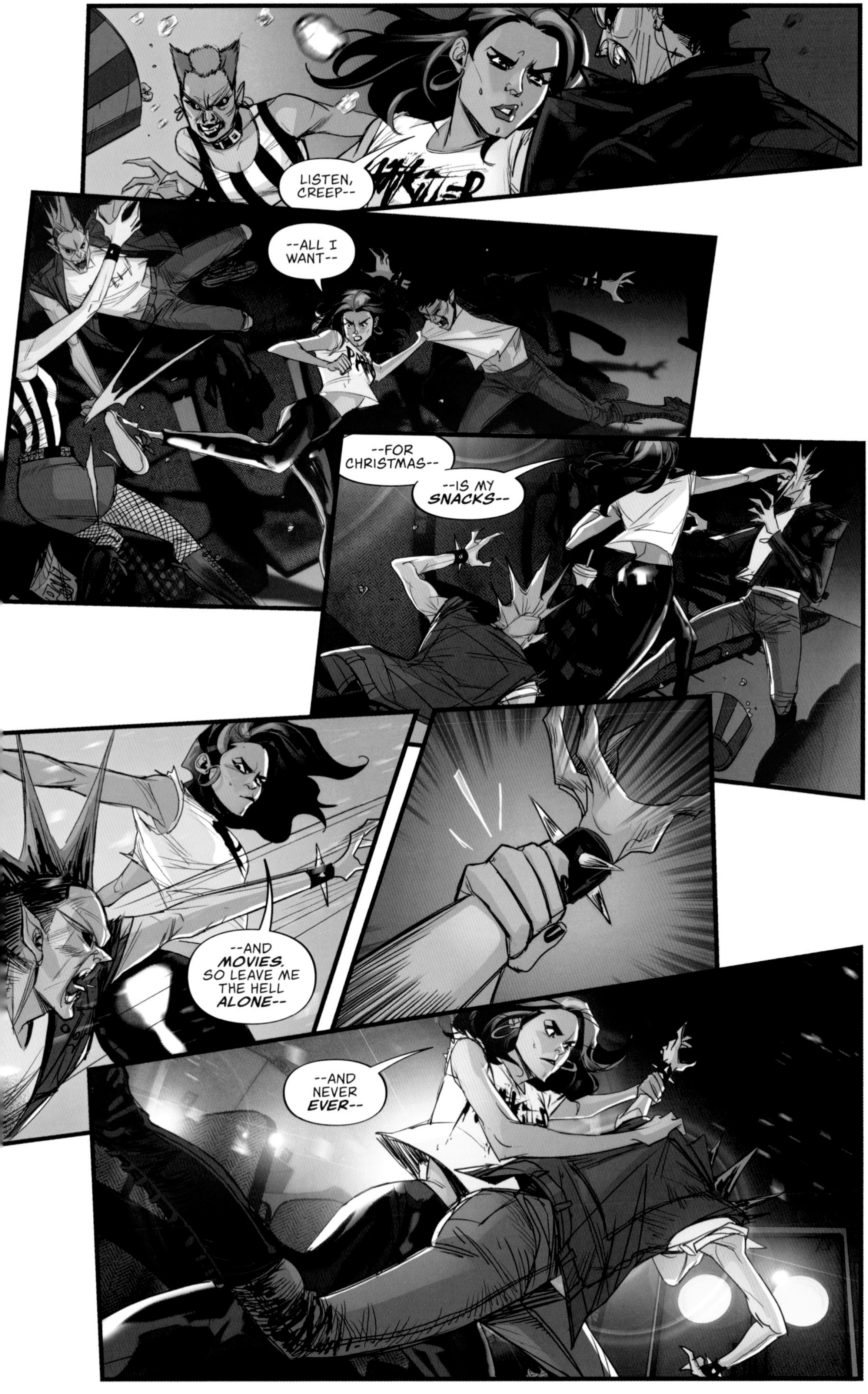
LISTEN, CREEP--
--ALL I WANT--
--FOR CHRISTMAS--
--IS MY SNACKS--
--AND MOVIES. SO LEAVE ME THE HELL ALONE--
--AND NEVER EVER--

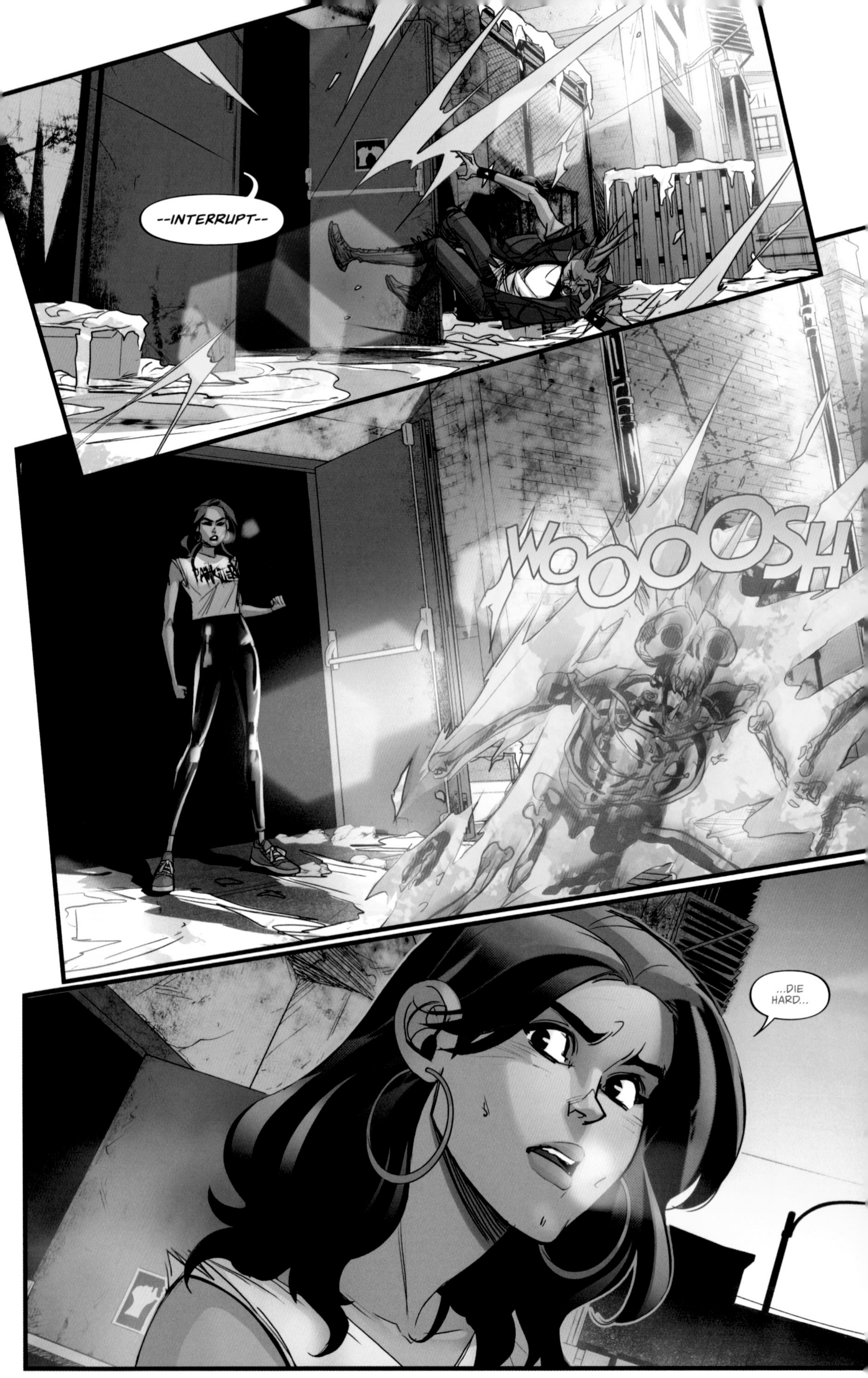
--INTERRUPT--
WOOOOOSH
...DIE HARD...

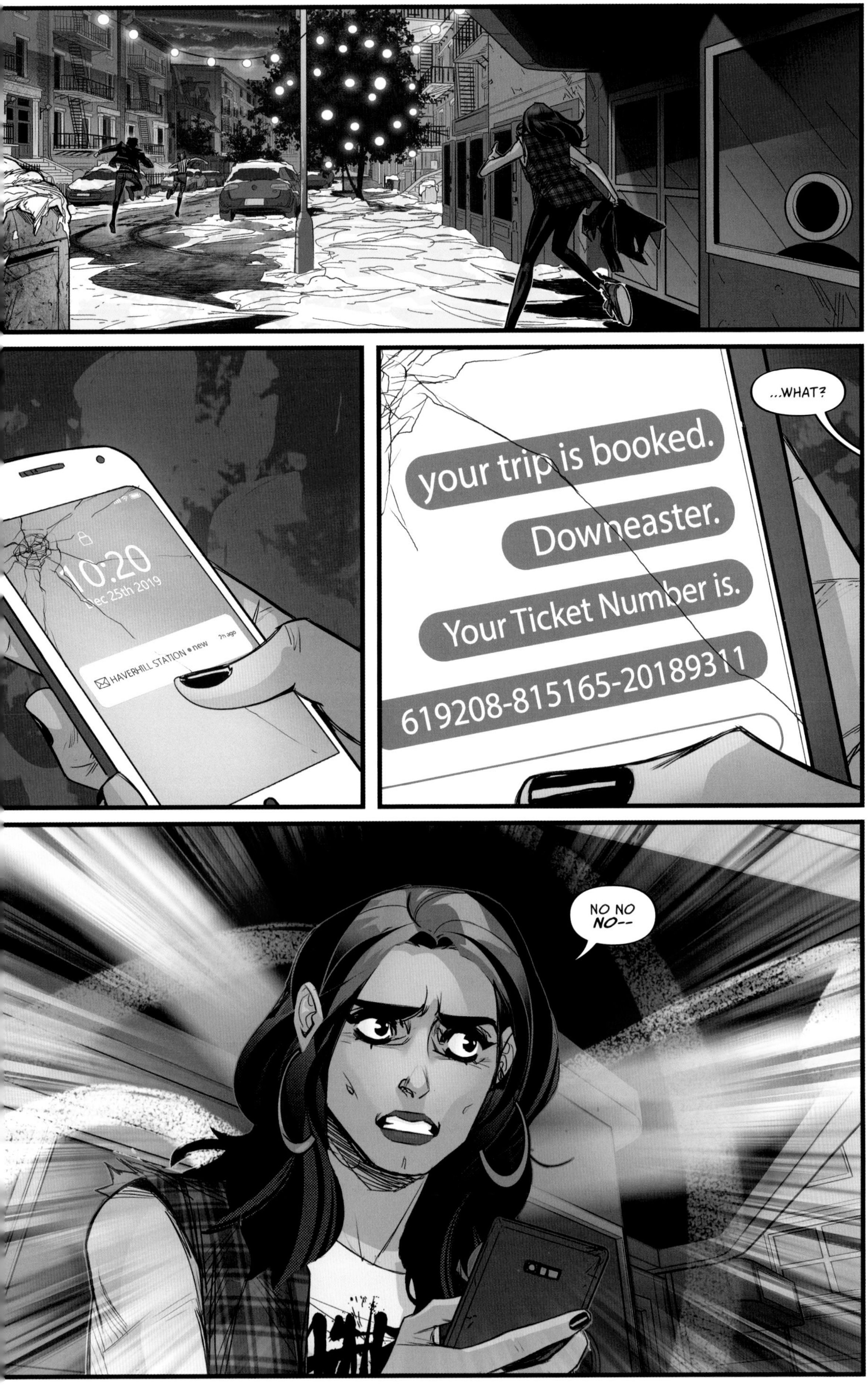
10:20
ec 25th 2019
HAVERHILL STATION • new
your trip is booked.
Downeaster.
Your Ticket Number is.
619208-815165-20189311
...WHAT?
NO NO
NO--

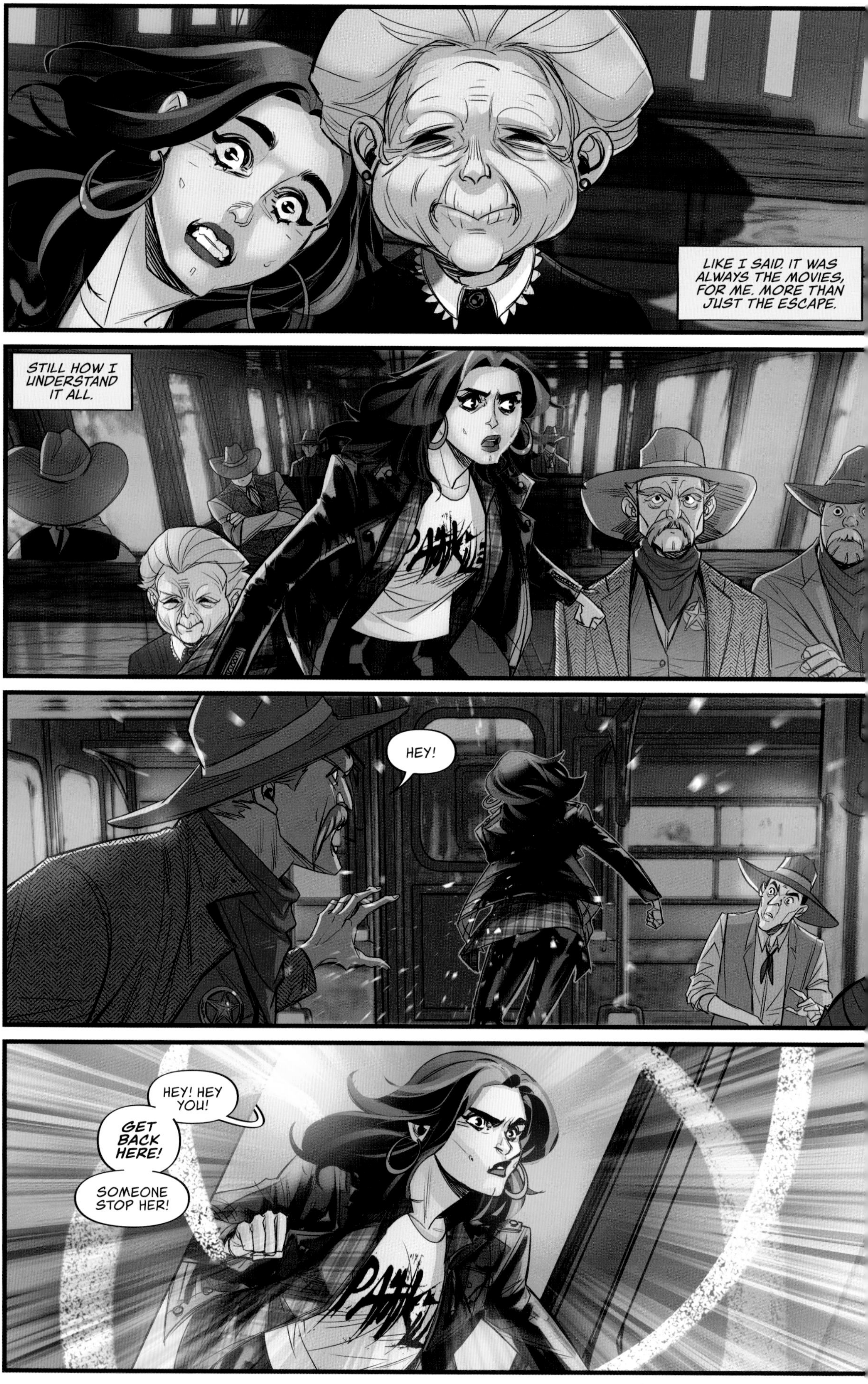
LIKE I SAID. IT WAS ALWAYS THE MOVIES, FOR ME. MORE THAN JUST THE ESCAPE.
STILL HOW I UNDERSTAND IT ALL.
HEY!
HEY! HEY YOU!
GET BACK HERE!
SOMEONE STOP HER!

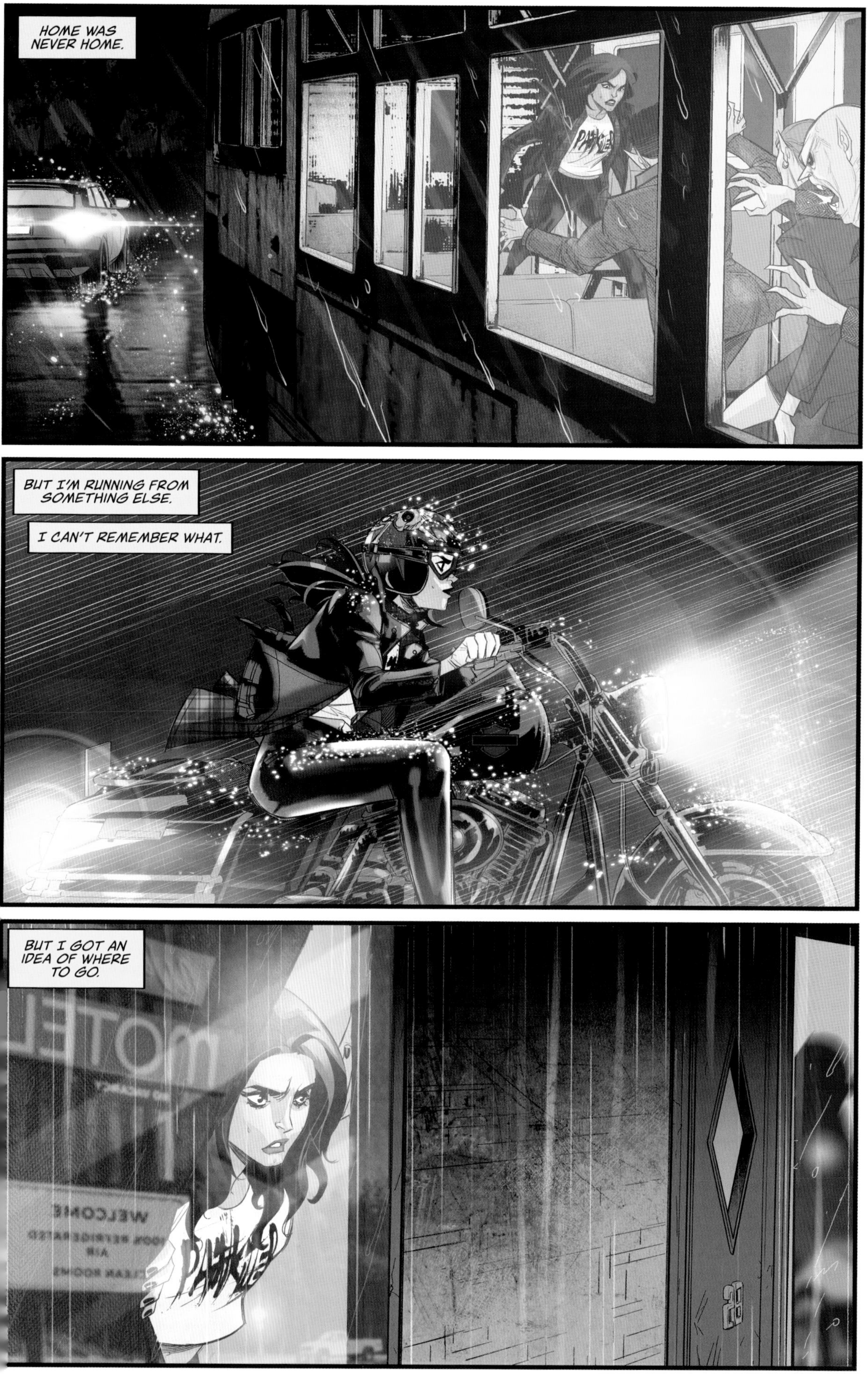
HOME WAS NEVER HOME.
BUT I'M RUNNING FROM SOMETHING ELSE.
I CAN'T REMEMBER WHAT.
BUT I GOT AN IDEA OF WHERE TO GO.

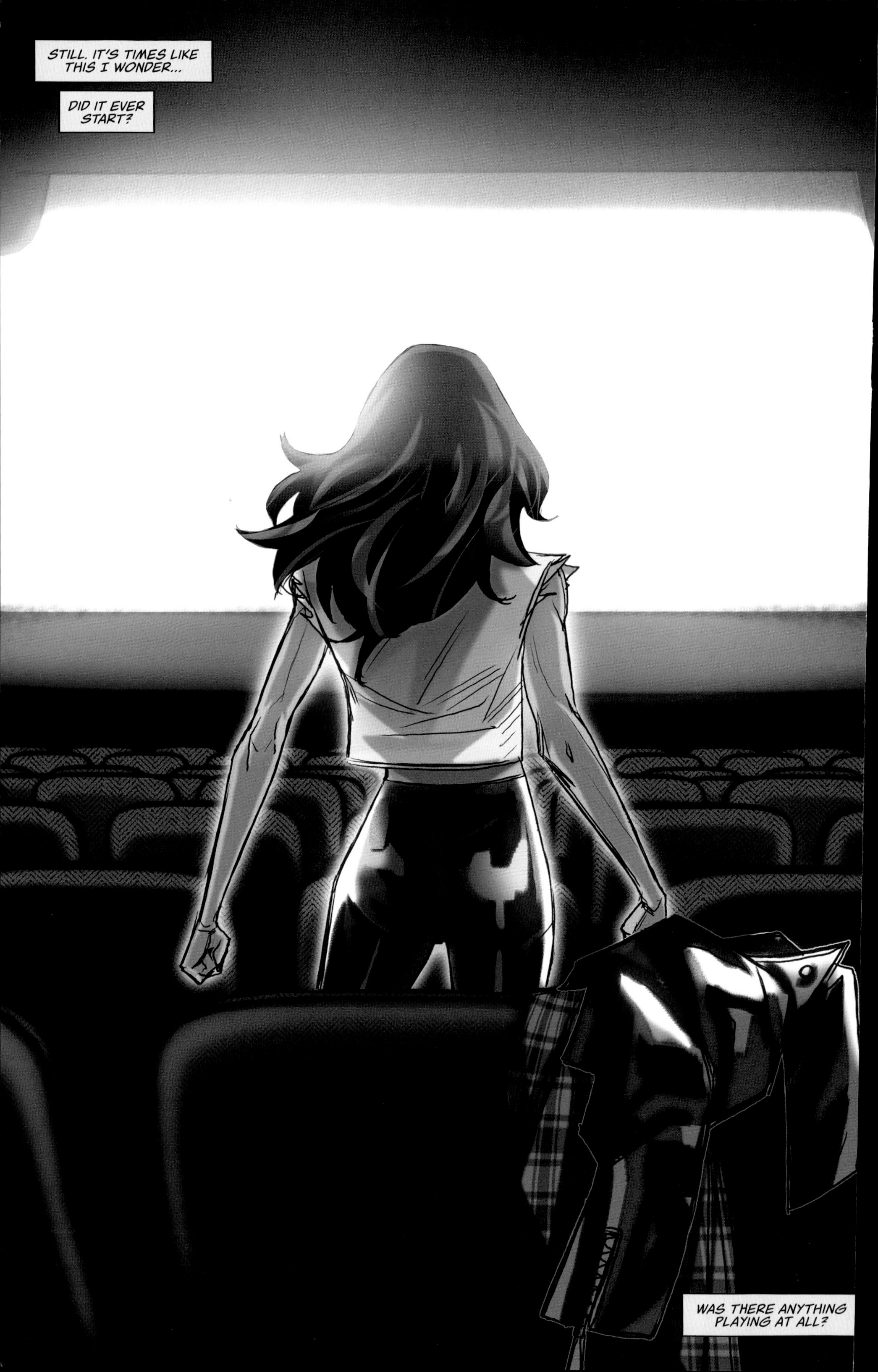
STILL. IT'S TIMES LIKE THIS I WONDER...
DID IT EVER START?
WAS THERE ANYTHING PLAYING AT ALL?

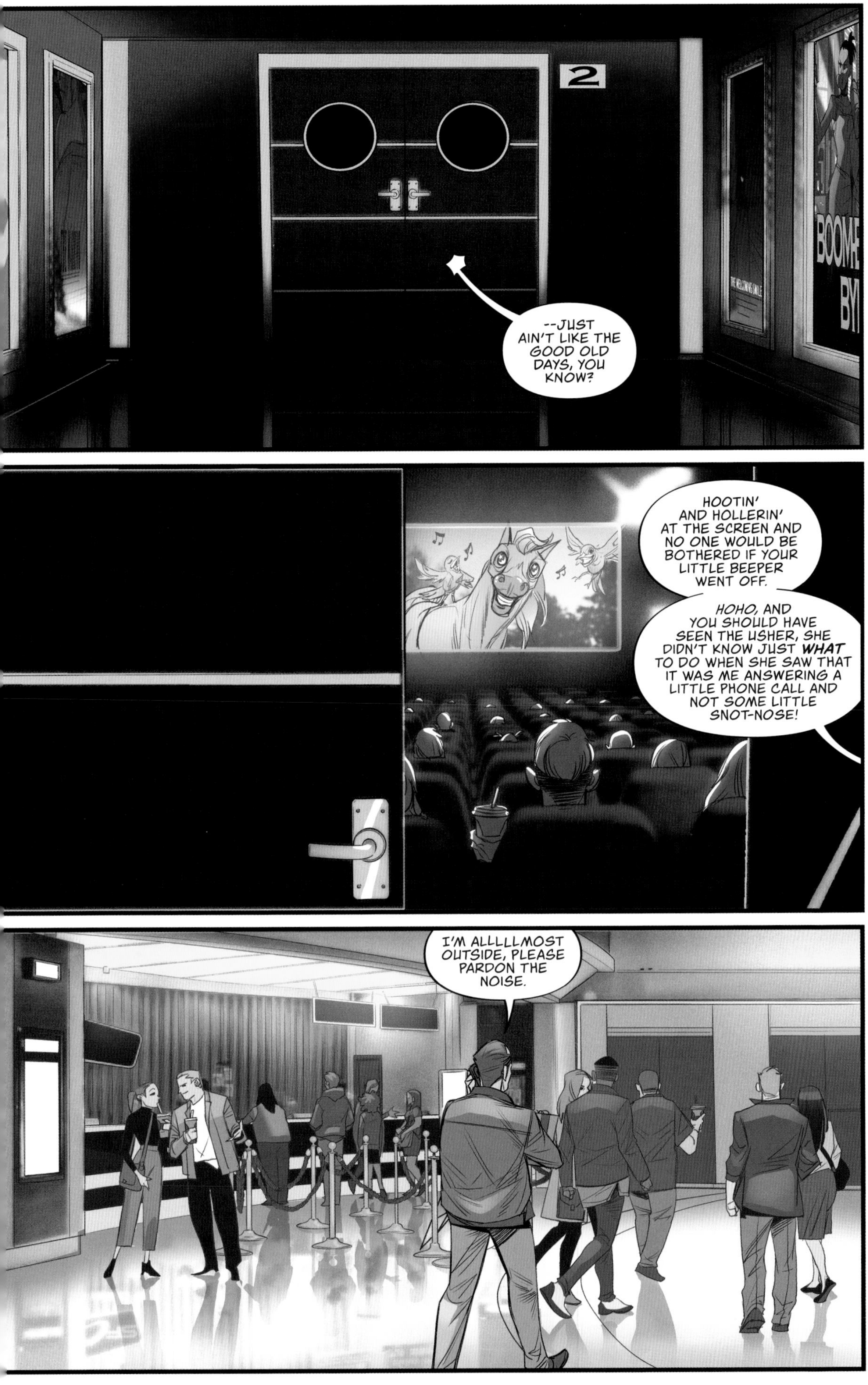
--JUST AIN'T LIKE THE GOOD OLD DAYS, YOU KNOW?
HOOTIN' AND HOLLERIN' AT THE SCREEN AND NO ONE WOULD BE BOTHERED IF YOUR LITTLE BEEPER WENT OFF.
HOHO, AND YOU SHOULD HAVE SEEN THE USHER, SHE DIDN'T KNOW JUST ***WHAT*** TO DO WHEN SHE SAW THAT IT WAS ME ANSWERING A LITTLE PHONE CALL AND NOT SOME LITTLE SNOT-NOSE!
I'M ALLLLLMOST OUTSIDE, PLEASE PARDON THE NOISE.

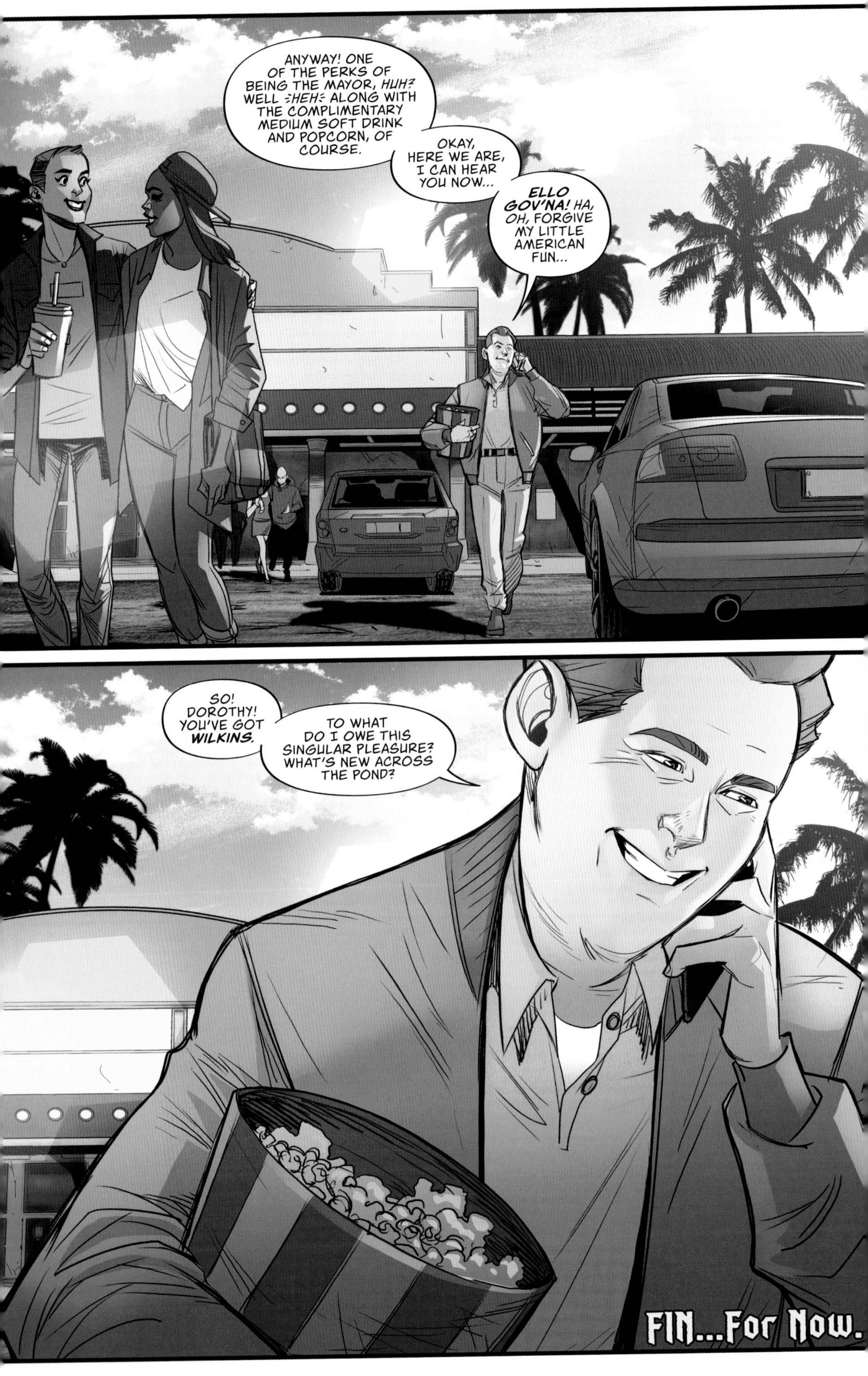
ANYWAY! ONE OF THE PERKS OF BEING THE MAYOR, *HUH?* WELL *=HEH=* ALONG WITH THE COMPLIMENTARY MEDIUM SOFT DRINK AND POPCORN, OF COURSE.
OKAY, HERE WE ARE, I CAN HEAR YOU NOW...
ELLO GOV'NA! *HA, OH,* FORGIVE MY LITTLE AMERICAN FUN...
SO! DOROTHY! YOU'VE GOT **WILKINS.**
TO WHAT DO I OWE THIS SINGULAR PLEASURE? WHAT'S NEW ACROSS THE POND?
FIN...For Now.

LOL.
LMK

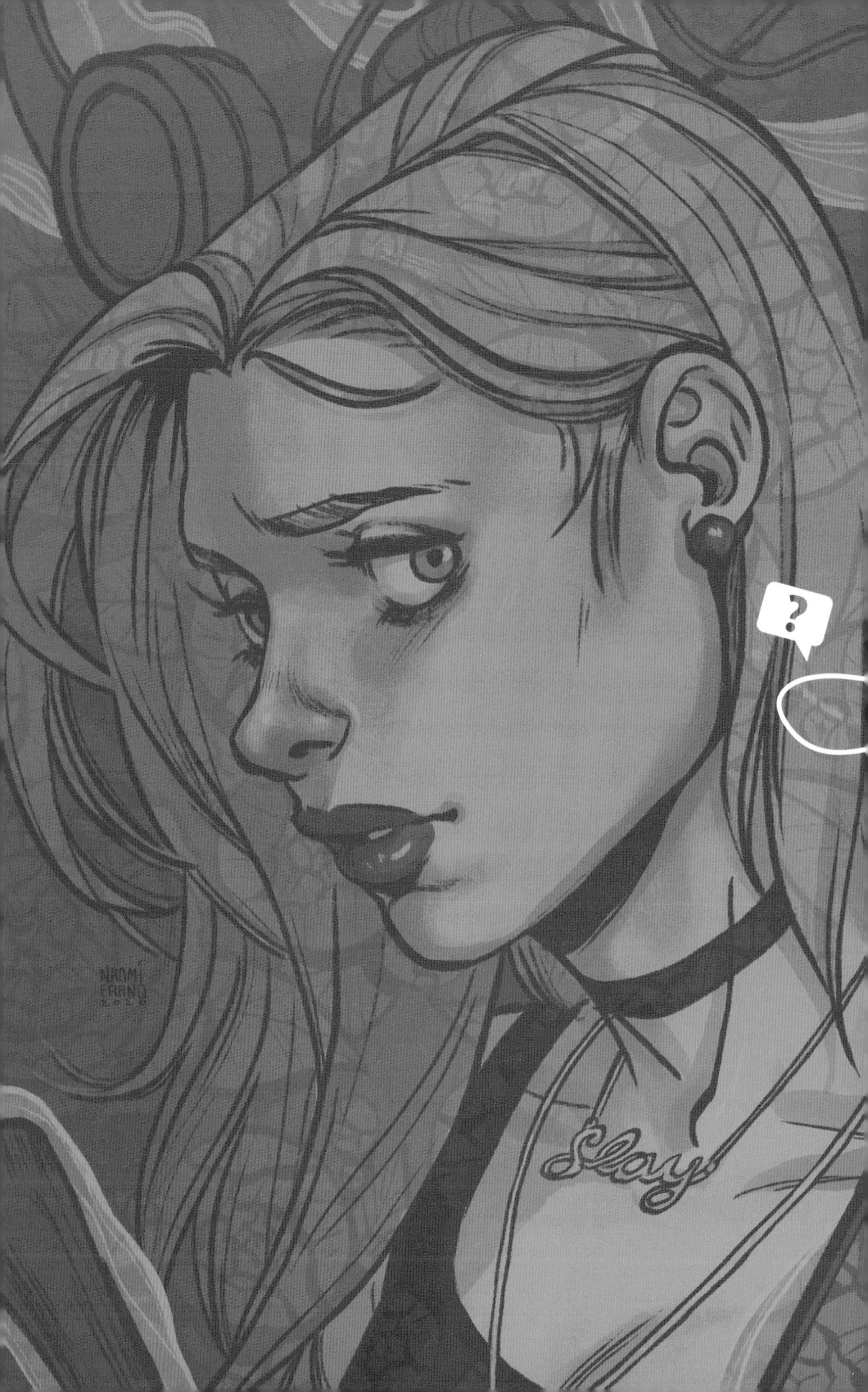
?
Slay

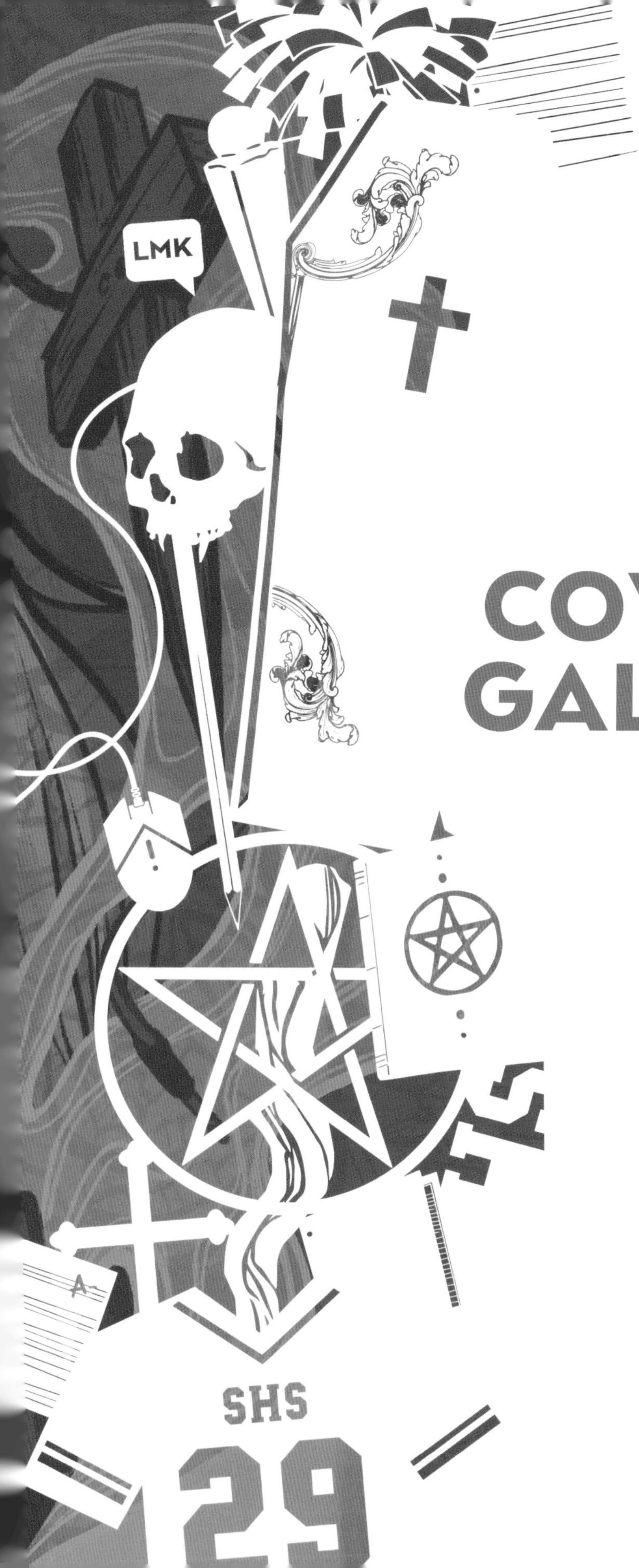
LMK
SHS
29

COVER GALLERY

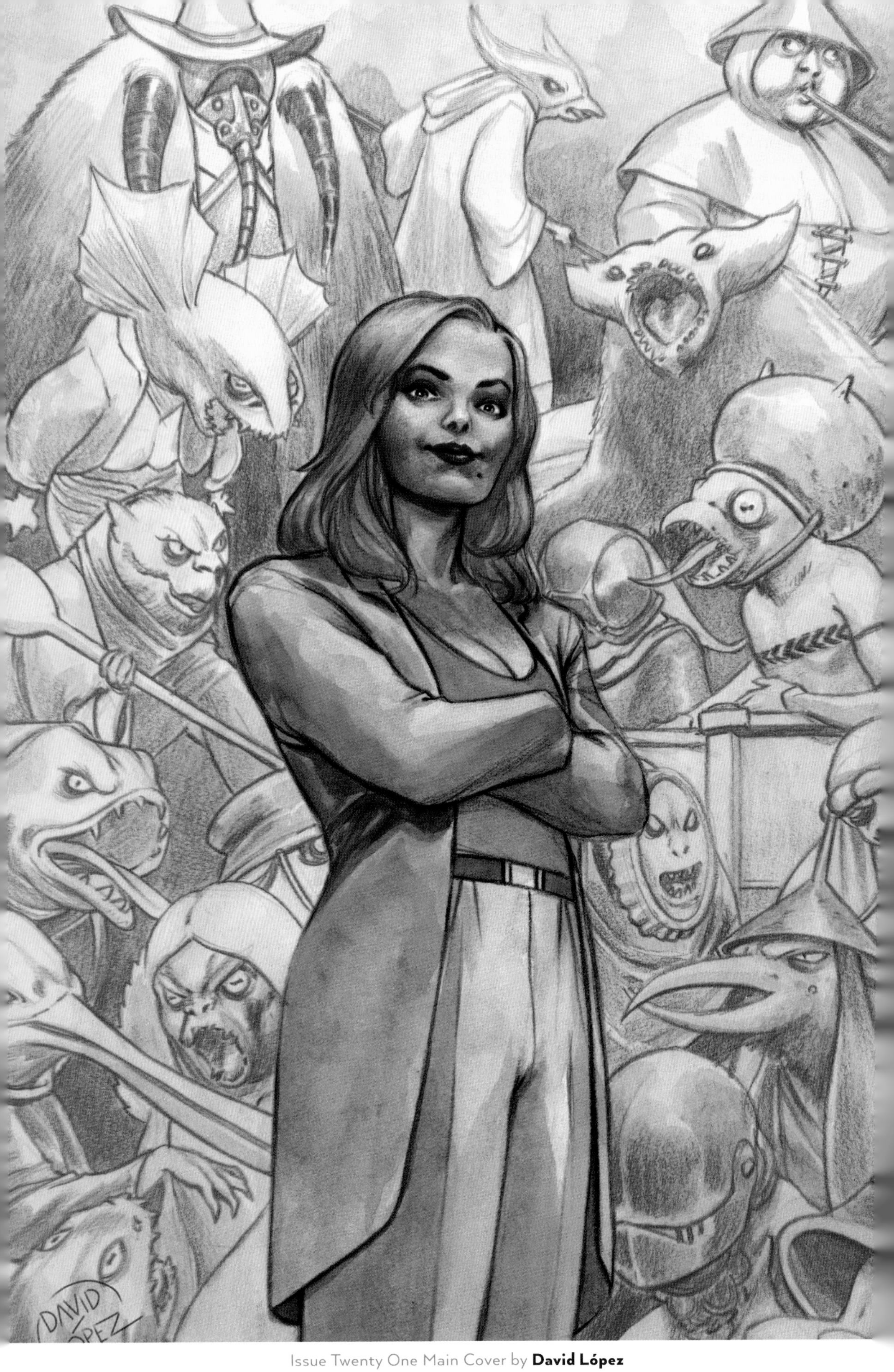
DAVID LÓPEZ

Issue Twenty One Main Cover by **David López**

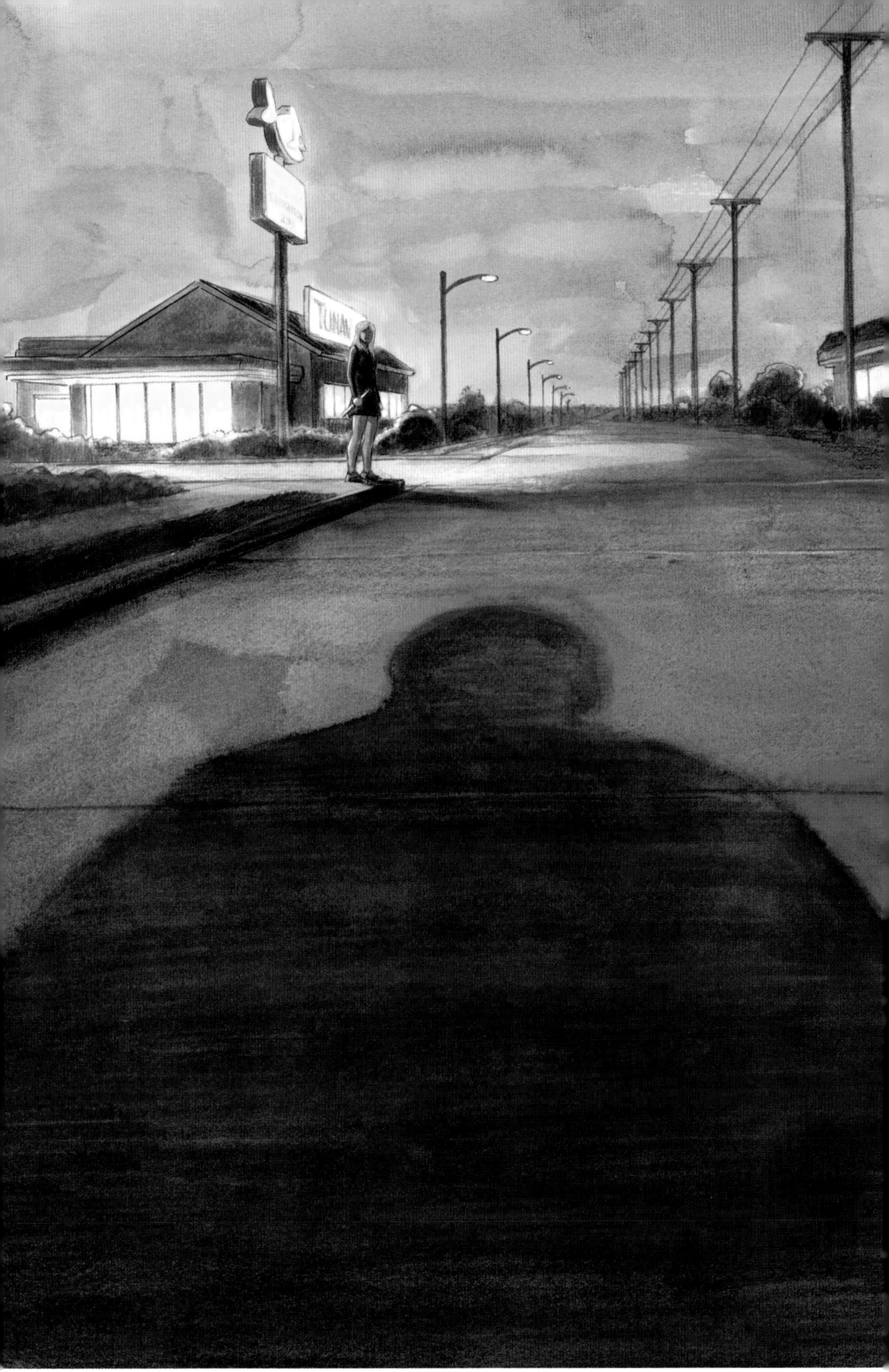

Issue Twenty Two Main Cover by **David López**

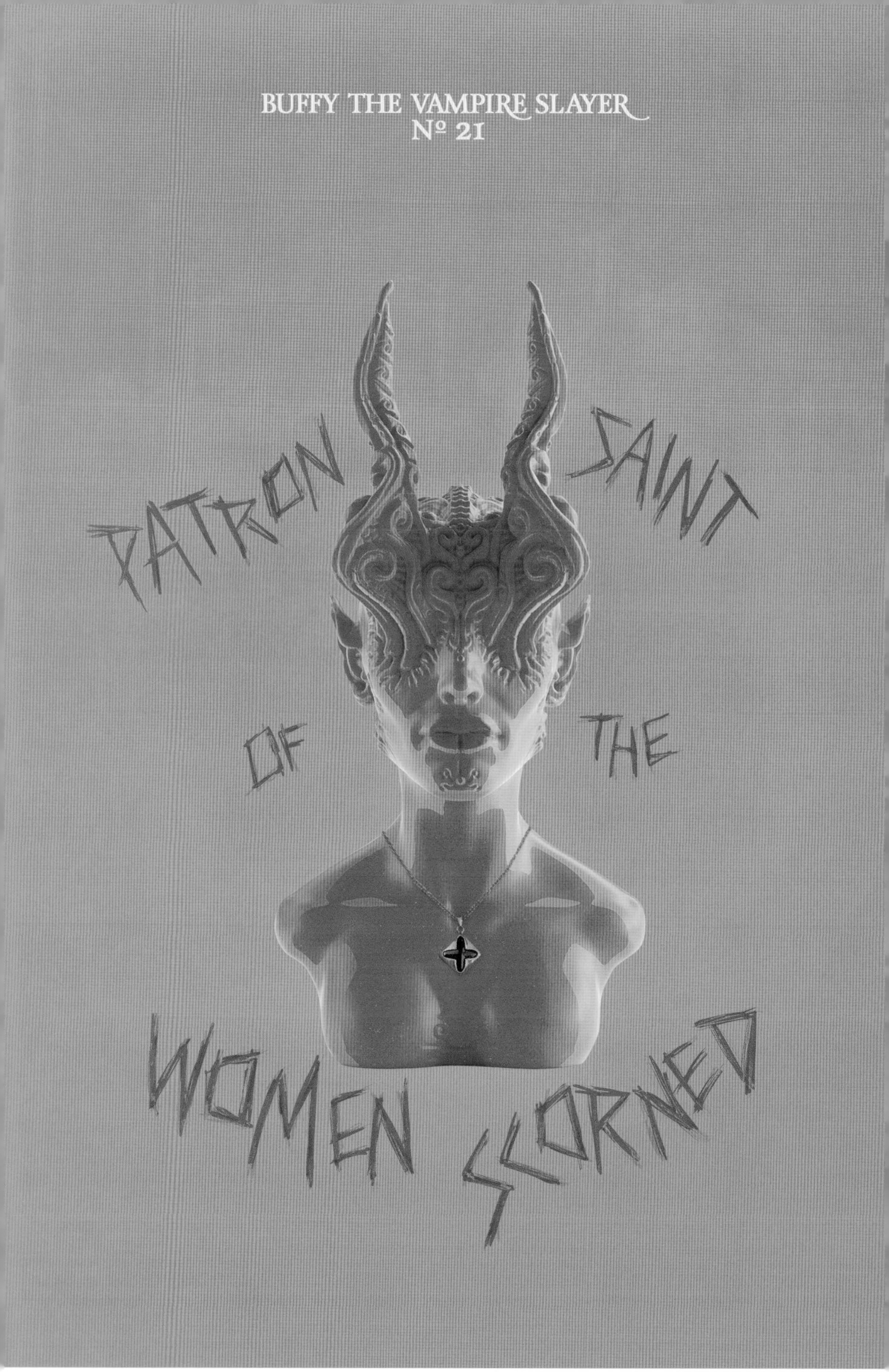
BUFFY THE VAMPIRE SLAYER
Nº 21
PATRON SAINT
OF THE
WOMEN SCORNED

Issue Twenty One Ring of Fire Cover by **Becca Carey**

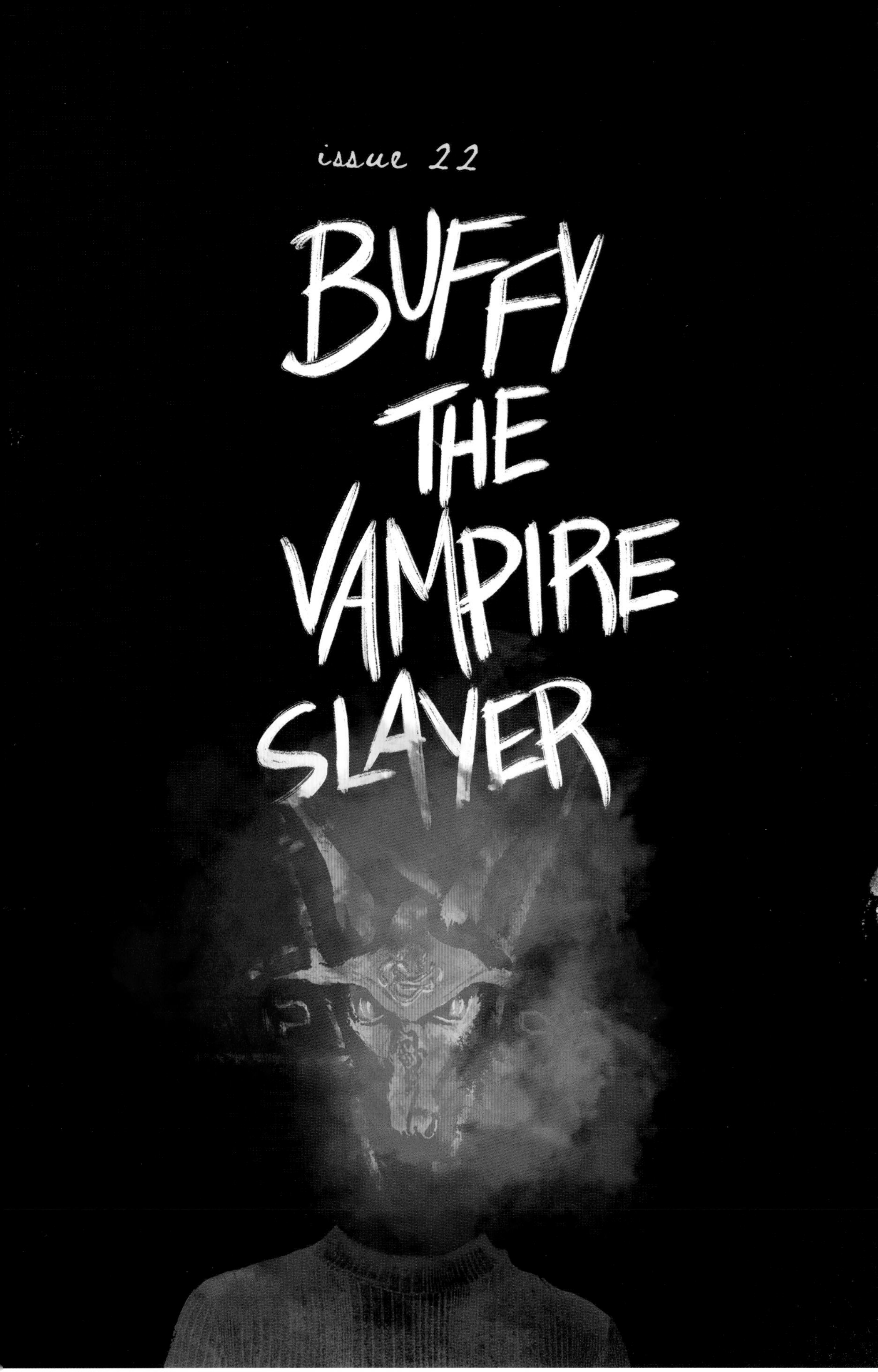
issue 22
BUFFY
THE
VAMPIRE
SLAYER

Issue Twenty Two Ring of Fire Cover by **Becca Carey**

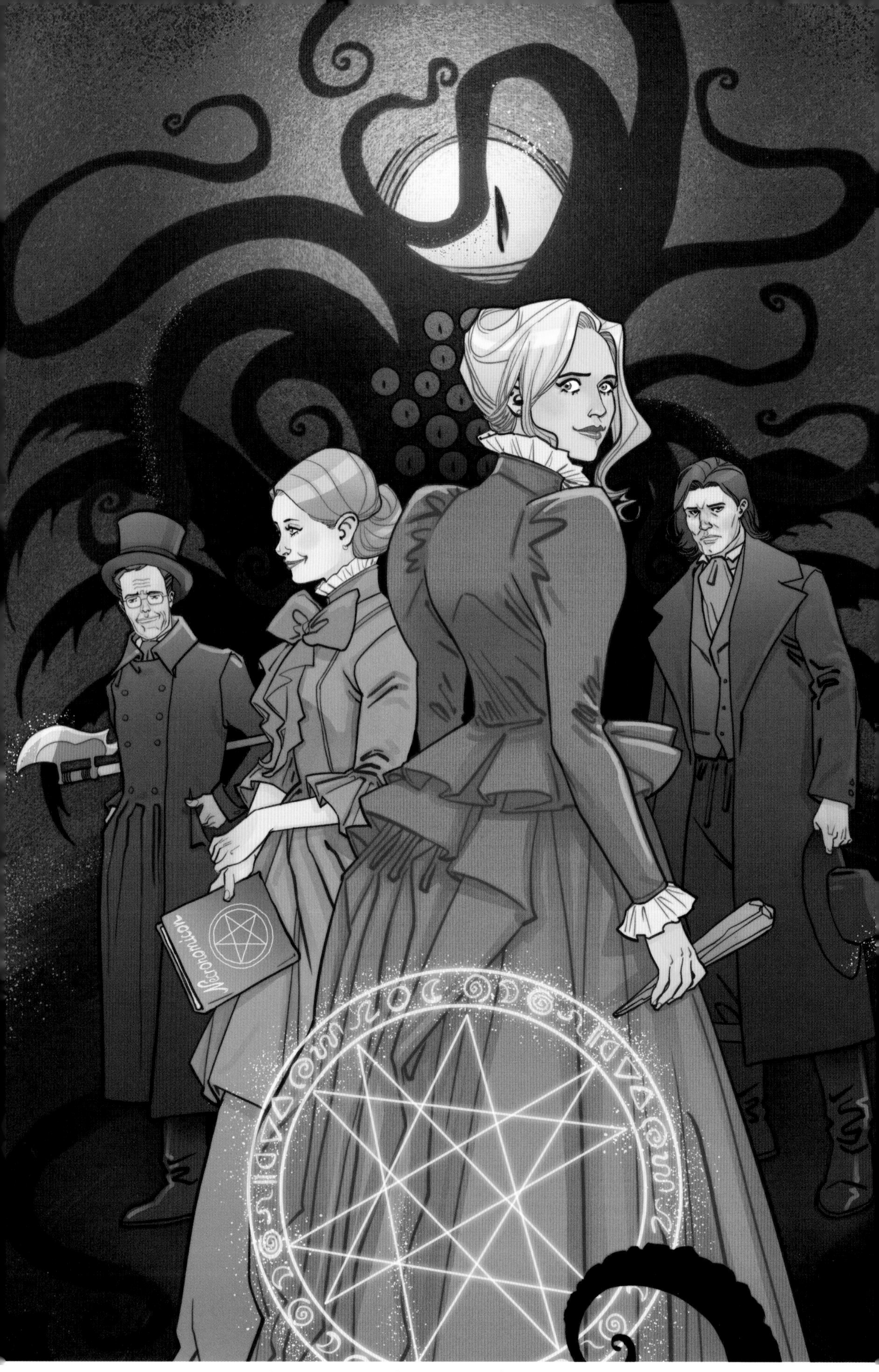
Necronomicon

Issue Twenty One Multiverse Cover by **Marguerite Sauvage**

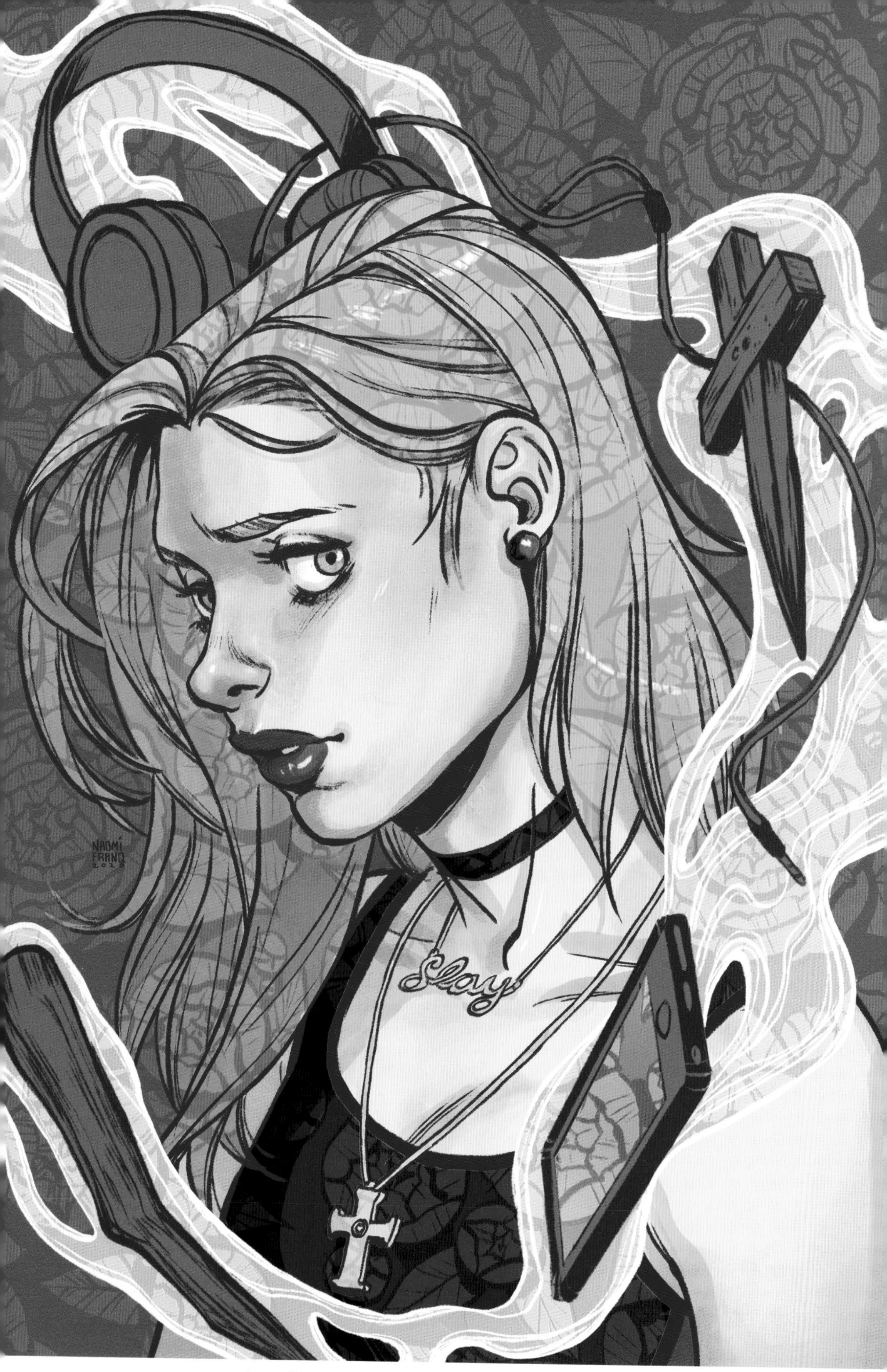
Slay

Issue Twenty Two Variant Cover by **Naomi Franquiz**

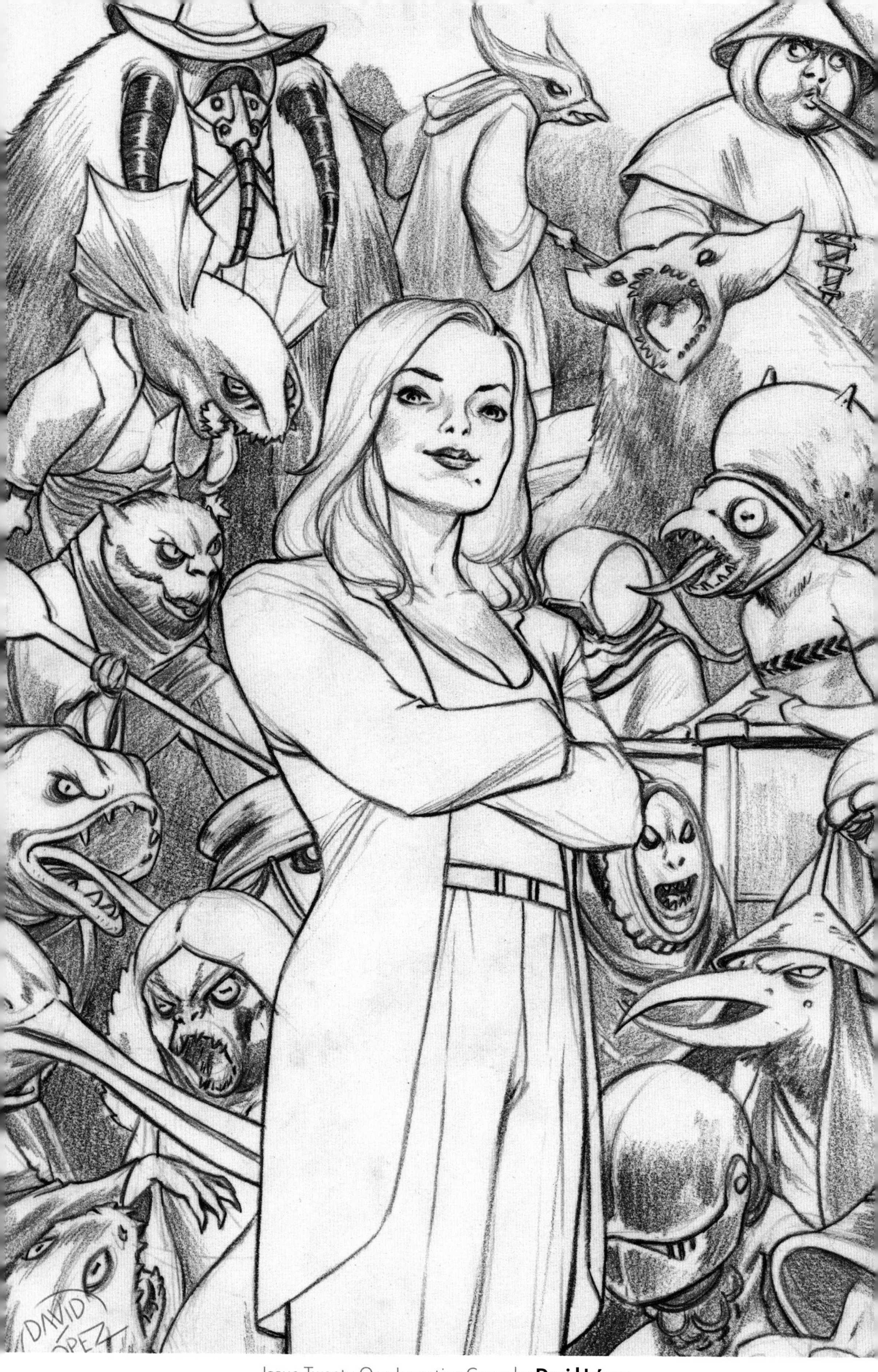

Issue Twenty One Incentive Cover by **David López**

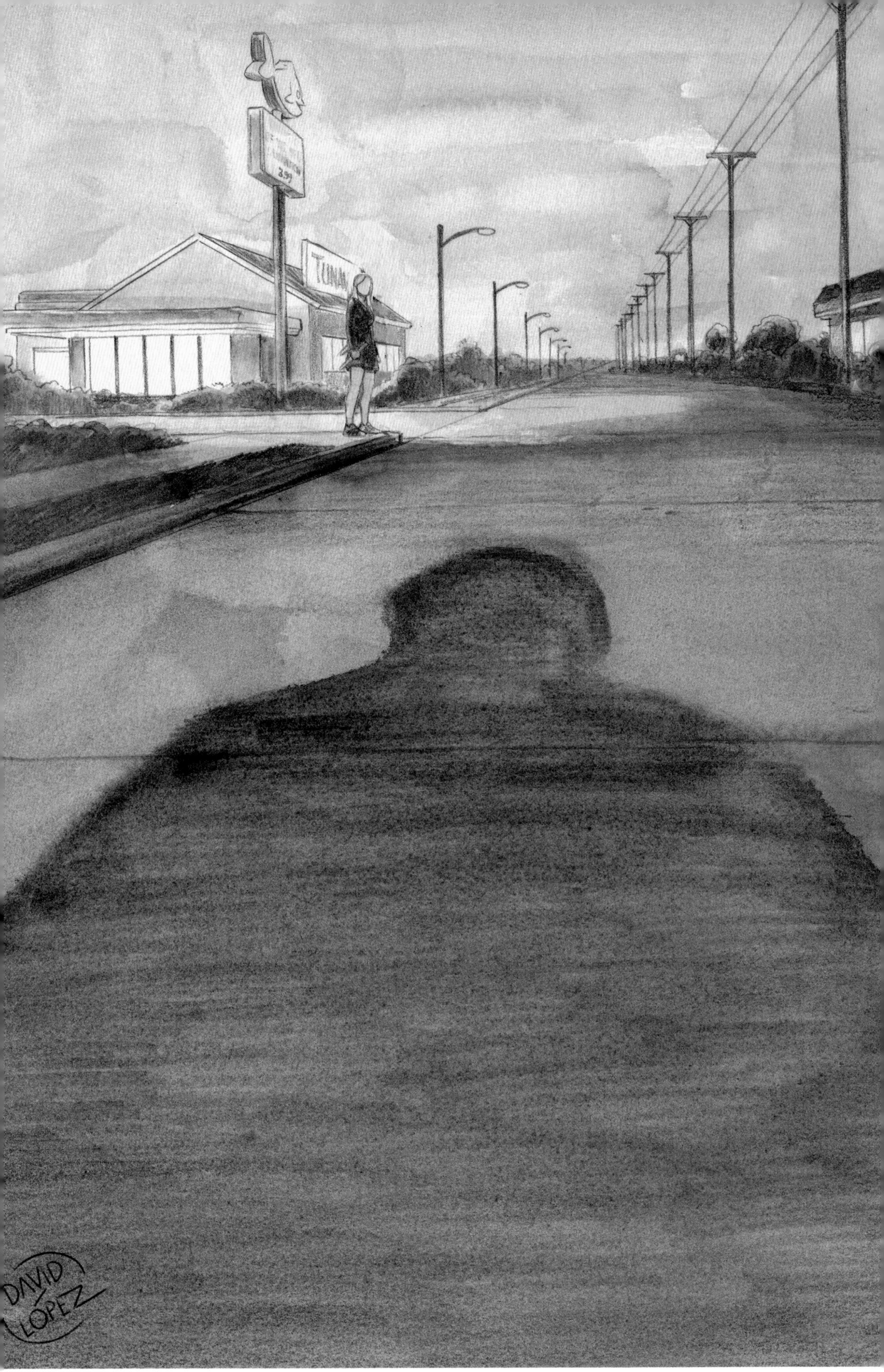
TUNA
DAVID LÓPEZ

Issue Twenty Two Incentive Cover by **David López**

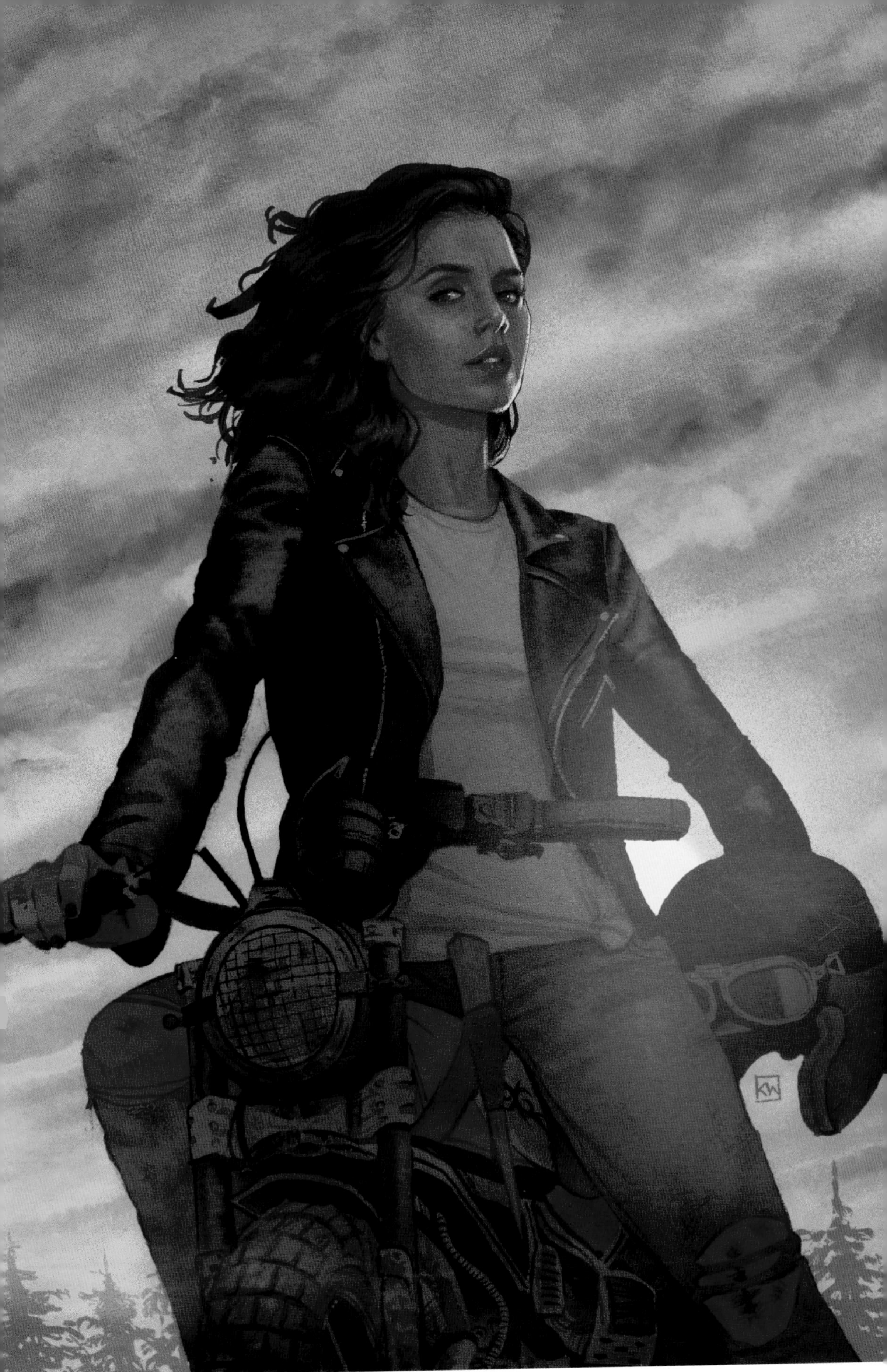
KW
Buffy the Vampire Slayer: Faith Special Main Cover by **Kevin Wada**

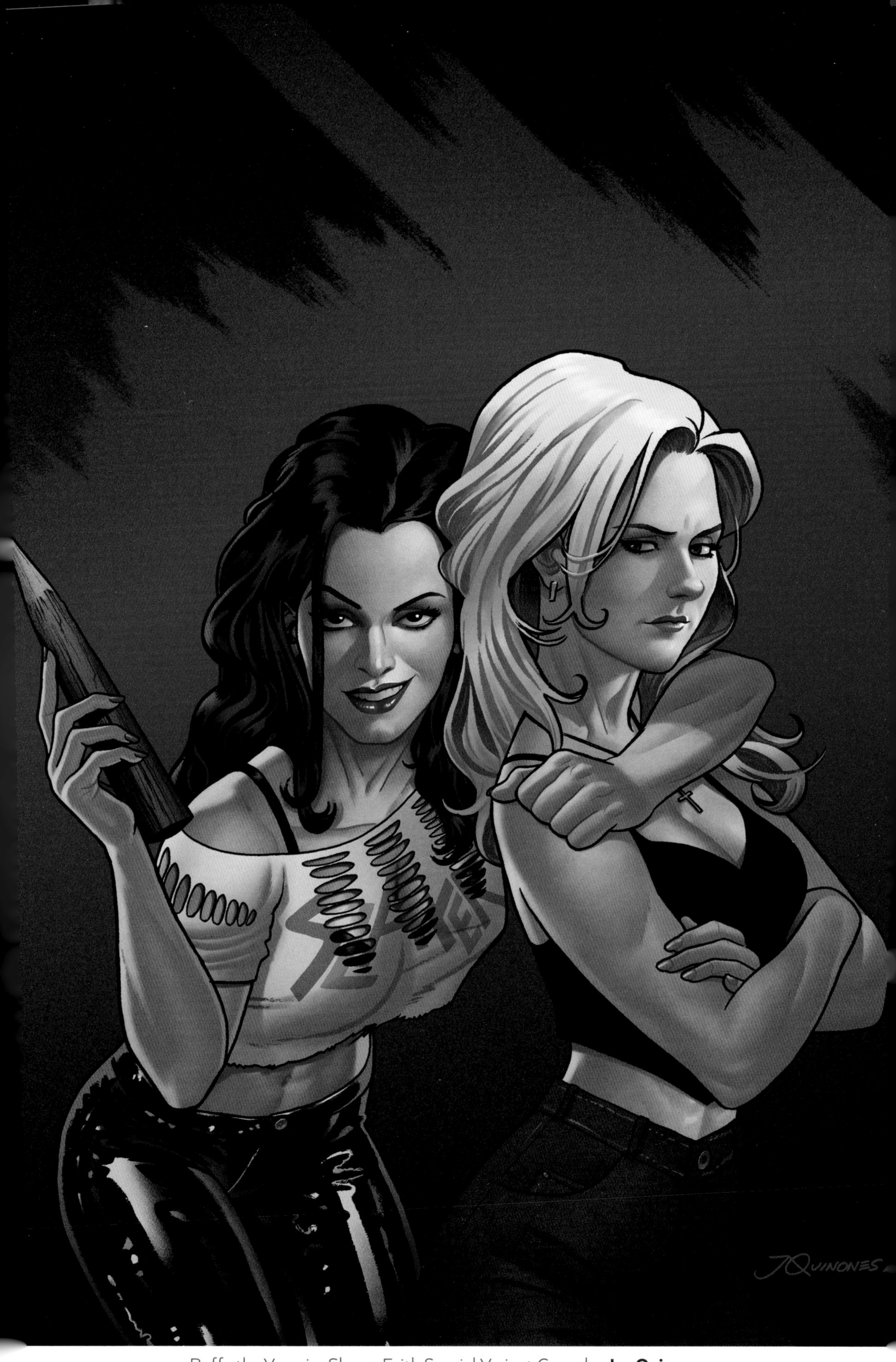
JQUINONES

Buffy the Vampire Slayer: Faith Special Variant Cover by **Joe Quinones**

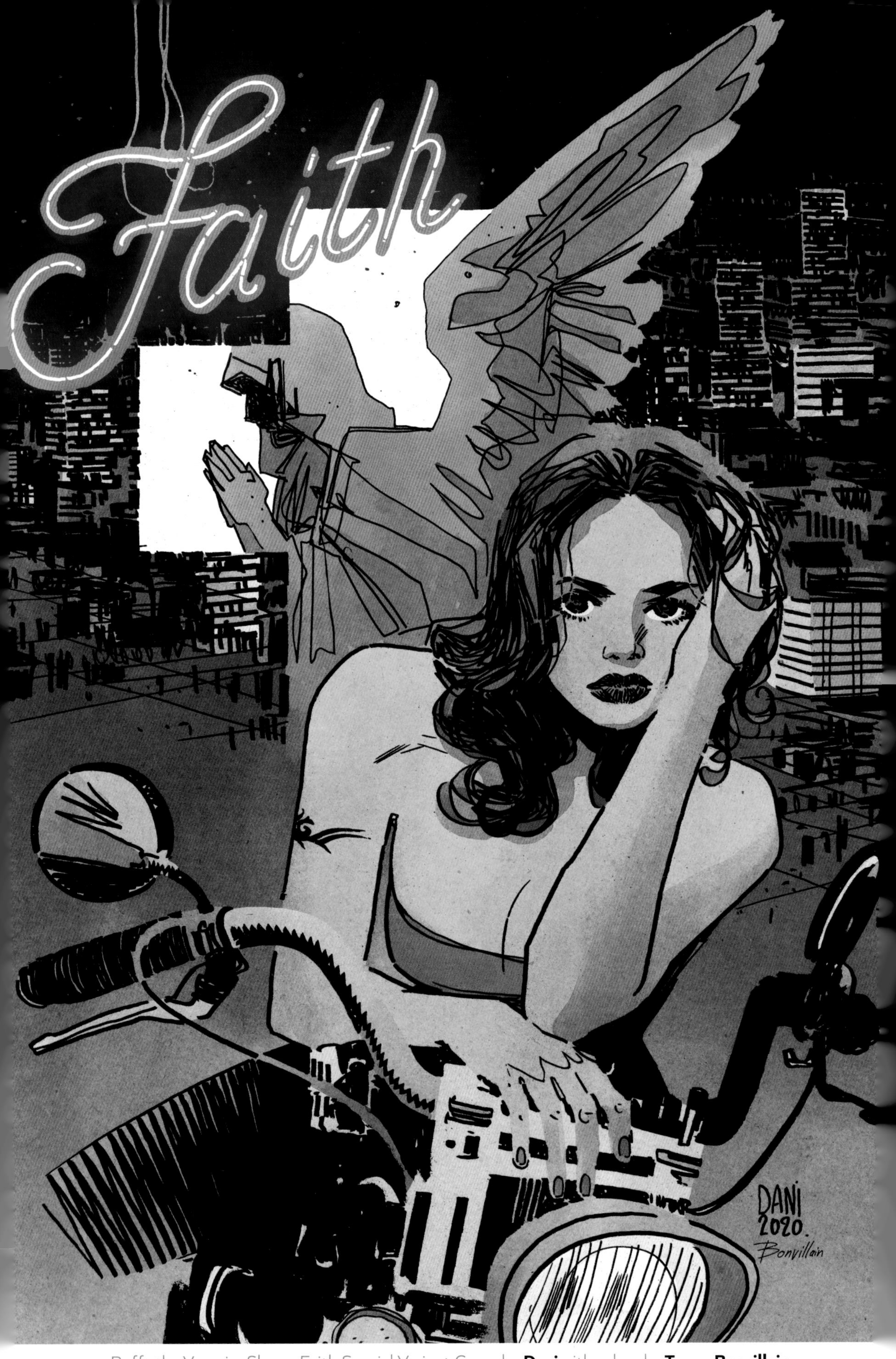
Faith
DANI
2020.
Bonvillain

Buffy the Vampire Slayer: Faith Special Variant Cover by **Dani** with colors by **Tamra Bonvillain**

Buffy the Vampire Slayer: Faith Special Variant Inks Cover by **Joe Quinones**

FAITH CHARACTER DESIGNS BY
ELEONORA CARLINI

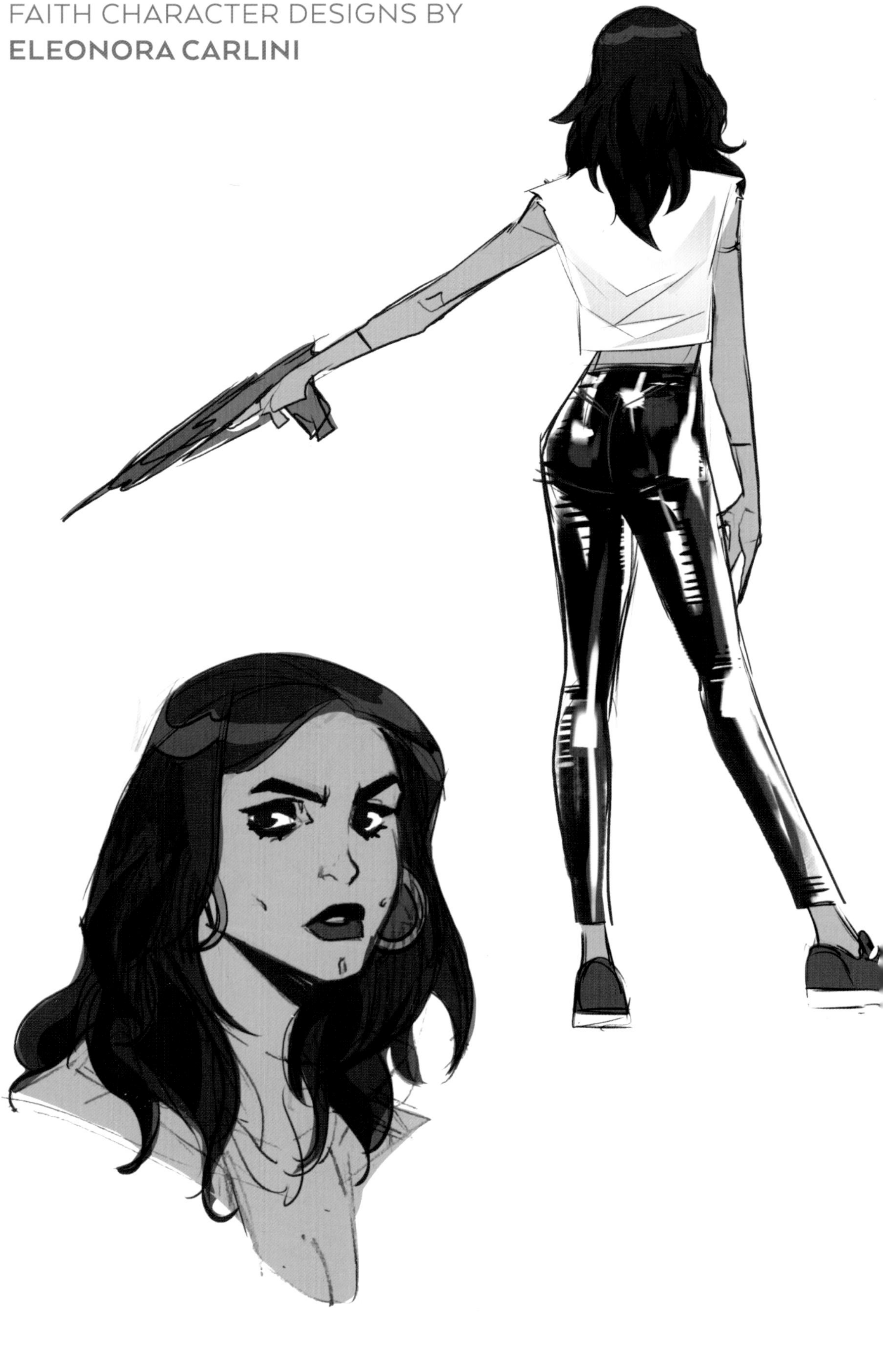